The Essential
Greek Mythology

Editor: Sofia N. Sfyroera
Translation: Diane Shuggart

Cover: Kostas Houhoulis
Photographs: Studio Kontos Photography

Copyright © 2003 «ELLINIKA GRAMMATA»

All rights reserved. No part of this publication may be reproduced, stored in a retrieval system, or transmitted in any form or by any means, electronic, mechanical, photocopying, recording or otherwise, without permission in writing of the Coeditors.

Ellinika Grammata Publ.
59, Emm. Benaki Str., 10681 Athens
tel. 2103891800, fax 2103836658
www.ellinikagrammata.gr
183, Monastiriou Str., 54627 Thessaloniki
tel. 2310500035, fax 2310500034

Distribution
Ellinika Grammata Publ.
6, Gennadiou Str., 10678 Athens
tel.-fax 2103817826

ISBN 960-406-357-X

Sofia N. Sfyroera

The Essential Greek Mythology

ELLINIKA GRAMMATA
ATHENS 2003

Contents

Introduction 11

THE THEOGONY
THE CREATION OF THE WORLD
- Chaos 13
- Orphic cosmogony 13
- Gaea 15

THE CHILDREN OF URANUS
- Titans – Cyclopes – Hecatoncheires 16
- How Uranus was deposed 17

CRONUS AND RHEA 17

THE CLASH OF THE TITANS
- The fate of the defeated Titans 18
- Atlas's punishment 18

THE BATTLE OF THE GIANTS 20
- Typhoeus 21

THE CREATION OF MAN
THE MYTH OF PROMETHEUS 23
PANDORA 26
DEUCALION AND PYRRHA 27

THE OLYMPIAN GODS
- Zeus 29
- Hera 36
- Poseidon 40
- Athena 51
- Demeter 57
- Aphrodite 63
- Hephaestus 77
- Hestia 81
- Ares 83
- Apollo 89
- Artemis 102
- Hermes 104
- Hades 110

DIONYSUS & THE DIONYSIAN GODS
DIONYSUS 113
SATYRS AND SEILENI 123
MAENADS 125
PAN 126
PRIAPUS 129
CENTAURS AND LAPITHS 130

THE LESSER GODS
LESSER GODS OF URANUS
- Iris 133
- Charites (Graces) 134
- Horae 134
- Muses 135
- Helius 136
- Phaethon 139
- Eos 139
- Selene 140

LESSER GODS OF THE SEA
- Nereus and the Nereids 142
- Proteus 143
- Glaucus 143
- Phorcys 144
- Triton 144
- Sirens 145
- Scylla and Charybdis 146
- Oceanus 146
- Oceanids 147
- Nymphs 147

GODS OF LOVE
- Eros 148

GODS OF THE UNDERWORLD
- Dike 149
- Ate 149
- Nemesis 150
- Keres 151
- Harpies 151
- Erinyes (Furies) 152
- Charon 153

GODS OF FIRE
- Cabeiri 154
- Telchines 156

GODS OF HEALING
- Asclepius 157

HERACLES 161

MYTHS ABOUT ATHENS
- Cecrops 179
- Aglaurus 180
- Erichthonius 181
- Erechtheus 182
- Cephalus and Procris 183
- Procne and Philomela 184
- Boreas and Oreithyia 184
- Aegeus 185

THESEUS 187

GODS OF THESSALY
- Peleus 195
- Jason and Pelias 197
- Phrixus and Helle 197

THE EXPEDITION OF THE ARGONAUTS 199

MYTHS ABOUT AEGINA
- Aegina and Zeus 207
- Aeacus and his Descendants 208

MYTHS ABOUT CRETE
- Minos 211
- The Minotaur 213
- Daedalus and Icarus 214
- Rhadamanthys and Sarpedon 216
- Talus 217

THE THEBAN CYCLE
- Cadmus 218

THE DESCENDANTS OF CADMUS
- Ino and Athamas 220
- Semele 220
- Agave 221
- Actaeon 221

THE ROYAL HOUSE OF THEBES
- Labdacus 222
- Laius and Oedipus 222
- The Seven Against Thebes 225
- Antigone 226
- The Sons of the Seven Champions 226

BOETIAN TRADITION
- Alcmaeon 229
- Zethus and Amphion 230
- Niobe 231

THE ARCADIAN CYCLE
- Atalante 232

MYTHS ABOUT THE PELOPONNESE

CORINTHIAN HEROES
- Sisyphus 233
- Glaucus 234
- Bellerophon 234

THE ARGOS CYCLE
- Inachus – Phoroneus – Io 235
- Danaus – Danaidae 236
- Proetus and the Proetidae 237
- Acrisius and Danae 238
- Perseus 239
- Tantalus 240
- Pelops 241
- Atreus – Thyestes 242
- Tyndareus and Leda 243
- Dioscuri 244
- Helen 245
- Clytemnestra 247

THE TROJAN WAR
- Myth and History 249

THE HEROES OF THE TROJAN WAR

THE GREEKS
- Agamemnon 253
- Menelaus 254
- Achilles 254
- Ajax of Telamon 257
- Ajax of Locris 258
- Diomedes 258
- Odysseus 259
- Nestor 260
- Idomeneus 261
- Philoctetes 261

THE TROJANS
- Alexandros-Paris 262
- Hector 262
- Aeneas 264
- Glaucus 264
- Sarpedon 265
- Helenus 266

THE ODYSSEY

- The return of Odysseus 267
- The Lotus Eaters 268
- Polyphemus, the Cyclops 268
- The island of Aeolia 269
- The Laestrygonians 269
- The island of Circe 270
- Odysseus in the Underworld 270
- The Sirens – Scylla – Charybdis – The cattle of Helius 271
- Odysseus on Ogygia 273
- The land of the Phaeacians 273
- Odysseus at Ithaca 274
- The death of Odysseus 275

Introduction

People, young and old, always love hearing stories. People would tell stories long before they invented writing and have never stopped telling stories since.

In cold countries, stories are told around the fireplace. In countries blessed with mild temperatures, stories are told outdoors, on long, warm nights. Storytellers traveled from island to island in the Aegean and the Ionian. They followed paths that snaked up the opes of the mountains of Crete and the Peloponnese. They wandered far and wide, to Asia and the Black Sea coast. They were warmly welcomed in villages. No village feast, or *paniyiri*, was complete unless the storyteller's voice was heard. There was always a place for these storytellers, even at athletic competitions where youth wrestled or tested their strength in the javelin throw, archery, or chariot racing. When everyone was flushed from the heat and runners' throats were parched from the dust kicked up by the horses, the rhapsodist would begin to recount some old legend while strumming the lyre in accompaniment. Years and centuries thus passed, sometimes peacefully and sometimes torn by violence as kings of city-states which have long disappeared succeeded one another: Tiryns, Mycenae, Argos, Iolcus, Calydon, and many others.

Back then, every little thing was grist for the storyteller's mill: the weather, the wars, the misfortunes that befell the ruling families, the rise and fall of city-states. A legend or tale explained everything, from the shape of some cliff or rock to the sacrificial rituals. Nothing under the sun was left to mystery.

In an age when language could not yet express abstract ideas, the ancient Greeks expressed their thoughts and innermost feelings by creating myths. Their admiration of heroes, their need for role models, and their efforts to understand the mysteries of life and death, the philosophical questions that torment the human mind, the desire to learn about the world around them, created a poetic mythology that did transcended rational or conventional morals.

Ancient tales have survived through mythology, which has preserved accounts of odd habits and events, created an anthropomorphic concept of astral bodies, as well as fused old cults and habits with newer ones. Generations upon generations were raised in antiquity with the tales of this extraordinary world created in mythology. Today, Greek mythology reveals a spectacular world and amazing civilization that has been, is, and will be an inexhaustible source of inspiration for artistic creation.

The Theogony

THE CREATION OF THE WORLD

Chaos

In the beginning, there was the immeasurable abyss Chaos, a nebulous material space that would later contain everything that comprised the universe. After Chaos, there was Gaea, the eternal and unshakeable support, and Eros, the omnipotent beginning, the power of evolution that united all the elements and thus became the origin of the creation of beings.

Chaos gave birth to Erebus (Darkness) –the underworld that was as far below the earth as the sky was above it– and Nyx (Night), who in turn gave birth to Aether (Air), which surrounds the earth, and Hemera (Day).

Orphic cosmogony

In the beginning, there was only Nyx in the dark. She later gave birth to an egg that split in two, then hatched. One half fell downwards and became the earth, while the other half floated upwards and became the sky. Eros, who is the source of every mortal and immortal creature, emerged from the egg. Eros and Nyx lay together, and so did heaven and earth, thus creating everything we see around us: the sun, the moon, darkness and light, land and sea, trees, flowers, mountains, plains, islands, animals, birds, and reptiles. At the end, a clan of immortal gods was born. These were the Titans, amazing giants whose every step shook the earth.

Zeus was the king of the gods. He transformed himself into a divine snake, then descended to the Underworld where he lay with Persephone. The new king of the world Zagreus, often identified with Dionysus, was born of this union. Zeus gave the child to the Curetes to raise. But the Titans put the Curetes to sleep then covered their faces with plaster. Thus disguised, the Titans approached the infant's crib and offered him presents: first, a diamond-shape that buzzed, then a top and clay dolls whose arms and legs moved, then a shiny ball, and, finally a mirror. As the

Classical-era clay love idols (Pella Museum).

Nyx. Scene from the battle with the Giants depicted on the frieze of the altar at Pergamus, 180 B.C. (Berlin Museum).

infant Zagreus was distracted by his reflection, the Titans grabbed him, but he changed forms to escape them.

First, he changed into a youth who looked like Zeus in an attempt to intimidate the Titans. He then changed into a horned snake, next a wild horse so he could buck them off, then a lion to attack them, and finally a bull. But the Titans raised their daggers and killed the bull. Afterwards, they lit a fire, roasted the bull, and ate him.

The smoke and burning gristle wafted to the sky and reached Zeus. When he saw that his child had been slain, he threw down a lightning bolt and burned the Titans. Demeter descended to earth, picked up the bull pieces, and joined them, thus bringing Zagreus-Dionysus back to life. He then ascended to the upper world. Mortals were then shaped from the killers' ashes. Thus, human beings have a dual nature: the killers' ashes have produced the dark side that represents the Titan nature of human beings; the other side is the immortal soul, which was produced by the blood of Zagreus-Dionysus that the Titans drank before they were killed. Throughout their lives, humans struggle to preserve their immortal or divine nature and drown their murderous, Titan impulses.

According to this Orphic view of cosmogony, Zeus transferred his power and rule over the world to the bright Zagreus-Dionysus. The world then split from Darkness, which had created Cronus and Aether, by activating a birth-giving process. From Aether, Cronus created the Cosmic Egg from which the primal form of Fanitas-

Young and aged Lapithys from the western pediment of the Temple of Zeus at Olympia, 460 B.C. (Olympia Archaeological Museum).

Dionysus (Dionysus the Bright) emerged, the bright creator of everything. He then lay with Persephone, who gave birth to the second Dionysus that was devoured by the Titans. But Athena saved his heart, which Zeus swallowed. After destroying the Titans with his lightning bolts, Zeus united with Semele, who gave birth to a third Dionysus, while using the ashes of the Titans – which also contained elements of the devoured Dionysus – to create human beings. Thus humans have a dual nature, are made of dust, but are also divine.

Gaea

Gaea or Ge (Earth) is the mother of everything, nurturer of all beings, provider of all goods. She gave birth to gods and humans and embraces whatever she has nourished and gives it new birth.

Her first child – and her equal – was Uranus. He wrapped himself around her and became the home of the immortal and blessed gods. Gaea (Mother Earth) united with Uranus (Father Heaven), producing rain, from which sprung the first dynasty of gods. After Uranus, Gaea gave birth to Ourea (mountains) and the deep sea, Pontus.

After uniting with Uranus, Gaea gave birth to the Titans, the Cyclopes, and the Hecatoncheires. From her union with Nereus, Gaea gave birth to Thaumus, Phorcys, Eurybia, and Ceto; from her union with Tartarus, Gaea gave birth to the monster Typhoeus or Typhon.

In older Orphic theogony, Ge, Uranus, and Oceanus are born from the power of Eros who miraculously united them. In more recent Orphic theogony, Uranus and Ge are created when the Great Being born to Chronus (Time) was torn into two hemispheres.

The worship of Gaea has deep roots in ancient Greece. At Dodona, she was worshipped with Zeus as *"fruit-bearer and mother."* The Oracle of Delphi was originally consecrated to Gaea, while temples dedicated to Gaea have been found throughout Greece.

An ovoid sacred stone marked the "navel of the earth" – the spot where two eagles released into the air by Zeus met. The myth was likely devised by the sanctuary's priests and originally indicated the burial spot of Gaea's son Python. Apollo introduced the cult of Python at Delphi after killing him. The shape of the omphalos (navel) is similar to that embellishments over burial mounds.

THE CHILDREN OF URANUS

Titans – Cyclopes – Hecatoncheires

The second generation of gods was born from Gaea's union with Uranus. These were the twelve Titans. The six male Titans were Oceanus, the god of the river Oceanus; Coeus, father of Leto; Crius; Hyperion, father of Helius (Sun), Selene (Moon), and Eos (Dawn); Iapetus, father of Prometheus; and Cronus. They had six sisters: Tethys, wife of Oceanus; Theia, wife of Hyperion; Themis, goddess of justice and law; Mnemosyne, the goddess of memory; Phoebe, mother of Leto; and Rhea, mother of the Olympian gods.

The Cyclopes were also children of Gaea and Uranus: Brontes, who represented the thunderclap; Steropes, who held lightning; and Arges, the master of the lightning bolt. The Cyclopes had a single eye located in the middle of their foreheads, and were considered selfish and arrogant.

The Hecatoncheires were another group of children born to Gaea and Uranus. The names of these powerful, hundred-handed giants were Aegaeon or Briareus, Cottus, and Gyes.

The birth of Aphrodite, 460 B.C. (Museum of Rome).

THE THEOGONY

How Uranus was deposed

Uranus and Gaea kept having children, but knowing that he was in danger of being overthrown by one of them, Uranus would toss them to Tartarus, a dark region beneath the Underworld.

Filled with despair at the fate of her children, Gaea decided to avenge them by castrating Uranus. All of her children except Cronus refused to help her. So, when Uranus, filled with amorous intentions, came with Nyx to lay with his wife Gaea, Cronus immobilized him and cut off his genitals, which he then tossed into the sea. Aphrodite rose from the white foam at that very spot, while the Erinyes (Furies), the Giants, and the Melic nymphs sprung from the blood that dripped from his wound.

Uranus did not die from the wound. His powers were limited, but he retained the ability to predict the future.

CRONUS AND RHEA

After deposing his father Uranus, Cronus became the ruler of the gods. He then married his sister Rhea, with whom he had Hestia, Demeter, Hera, Hades, and Poseidon. But because his father had predicted that Cronus would be deposed by one of his children, he swallowed each one after their birth. Desperate, Rhea, who was then carrying Zeus, sought the aid of her parents who advised her to go away and give birth to her child in secret on Crete, then return and pretend to give birth.

Rhea followed their advice and when it came time for her to give birth, she presented Cronus with a rock wrapped in swaddling clothes. He swallowed the rock, thinking he had again managed to thwart his fate. But when his son Zeus grew up, he deposed Uranus, and then forced him to regurgitate his other children.

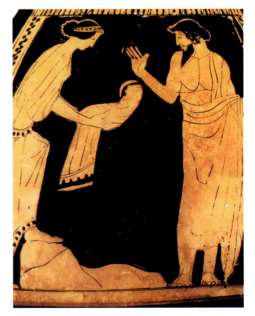

Rhea offers Cronus a stone wrapped in swaddling instead of the newly born Zeus (red-figure pelike, 460 B.C., Metropolitan Museum of New York).

THE CLASH OF THE TITANS

When Zeus took charge, he found himself opposed by the older gods who took Cronus's side in the battle between father and son. The first to revolt were the Titans, who had been freed from their shackles and refused to submit to the rule of the later Olympian gods. Their clash was tough, long, and seemed endless.

Counseled by Gaea, Zeus freed the Cyclopes –Brontes, Steropes, and Arges– from Tartarus by killing the monster Campe who was guarding them. Grateful to be released, the Cyclopes gave Zeus the gifts of thunder and lightning. They also gave Poseidon a trident and Hades a cap that made him invisible. The Cyclopes also granted the gods another gift: a mantle so that their enemies could not see the lightning flash and an altar on which the gods could take their vows before battle.

Zeus also freed the other three sons of Uranus and Gaea, the Hecatoncheires, whose incredible strength helped tilt the battle to the Olympians' side as they buried the Titans under 300 rocks they simultaneously hurled at them.

The fate of the defeated Titans

The defeated Titans were tossed to Tartarus, which was as far from the earth as it was from the sky. Indeed, if a bronze anvil fell from the sky, it would take ten days to reach the surface of the earth and take ten more days to reach Tartarus. Even the immortal gods feared this vast, dark area. It is where the palace of Nyx was located, surrounded by dark clouds. This is where the enemies of Zeus were incarcerated behind a bronze wall whose entrance was blocked by an enormous gate made by Hephaestus. Three giants who never slept guarded the Titans: Gyes, Cottus, and Briareus.

Atlas's punishment

Atlas was among the Titans severely punished for their revolt against Zeus. Atlas was exiled to the far ends of the earth. His western kingdom was located at the edge of Chaos, in front of the house of Nyx, where the origins of Gaea, Pontus, Uranus, and Tartarus could be found. The Hesperides who guarded the golden apples also lived here. Atlas was condemned to supporting the earth on his shoulders for all eternity. But from his position he also learned all the secrets of heaven and sea, and was the first one to know that the world was a large globe.

Zeus also punished three other Titans after defeating them. Menoetius and Epimetheus were blasted into Erebus, while Prometheus was chained to the highest peak of the Caucasus Mountains with unbreakable nails and was visited every day by an eagle, sent by Zeus, to eat his liver, which grew again during the night.

According to a different account, Atlas was the son of the Titan Iapetus and the oceanid Clymene or Asia. In other accounts, his parents are Uranus or Aether and Gaea or Libya or Hemera. Meanwhile, Plato, in the myth of Atlantis (Critias), presents Poseidon and Cleito as the parents of Atlas, while his tough punishment is attributed to his role in the dismemberment of Dionysus.

With Pleione, Atlas had seven daughters known as the Pleiades. Atlas is also believed to have fathered the Hesperides, Calypso, Dione, Maia, Hesperis, Ayson, and the Hyades. Through his children, he thus became the forefather of several rulers.

Roman statue of Atlas holding up the earth (National Museum of Naples).

THE BATTLE OF THE GIANTS

After defeating the Titans, Zeus still had to face quite a number of enemies. These included the Giants, who sprung from the blood of the castrated Uranus and were born with shiny armor. Super-human monsters, they had long hair and beards that covered their reptilian scales. There were more than one hundred Giants, but unlike the Titans they were not immortal. Gaea felt sorry for them and, enraged at the punishments meted out to the Titans, urged the Giants to fight Zeus and the Olympian gods.

Although the clash with the Giants is depicted on a number of pieces of pottery, it is only mentioned once in ancient texts by Apollodorus. Evidently, its narration is based on some lost, third-century-B.C. epic, as the works of neither Homer nor Hesiod contain any references to it.

According to this myth, Gaea was aware of an old prophecy that said the Giants would be defeated if the gods allied themselves with a mortal. She thus sought a magic herb that would grant them immortality. But Zeus forbade Eos, Helius, and Selene from rising, then went out in the darkness and found the herb, which he destroyed with Athena's help and then formed an alliance with Heracles.

The clash with the Giants took place in Phlegra, an area of the northern Halkidiki peninsula, but the Giants' fate had been sealed before the battle. Heracles killed Alcyoneus, who would enjoy immortality as long as he never set foot on the land where he had been born. Seeking to avenge his brother's death, Porphyrion tried to rape Hera, but was mortally wounded by one of Heracles's arrows. According to another account, Aphrodite used her beauty to lead the Giants to a cave,

The Clash of the Giants: Hera, Athena, Ares, Hermes, and Poseidon battle the Giants, 525 B.C. (Delphi Museum).

where Heracles killed them; crushed beneath huge rocks, they exploded and caused volcanic eruptions.

Athena's role in the battle of the Giants was decisive as she pinned down Enceladus beneath the island of Sicily. She also flayed Pallas, and used his skin to make her shield. Polybotes suffered a similarly grim fate at the hands of Poseidon, who chased the Giant to the island of Cos. There, he seized a piece of the island –Nissyros– and struck Polybotes down with it.

In other accounts of the battle with the Giants, Dionysus played an important role. He rode into battle on donkey-back, accompanied by the satyrs and seileni. When the donkeys saw the Giants, they were frightened and began to bray. Mistaking the donkeys for strange monsters, the Giants were frightened and fled.

Typhoeus

Zeus was finally left with one enemy: the monster Typhoeus, Gaea's last child from her union with Tartarus. Omnipotent and brave, Typhoeus was a hundred-headed dragon that spewed flames and let out high-pitched cries. He was taller than the highest mountains and his entire body was covered in feathers. When he stretched his arms, one hand would touch the east and the other would touch the west, while snakes poked out of his thighs, slithering around his body and making horrible, whistling sounds.

Typhoeus was married to Echidnea, a monster who was half nymph and half snake. She gave birth to their monster-children, the Chimaera, the Lerna Hydra, and the hounds Orthus and Cerberus.

Typhoeus attacked the Olympian gods who fled to Egypt where they changed into animals to escape the hideous Giant. Zeus fended him off using a lightning bolt and a diamond scythe, then chased Typhoeus all the way to Syria where the two wrestled. Typhoeus squeezed Zeus with his snakes, then neutralized him by cutting the sinews of his hands and feet, before tossing him into a cave in Cilicia wrapped in a bear skin. The god Hermes then appeared in the cave and helped restore Zeus. Together, the two gods climbed into a chariot driven by winged horses; they chased Typhoeus and attacked him with lightning bolts. The Giant responded by hurling mountains back at them. Typhoeus soon became exhausted. After the crossing the sea, the monster ended up in Sicily, where he was crushed under Mount Aetna.

Bronze statue of Zeus throwing a thunderbolt (Olympia Archaeological Museum).

The Creation of Man

THE MYTH OF PROMETHEUS

The myth of Prometheus represents humankind's passage to civilization. It is found in all mythologies, but is mostly vividly represented in Greek mythology where learning reached its peak.

The name Prometheus is rooted in the words *pro* and *mytheus* (or, in Doric Greek, *matheus*), which means forethought or someone who looks and plans ahead. According to another account, Prometheus's name was rooted in the Greek corruption of the Sanskrit word *pramantha*, or the fire bore that he supposedly invented as the Thurians worshipped a Zeus Prometheus who held a fire bore. Prometheus thus symbolizes the strong man who rises above the fate of mortals and touches the divine, thus opening the road for humans to prevail in a hostile environment. As the bearer of fire, he became the personification of knowledge and the creator of civilization. His tragedy also makes him a model for the tragic and civic-minded human, the ideal citizen who puts forth the powers of the mind and of the will, the person who can stand up to fate and defeat it with logic. According to the most prevalent mythological accounts,

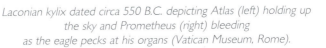

Laconian kylix dated circa 550 B.C. depicting Atlas (left) holding up the sky and Prometheus (right) bleeding as the eagle pecks at his organs (Vatican Museum, Rome).

Prometheus was the son of the Titan Iapetus and the oceanid Clymene and the brother of Atlas, Menoetius, and Epimetheus. Aeschylus presents Prometheus as the son of Themis, that is, of justice and the law. A symbol of logic, intellect, and ingenuity, Prometheus is the independent hero who stood up to the blind tyranny of power. He thus incurred the wrath and hatred of Zeus, who punished Prometheus in a merciless manner for becoming the benefactor of the human race, which, according to some myths, he created.

Pausanias writes that the inhabitants of Phocis would point out rocks that smelled like humans and which they claimed were clumps of leftover mud from which Prometheus had made man. Indeed, Aesop says that humans were made of dirt and Prometheus's tears. But Plato, in *Protagoras*, claims the gods shaped animals and humans, but assigned Prometheus and Epimetheus to embellish them with the traits and characteristics that distinguish each creature. Epimetheus, who symbolizes afterthought, asked Prometheus to let him hand out these traits alone. Thus, Epimetheus gave some animals speed, others strength, others feathers or talons. When he came to humans, Epimetheus had run out of gifts, so he just left them naked unarmed, and helpless. Prometheus took pity on humans, and in order to provide them with strength and the ability to defend themselves, stole craftsmanship from Athena and fire from Hephaestus (as craftsmanship would be useless without fire.) By giving humans the art of politics, which he stole from Zeus, Prometheus incurred the god's wrath and was punished.

Hesiod writes that Prometheus first enraged Zeus by deceiving him at a meeting of gods and humans to discuss how the animals slaughtered for sacrifices would be shared. Prometheus, who was responsible for sharing out the meat, presented a slain bull that he had

"In the beginning, seeing they saw amiss, and hearing heard not, but, like phantoms huddled in dreams, the perplexed story of their days confounded; knowing neither timber-work nor brick-built dwellings basking in the light, but dug for themselves holes, wherein like ants, that hardly may contend against a breath, they dwelt in burrows of their unsunned caves. Neither of winter's cold had they fixed sign, nor of the spring when she comes decked with flowers, nor yet of summer's heat with melting fruits." (Prometheus Bound, Aeschylus). Prometheus then took pity on mortals and "I the rising of the stars showed them, and when they set, though much obscure. Moreover, number, the most excellent of all inventions, I for them devised, and gave them writing that retaineth all." Thus, he harnessed animals to the yoke and invented the chariot, as well as boats so they could sail the seas, and the art of prophecy, how to make sacrifices, and how to extract metals. He thus became the great benefactor of humankind, as he also gave mortals the medicines to heal their diseases and erased their fear of death. Hesiod says that Prometheus also stole fire from the gods by hiding a flame inside a plant stalk so he could give it to mortals. According to the most prevalent myths, this theft took place at Hephaestus's workshop on the island of Limnos, although other accounts claim it took place on Mount Olympus. In one version of this myth, Prometheus lit the torch he gave to mortals from the wheels of the chariot driven by the sun-god Helius (Lapithus from the western pediment of the Temple of Zeus at Olympia, 470-456 B.C., Olympia).

divided by wrapping the meat and intestines in the animal's hide and wrapping the bones in the shiny fat.

Attracted by the fat's luster, Zeus chose the package of bones. Realizing that the Titan had tricked him in favor of the humans, Zeus became furious and vowed revenge. He thus took back the gift of fire, a basic tool for humankind's survival, and condemned humans to a life of toil and torment. *"They had eyes, but didn't see, they had ears but didn't hear, and their entire lives seemed like a hazy dream. They didn't know how to build dwellings, so they lived in sunless caves, and didn't know whether it was winter, spring, or summer,"* Aeschylus writes in his play *Prometheus Bound*.

Prometheus took pity on the mortals and showed them *"the way of the stars, the roads and points of the horizon, numbers, and the greatest wisdom, letters,"* Aeschylus informs. And so Prometheus helped mortals put beasts under the yoke, invent the carriage, build ships that floated on the waves, develop divination and sacrificial rituals, and mine ores. He became the great benefactor of the human race as he gave them medicine to cure illness and erased their fear of death. And, as Hesiod notes, Prometheus even hid a flame in the stalk of a plant, thus stealing fire back from the gods so he could give it to mortals again. According to the most prevalent accounts, Prometheus stole the fire from Hephaestus's workshop on the island of Lemnos. By other accounts, Prometheus stole the fire from Mount Olympus or lit a torch from the wheels of Helius.

Other ancient writers claim Zeus punished Prometheus because he knew a secret that was related to Zeus's power: that Zeus was trying to seduce the nereid Thetis but that a son would be born from that union who would depose Zeus.

For whatever reason, Prometheus was punished severely. He was chained to the highest peak of the Caucasus Mountains with unbreakable bonds made by Hephaestus. There, an eagle picked at his liver, which grew back during the night. Heracles released him from his bondage thirty years later, with the consent of Zeus. Prometheus and Zeus were reconciled, and Prometheus was invited back to Mount Olympus, where he took the place of the centaur Cheiron who relinquished his immortality for Prometheus.

Hera welcomes Prometheus to Mount Olympus (red-figure kylix, 480-470 B.C., National Library, Paris).

PANDORA

Angered by Prometheus's theft of the fire, Zeus ordered Hephaestus to create from dirt and water a maiden as beautiful as a goddess, but to give her a human voice and powers. Hephaestus obeyed. Athena and the Charites (Graces) endowed her with charms, while Hermes endowed her with a fickle character and the ability to lie and deceive. The girl was named Pandora ("all gifts") as the gods had given her everything. Hephaestus then presented the maiden to the Titan Epimetheus married her, flouting his brother's advice to never accept a present from Zeus.

Pandora had been given a box by the gods, who ordered her not to open it. But her curiosity got the better of her and she disobeyed the order. In an instant, all the troubles that have since plagued humankind spilled out of the box, and only hope remained shut inside.

The myth of Pandora thus symbolizes the beginning of the humankind's woes and humans' loss of immortality. It also represents the Dorians' patriarchal perception of a poor imitation of Gaea who provides her creatures with everything.

The goddess Athena and Hephaestus dress Pandora, whose name is given as Anesidora. (Kylix circa 470-460 B.C., British Museum).

DEUCALION AND PYRRHA

Zeus was not satisfied with the troubles Pandora unleashed upon mortals, so he decided to destroy them with a deluge as punishment for their lack of respect and wickedness. The only survivors were Deucalion, a son of Prometheus, and Pyrrha, daughter of Pandora and Epimetheus, who followed Prometheus's advice to build an ark and stock it with provisions. The couple hid in the ark and floated on the waves for nine days and nine nights.

On the tenth day, the ark ran aground on the peak of Mount Parnassus or at Mount Orthri in Thessaly, or on Mount Athos, or on Mount Aetna, where Deucalion and Pyrrha offered the gods a sacrifice to placate them. Zeus then sent his messenger, Hermes, to ask them what they wanted. Deucalion wished for the creation of a new human race. His prayer was heard and Zeus advised the couple to toss *"their mother's bones"* behind their heads. The couple interpreted Zeus's words as meaning they should toss stones behind them as they walked. They did; men sprung from the stones tossed by Deucalion and women sprung from the stones tossed by Pyrrha. This is how a new people or *laos* was created from stone or *laas*. According to Hesiod, these people were the Lelegians. The true children of Deucalion and Pyrrha were Hellen, the eponym of the Hellenes or Greeks, Amphictyon, and Protogeneia. Pandora, Thyia, Candebus, and Melantho are also mentioned as their children.

Hellen's sons became the eponyms of the Dorians, Aeolians; through a third son, Xuthus, Hellen's grandsons became the eponyms of the Achaeans and the Ionians. All four branches of the Hellenes were thus descended from Deucalion; the Greeks' heroes and royal dynasties are also mentioned as his direct descendants.

The ancient Greeks paid great tribute to Deucalion, whom they considered the purest and most respectable of men, the first founder of cities and temples, as well as their first king (Apollodorus). According to Aristotle, the deluge occurred in the region of Dodona and the Achelous River, while by some traditions Deucalion took those who had survived the flood to Dodona. Other accounts claim that Deucalion and Pyrrha lived in Opuntian Locris on the mainland side of the Euboean Sea, (Pindar) the fortified harbor at Cyno (Strabo), where Pyrrha is also said to have been buried. But Athenians believed that Deucalion's grave was next to the Temple of Olympian Zeus that he had founded (Pausanias), while Plutarch places Deucalion's grave at Delphi.

The Olympian Gods

ZEUS

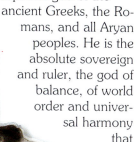

Zeus or Jupiter, the father of the gods and of mortals –according to Homer– is the supreme god of the ancient Greeks, the Romans, and all Aryan peoples. He is the absolute sovereign and ruler, the god of balance, of world order and universal harmony that emerged after a long period of cosmogonic changes and upheavals.

The initial character of the "king of kings" derives from his name, which in Greek is *Dias*. In all Indo-European languages, *dias* derives from the root *div* (or divine) that expresses the common need for a deity created by the sight of the sky and all the heavenly bodies. Thus, Zeus lives above the earth in eternal light, among the clouds. In Greek, he is sometimes referred to as *nepheleigeretis* or *kelaenephis* from the *nephelai* (clouds). He is master of storms and ruler of winds; Zeus also rules thunder, lightning, and rain, fertilizes the earth, and watches over the universe.

Prudent and profound, Zeus is omniscient, but his decisions were inscrutable even by the other gods. He was a protector of strangers (*Xenios Zeus*, from the Greek *xenos* or foreigner), as well as a protector of vows; he was an avenger, but he was also benevolent and created for code of ethics his worshippers through which he emerges as the perfect being, the ultimate God.

Zeus lives above the earth, bathed in eternal light and lord of the clouds, ruler of the storms and the winds. He also reigns over thunder and lightning, sends the rains, fertilizes the earth, and oversees the workings of the universe.

The birth of Zeus

In antiquity there were several myths, including local variations, about the birth of Zeus as every Greek city sought to claim the honor of being his birthplace. But according to the prevalent account, when Rhea gave birth to Zeus she sent the infant to Crete and entrusted him to the care of the nymphs Ida and Adrasteia, while deceiving Cronus by giving him a stone to swallow.

Zeus was raised in the Idaean Cave, where he was fed honey and milk from the goat Amaltheia, an animal that had been reared in the land of Helius. Zeus later used the goat's impenetrable hide in his battle against the Titans and it became a symbol of his power. One of Amaltheia's horns, which was broken either by Zeus or by accident, also became a symbol of abundance, as it would magically fill with foods and other goods.

Other accounts claim the young god was raised on ambrosia brought to him by pigeons and nectar pumped from a rock by an eagle. The Curetes were charged with guarding the cave, and their war whoops and dances covered the infant's cries. When Cronus discovered their collusion in the plot to deceive him, he punished them by changing them into lions. Zeus, however, showed his gratitude by later making the lion the king of animals.

Cronus deposed

When Zeus was grown, Metis, a daughter of Oceanus, gave him an emetic herb. Zeus used this herb to force Cronus to regurgitate his other children, which he had swallowed. Zeus then enlisted the help of his siblings and the Cyclopes in fighting his father, whom he overthrew after a battle of ten years. He later defeated the Titans and the Giants, gods who represented the old order and symbolized the primitive, destructive forces of nature and geological disruptions. Having emerged as ruler of the bright sky and all gods – except Moira (Fate), a mysterious power that was stronger than the gods – and humankind, Zeus then imposed order and harmony, by dissolving the demons of darkness.

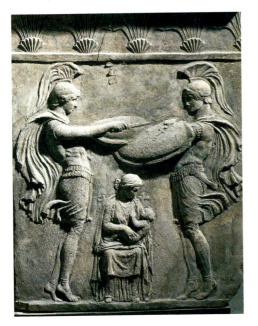

The birth of Zeus. The Curetes bang their shields to make noise and cover the cries of the newly born god cuddled by the nymph Amaltheia (Louvre Museum).

The god's loves and children

According to the Homeric tradition – which was accepted throughout the Greek world – Zeus's only legal bride was his sister, Hera, with whom he had Hephaestus. Other myths recognize Zeus as the father of several of Hera's children: Ares, Eileithyia, and Hebe.

Zeus had countless amorous adventures with goddesses and mortal women since mythology did not only provide an allegorical description of the natural elements but also expressed Greeks' desire to claim a genealogical link with the king of the immortals.

Thus, some ancient writers claim that Zeus wed Metis, the daughter of Oceanus and Tethys. Metis personified wisdom and science, which Zeus absorbed by swallowing her while she was pregnant because Uranus had predicted that she would give birth to a child that would be more powerful than his father. As a result, Athena sprung from Zeus's head.

Zeus was later said to have wed the Titan Themis, the personification of law, as well as natural and moral order. The children born from this union were the Horae (Seasons) –Eunomia (Order) and Dike (Justice)– and the Moerae, who were charged with dispersing fortune and misfortune to mortals.

Zeus's third bride was Themis's sister, Mnemosyne (Memory), with whom he lay for nine nights so that she gave birth to the nine Muses (sources of inspiration). With Demeter, Zeus had Persephone (the vegetation that is born in spring and dies in autumn). He also lay with Leto, daughter of the Titans Coeus

The abduction of Europa by Zeus disguised as a bull (British Museum).

and Phoebe, with whom he fathered Apollo (light) and Artemis (moon). With Oceanus's daughter Eurynome, Zeus fathered the Charites (Graces).

Ever unfaithful, Zeus could not resist the charms of the nymphs and beautiful mortal women. Thus, he fathered many of Greece's heroes, rulers, and kings:

- in Laconia, by turning himself into a swan, Zeus lay with Leda, who gave birth to the twins Castor and Polydeuces (Pollux), and Helen of Troy;
- with the nymph Taygete, Zeus fathered Lacedaemon, a king and hero of the Lacedaemonians;
- in Boeotia, Zeus in the form of a satyr lay with Antiope, daughter of the river-god Asopus, and fathered the Theban dioscuri, Amphion and Zethus;
- with Alcmene, before whom he appeared in the guise of her husband Electryon, he fathered Heracles;
- disguised as an eagle, he lay with Aegina, daughter of the river-god Asopus, and fathered Aeacus, eponym of the Aeaceians;
- in Arcadia, Zeus lay with the nymph Callisto and fathered Arcas, king and eponym of the Arcadians;
- in Cyllene, Zeus lay with Maia, one of the Pleiades and daughter of Atlas and Pleione, who bore him the god Hermes;
- with Niobe, daughter of the Peloponnesian king Phoroneus, Zeus had the Argus, hero of the eponymous city-state;
- disguised as a bull, Zeus abducted Europa and took her to Crete, where he lay with her and fathered Minos and his brothers;
- with Io, daughter of the river-god Inachus, Zeus fathered the Egyptian king Epaphus;
- Dione, daughter of Aether and Gaea, bore Zeus a daughter, the goddess Aphrodite;
- transformed into a shower of gold, Zeus united with Danae and fathered Perseus;
- with Electra he fathered Dardanus;
- Zeus lay with Semele, who bore him Dionysus;
- with Elarus, he fathered Tityus.

Zeus fathered children with countless women, but was also smitten by the beauty of Ganymede, whom Zeus kidnapped and installed on Olympus as the gods' cupbearer.

Naturally, his legal bride Hera did not accept his adventures passively, and Zeus was frequently the target of her rage and jealousy. Yet in spite of their terrible quarrels, Zeus was considered by the ancients as the protector of marriage and known as *Gamilios Zeus*.

Zeus seizes the handsome Trojan youth Ganymede, son of Tros and Callirhoe, 480-470 B.C. (Olympia Archaeological Museum).

The cult of Zeus

Sanctuaries where the Greeks made offerings to the father of the gods can be found on almost all the mountaintops in Greece. But the most important sanctuaries dedicated to the god were the Oracle at Dodona, the Temple of Zeus at Olympia, and the Temple of Ammon in an oasis on the east bank of the Nile.

The Oracle of Dodona

Located in the Epirus region, about 22 kilometers northwest of the city of Ioannina, the Oracle of Dodona is believed to be the oldest oracle of ancient Greece. Hesiod mentions being told by three priests of the Thebans in Egypt that two black doves founded the temples of Zeus at Dodona and Karnak. The priests of Dodona claimed a slightly different story: that two old women abducted from Thebes by the Phoenicians had been responsible for establishing the cult of Zeus in both countries.

Nonetheless, even though there is no archaeological evidence to support a link between the two sanctuaries, a coin dated to 300 B.C. that depicts three doves on one side – two of them on the ground and one resting on the sacred oak – have been unearthed. Hellos, eponym of the prehistoric tribe of Helloi or Selloi of Dodona, had wanted to remove the oak because it had revealed his theft of an animal. But he was deterred from chopping down the tree by a dove nesting in the oak's branches. It's obvious, therefore, that myths surrounding Dodona have

Bronze bust of Zeus, early fifth century B.C. (National Archaeological Museum, Olympia, bronze collection).

assimilated the practices of prehistoric cults of the Selloi –which symbolized the worship of Gaea– the oak, and Zeus.

Yet it seems that the cult of Gaea was older, as the Oracle of Dodona has all the characteristics of chthonic worship: the simple temple that included a pit into which sacrificial hogs were thrown, the Naiad spring, and the divinatory oak.

Following the appearance of the first Greek tribes in Epirus (circa 1900-1800 B.C.), the worship of Gaea was replaced by the Indo-European cult of the oak. This lasted until roughly 1300 B.C., when the cult of the patriarchal deity of the Pelasgic Zeus was introduced to Dodona, possibly via Thessaly. Gaea was then transformed into a divine bride named Dione and the sacred oak became the shelter of the

THE ESSENTIAL GREEK MYTHOLOGY

Bronze statue of Zeus holding thunderbolt (Olympia Archaeological Museum).

two deities. Thus, the rustling of tree's leaves, the clinking of the copper pots hung on its branches, and the cooing of the doves nesting in these branches, were believed to reveal the wishes of the gods. The sanctuary's priests, the Peleiades, interpreted these divine messages. The Selloi, priests of Zeus, also served at Dodona, where they slept on the ground and never washed their feet – another sign of an earlier chthonic cult. Until the conversion to Christianity around the end of the fourth century, Zeus and Dione remained the primary deities at Dodona until the ruler of Epirus, the Molossian king Pyrrhos, introduced the cults of Heracles, Aphrodite, and Aeneas.

The Sanctuary at Olympia

The impressive Temple of Zeus was located in the middle of the Altis, or sacred grove, in the most beautiful site of ancient Greece: Olympia. Before the cult of Zeus was introduced into the area, the cult of Gaea had been prevalent and an oracle consecrated to Gaea, known as the Gaeon in antiquity, was located at the northwestern foot of Cronius, the hill that forms the sanctuary's northern boundary. Rhea and Cronus had also been worshipped at this shrine. The earlier prevalence of female fertility deities at Olympia can be seen in the ancient cult of Hera in the sacred grove, as well as in the altar dedicated to the goddess in the stadium and the prominent role of the priestess *Demeter Chamyne*.

The famed Temple of Zeus was built from limestone in the Doric style by the Eleians in the fifth century B.C. and designed by the Eleian architect Libon. A chryselephantine statue of Zeus sculpted by Pheidias stood at the temple's center, and its elliptical pedestal was discovered slightly northeast of the temple.

Even in antiquity, Olympia was not known just for its Temple of Zeus but also renowned for the Olympic Games, the panhellenic athletic competition held in the god's honor every five years during the second or third full moon after the summer solstice. The games were held during the eighth lunar month, Apollonius or Parthenius (July-August) of the Eleians. A truce was called during the Games, in which only Greeks who had been born free to free parents were allowed to compete.

Athletes arrived at Olympia a month before the Games, accompanied by their coaches, their fathers, and their brothers. After taking an oath that they would compete fairly and had exercised for ten months, they competed naked for the prize of a branch of the sacred olive growing in the Temple of Zeus. Winners were deemed to be worthy, and were crowned with wreaths of olives while standing in front of the statue of the Olympian god while spectators covered them with flowers and leaves. These athletes were said to attain immortality and become eternal symbols of the good fight and of the victory of the spiritual over the material.

Aside from fame and honor, winners were also assured of a comfortable life, as they were elevated into heroes, reflecting fame on their birthplace. This, in turn, helped maintain a stable, strong core of citizen-warriors that could safeguard the city-state in a competitive environment.

The Temple of Ammon

The temple and sanctuary of Ammonas at Thebes (Karnak) in Egypt was founded during the 12th dynasty. Ammon, whom the Egyptians worshipped as king of the gods, was depicted with the head of a ram or as a man with a ram's horn. Inside the temple dedicated to Ammon, priests kept a ram, which they considered to be a representative of the god. Alternatively, Ammon was depicted as a head covered by a solar disk and two long feathers.

The ancient Greeks, who identified Ammon with Zeus, called him *Zeus Ammonas*. His worship spread to Greece, especially at Pellene in Macedonia and in Boeotian Thebes.

Ammon also appears in Cretan mythology. He is said to have ruled Crete and married Rhea, who subsequently deserted him to marry her brother Cronus.

The oracle at Ammon was one of the most important seers of antiquity. The god's messages were divined from various points on his statue, the flight of the birds, the rustling of leaves, or the gurgling of a spring. It is worth noting that many ancient Greek cities dispatched ambassadors to receive the prophecies of Ammon from the priests. Alexander the Great made a historic visit to the temple where he was received as the son of Zeus Ammonos.

*Zeus, 470 B.C.
(Olympia Archaeological Museum).*

HERA

The queen of the gods, bride, and sister of Zeus, Hera was one of the greatest deities of the ancient Greeks and later of the Romans. She was a daughter of Cronus and Rhea, and like their other children was swallowed by her father, only to be spit out again when Cronus was given an emetic herb by Zeus.

Naturally, many Greek cities vied for the honor of being recognized as the birthplace of the great goddess. According to various local myths, Hera was born in Argos and delivered to the daughters of the river-god Asterion, on Euboea, in Akraia, and in Procymna. In other accounts, the goddess was born on the island of Samos, in the Peloponnesian provinces of Arcadia and Corinth, and elsewhere.

The origins of Hera's name have never been quite clear, although it has been suggested that it was an Aeolian corruption of the Sanskrit word *swar*, which means sky. It's also worth noting that it Latin, Hera shares the same root with the German *herus* and *herr*, meaning woman.

In any case, it is certain that Hera is a genuine Greek goddess, patron of agriculture and vegetation – an identity she acquired after her union with Zeus, when she became the queen of the heavens.

Hera, bride of Zeus and mother of gods

There are numerous and varied myths about where Hera and Zeus united the first time. Homer (*The Iliad*, 296) claims their union took place in the land of the Hesperides, while Pausanias claims Zeus disguised himself as a cuckoo to seduce Hera on Euboea, then whisked her off to Mount Cithaeron.

Hera was the ideal woman –beautiful, modest, and completely dedicated to her husband. She never became involved in another relationship, and thus demanded that her husband be faithful, too. But his countless romantic adventures made her jealous and their quarrels became frequent and intense. In one such moment of frustration, Hera gave birth by herself to the war-god as a result of a simple contact with a flower.

According to other myths, she also gave birth to Hebe, the goddess of eternal youth, after simply dining on lettuce. Eileithyia, a goddess of

Bust of Hera from Argive Heraion, 420 B.C. (National Archaeological Museum).

childbirth, and the hundred-headed monster Typhoeus were also born this way.

Of course, other myths attribute many children to Zeus and Hera, and suggest that Hephaestus was the fruit of their pre-marital relationship, while Ares and Angelos were born after Zeus and Hera married. Angelos attached herself to the souls of the deceased and became a deity of the Underworld after her relationship with Hera was disrupted by the theft of a face cream.

Hera's rage at her husband's infidelities knew no bounds. She even conspired with Athena and Poseidon to overthrow him, and would have succeeded if Thetis had not rushed to his assistance by bringing the hideous Hecatoncheiras Briareus (called Aegaeon by mortals) to Mount Olympus and seating him next to Zeus, thus scaring off the rebels and forcing them to cancel their plans.

Hera then trained her rage on the nymphs as well as on Zeus's mortal lovers and their children:
- delayed Alcmene's childbirth by nine days, then sent a serpent to strangle the infant Heracles;
- she persuaded the pregnant Semele to demand that Zeus appear before her in his godly form and sent the Titans to dismember Dionysus;
- she drove Ino and her husband Athamas mad because they agreed to raise the infant Dionysus;
- she relentlessly pursued Leto making it impossible for Leto to rest for a minute to give birth. Hera then sent a snake to attack Leto;
- she turned Callisto into a bear and sent Artemis to kill her;
- she chased Io, who had been changed into a cow, and then had the many-eyed dog Argo guard Io.

Hera's vengefulness was not exhausted with these actions and she punished anyone who dared challenge her. A prime example was the crisis precipitated by Paris, who chose Aphrodite over Hera as the greater beauty. Thus, in the Trojan campaign Hera took the side of the Achaeans and brought many calamities to the Trojan camp. She was equally harsh in her punishment of the daughters of Proetus, either because they claimed to be more beautiful than Hera or because they ridiculed the sparseness of her sanctuary at Argos.

Yet in spite of his dalliances, Zeus did not allow anyone to covet his bride, which is why he punished Endymion, a king of Elis, by putting him to eternal sleep and deceived Ixion, a Thessalian king, by shaping a cloud in Hera's likeness.

Hera and Zeus. Hera, ready for marriage according to one interpretation of the shape of her mouth, is the model of a woman who devotes herself to a single man. She thus personifies the institutional and legal aspects of marriage, without overlooking the sexual aspects of her marital duties.

The cult of Hera

Hera was worshipped in all Greek cities and foreign colonies. Indeed, the Temple of Hera at Lacinia near Croton was the center of a massive celebration; the head of the statue of Hera Lacinia was the symbol of the alliance formed by the Greek cities of Lower Italy and Sicily. In the Greek world, the main centers for the worship of Hera in Homeric times were at Argos, Sparta, and Mycenae, while in historic times, there were temples dedicated to Hera – known as *Heraion* – at Argos and on the island of Samos.

Grand festivals were held in honor of the goddess throughout Greece. These festivals were known as *Heraia* and included athletic competitions, processions, dancing, and animal sacrifices known as Hecatombaea. It is worth noting that girls also took part in the footraces held every five years at Olympia at the *Heraion*. The winners were crowned with an olive branch and had the right to place their image in the sacred grove or Altis.

Hera's gold throne, scepter, and crown were the symbols of her power. Her favorite animals and birds were the cow, the peacock, and the cuckoo, while her favorite plants were the lily and the pomegranate.

Heraion on the Corinthina Gulf near Loutraki.

Stone head, possibly from cult statue of Hera in the Olympia Heraion, 600 B.C. (Olympia Archaeological Museum).

Argive Heraion
The famed sanctuary dedicated to Hera was located at Argos on a hillock once known as Euboea. Excavations of the site at the end of the 19th century unearthed several structures including a temple, stoa, and palaistra. The most impressive was the Heraion, or main temple, that was built over an early structure dated to the eighth century B.C. and destroyed by fire (423 B.C.).
The Argive Eupolemus is believed to have been the architect of the Doric peristyle, which contained a chryselephantine (gold and ivory) statue of Hera by Polykleitos who depicted the goddess sealed on a throne clasping a scepter.
Polykleitos's brother Naukides later made a chryselephantine statue of Hebe that was placed next to the statue of Hera. Unfortunately, neither statue has survived.

POSEIDON

Poseidon, god of water and the sea, was an important deity of the seafaring Greeks. He lived at the bottom of the Ocean and used his trident –a gift from the Cyclopes or the Telchines– to rule the waves, alternately whipping up the waves or calming them. He was also the god of earthquakes and could rock the earth, which he also kept floating on the sea; he used his trident to create straits, ports, islands, and springs.

A son of Cronus and Rhea, Poseidon was considered by some ancient writers as being older than Zeus, thus he never forgave his brother for snatching power. By other mythological accounts, Poseidon was younger than Zeus and spared his father's bulimia because his mother hid him among a flock of sheep grazing near the Arni spring in Mantineia.

Myths about how Poseidon was raised are similar to those myths about Zeus's infancy and childhood. Just as the Curetes raised Zeus on Crete, Poseidon was raised by the Telchines and the oceanid Capheira on the island of Rhodes. Poseidon later lay with the Telchines' sister Halia, who bore him six sons and one daughter, Rhode.

Bronze statue of Poseidon of Artemision, 460 B.C. (National Archaeological Museum).

Poseidon and the other Olympian gods

Poseidon and Zeus

Despite his initial negative reaction to Zeus's assumption of power over the world, Poseidon submitted to Zeus's rule. And even though both vied for the love of Thetis –but backed away from their amorous pursuits when they learned that the child she bore would overthrow his father– Poseidon allied himself with Zeus in the battles against the Giants and repeatedly helped Zeus's lovers. For example, he calmed the sea so Zeus, disguised as a bull, could cross it with Europa. He also gave refuge to Leto, raising the island of Delos from the sea, and assisted Io who was pursued by Hera across the sea.

Nereid and sea monster on gold medal from Olympic Games, 225-250 B.C. (Thessaloniki Museum).

Poseidon and Hera

Poseidon and Hera collaborated to overthrow Zeus, then found themselves opposing each other over rule of Argos. Their dispute was settled in court, which ratified Hera's jurisdiction over the area. Angry, Poseidon punished the Argives by drying the rivers, then sending a huge tidal wave to flood the land. To mollify the god, the Argives built a temple in honor of *Poseidon Proclysteios* (or Poseidon who brings the flood).

Poseidon and Athena

Poseidon's application to become the patron of Athens was as unsuccessful as his bid for Argos. The Athenians chose Athena, who had given them the gift of the olive tree. Poseidon reacted in his usual way: by causing a flood. The deluge covered the Thriaecian plain and most of Attica. According to other accounts, Poseidon competed against several gods for patronage of a city-state, but always lost.

Poseidon's marriage and romances

Poseidon and Amphitrite

Amphitrite was Poseidon's legal bride. Hesiod writes in *The Theogony* that the sea goddess was a nereid, one of seven daughters born to Nereus and Doris. Apollodorus wrote that she was one of the oceanids, a daughter of Oceanus and Tethys, while Eratosthenes wrote that Amphitrite was a daughter of Atlas.

Poseidon had seen Amphitrite playing on Naxos with her sisters, fell in love with her, and kidnapped her. By one account, Amphitrite did not wish to unite with Poseidon, so she sought help from either Oceanus or Atlas, who hid her. Her hiding place was discovered by Delphinus, who led her to Poseidon. The grateful sea-god then immortalized the dolphin by turning him into a constellation and placing him in the sky among the other stars. Three children were born from the union of Poseidon and Amphitrite: Triton, Rhode, and Benthesicyme.

Although Poseidon had a number of extramarital adventures, Amphitrite was not jealous and never created a scene. She only intervened on one occasion, changing the beautiful nymph Scylla into a hideous monster. Amphitrite became queen of the sea and protectress of marine animals. Because of her marriage to Poseidon, she was named *Poseidonia* and her cult was widespread on the islands of Tenos, Syros, and Lesbos.

Poseidon and Demeter

Following the example set by Zeus, Poseidon fell in love with his sister Demeter, who changed into a mare and hid among the horses of Ogygus. But Poseidon turned himself into a stallion and took her by force. Enraged, the goddess of agriculture took the title Erinys (fury) and went to bathe in the Ladonas River to cleanse herself, thus acquiring the byname *Demeter Louseia*. From her union with Poseidon she bore a daughter, whose name was a secret revealed only at mysteries, and the divine horse Areion that had a human voice.

Poseidon and Medusa

Disguised as a horse, Poseidon lay with Medusa, who, according to one account was a beautiful Centaur. Because their union took place in the Temple of Athena, the goddess of virginity

Clay head of Medusa (Eretria Museum).

THE OLYMPIAN GODS

Trident drawing on ancient Greek coin (Numismatic Museum).

punished the sacrilegious Medusa by turning her beautiful head of hair into a head of snakes. Medusa bore Poseidon the two famous horses, Chrysaor and Pegasus, who sprang from her body after Perseus beheaded her.

Poseidon and Gaea

Poseidon also took Gaea as a lover. From their union was born the Giant Antaeus, who is mentioned as the king of the city of Isara in Libya. The larger-than-life Antaeus represents the indigenous people who were unfavorably disposed towards the Greek colonists, thus he appears in most myths as a tough and undefeated wrestler who fought every stranger who visited his land. Pindar writes that Antaeus drew his strength from the earth; he killed his opponents and used their skulls to build a temple to his father, Poseidon. But Antaeus was defeated by Heracles who, using a special wrestling technique, raised Antaeus over his head. Holding the giant above the earth, Heracles severed Antaeus's connection with the source of his power and strangled him.

Poseidon and Amymone

Amymone, a daughter of Danaus and Europa, was another one of Poseidon's lovers. She arrived in the Argolid with her father and fifty sisters. Their land was suffering from drought, and Danaus had dispatched his daughters to find water. On the way, Amymone shot a deer, but her arrow missed its target and hit a satyr. He tried to rape her, but ran away when Poseidon appeared. Having saved the young woman, the sea-god lay with her. Wishing to please her further, he struck his trident against the ground and made water flow from the spring of Amymone, later named the spring of Lerna. Amymone bore Poseidon a son, Nauplius, who founded the city of Nauplion.

Statue of Poseidon of Milos, 130 B.C. (National Archaeological Museum).

Sea horse and nymph, first century B.C., on mosaic from Rhodes.

Poseidon and Aethra

Poseidon also fell in love with Aethra, a daughter of Pittheus, the king of Troezen, and bride of Aegeus. The child born from their union was Theseus, although many ancient writers claim that this myth was made up by Aegeus himself to give his son a divine origin. Aethra's life ended in tragedy, as she was taken prisoner by the Dioscuri who gave her to Helen of Troy as slave. She was taken with Helen to Troy; after the city was sacked, her grandsons recognized her, but she took her own life on hearing of her son's death.

Poseidon and Melanippe

Melanippe, the daughter of Aeolus, bore Poseidon two sons: Aeolus the younger and Boeotus. To punish her for laying with Poseidon, her father had her eyes gouged out and left her children exposed in the wild, where they were rescued and raised by shepherds. Meantime, Theano, wife of Metapontus, king of Icaria, was having trouble conceiving. She found the twins and presented them as hers. Later, when she gave birth to her own children, she sought to get rid of Aeolus and Boeotus so she arranged a competition in which they were pitted against her own children. Aeolus and Boeotus defeated Theano's children and killed them, causing Theano to kill herself. The twins later avenged the blinding of their mother Melanippe. Poseidon then intervened and restored her sight. Melanippe then married Metapontus.

Poseidon and Mestra

Mestra was the daughter of the Thessalian king Erysichthon, who angered Demeter by cutting down trees in a forest consecrated to the goddess. As punishment, she condemned Erysichthon to eternal hunger. To sate his hunger, Erysichthon sold all his possessions to buy food. He even sold his daughter, with whom Poseidon was smitten. Thus the sea-god gave his beloved the power to change her shape so she could return home, where her father would sell her once more. Mestra changed into a mare, a deer, and a cow. She bore Poseidon one son, Ogygus.

Poseidon and Tyro

In *The Odyssey*, Homer narrates the tale of Poseidon's love for the beautiful Tyro, who was in love with the handsome river Enipeus. To lay with Tyro, Poseidon took the form of her beloved. Two children were born from their union: Pelias and Neleus. Pelias became the king of Iolcus and was the one who sent Jason on the quest for the golden fleece. Neleus settled in Messenia, where he founded the city of Pylos.

He had twelve children, one of which the sage Nestor – the only one who survived Heracles's rage when Neleus refused to cleanse the hero for the murder of Eyrytus.

Poseidon and Astypalaea

Astypalaea, a daughter of Phoenix and Peremide (a daughter of Peneus) and sister of Europa, was also one of Poseidon's lovers. She bore the sea-god a son, Ancaeus, captain of the Argos and the Lelegian king of Sami, on the Ionian island of Cephallonia. Ancaeus later colonized the Aegean island of Samos and married Samia, daughter of the river-god Maeander.

Aristotle writes that Ancaeus was an excellent viticulturist, but that he was very tough on his workers. While working in the vineyards, one of the slaves predicted that Ancaeus would never drink the wine made from a particular vine. Later, when the wine was ready and Ancaeus was about to open the barrel, he called the slave to him and reminded him of his prediction.

The slave responded that much could happen in the time that it took Ancaeus to raise the glass of wine to his lips. Indeed, just as he was ready to take a sip, he was informed that a wild bore was loose in the land. He put down his glass and went to hunt the beast, which killed him. The prophecy thus came true and inspired the ancient Greek adage that much can happen in the time that it takes to raise a glass to the lips.

Apollodorus, however, claims that Astypalaea bore Poseidon a son, Eurypylus, the mythical king of the Meropians of Cos who was the father of Heracles's wife, Chalciope.

Poseidon and Chione

Chione was a daughter of Boreas and Oreithyia and sister of Zetes and Calais. Poseidon seduced her and fathered her child, Eumolpus.

Poseidon's other children

Founders of cities

Since many of the Greek tribes claimed divine ancestry, Poseidon was named as the father of numerous children. These include Eurypylus, the king of Cyrene whom Poseidon fathered with Atlas's daughter Celaeno; Byzantus, the founder of Byzantium who was born from his union with the Ceroessa; Dyrraheios, the eponym of Dyrraheion in Elyria who was born of Poseidon's union with Epidamnus's daughter Melissa; Delphus, and the eponym of Delphi whom he fathered with Deucalion's daughter Melantho. Poseidon was also believed to be the father of Ialyssus, eponym of the Rhodian city; Calaurius, the hero and eponym of Calaureia (Poros), and Phocus, the eponym of Phocis.

Busiris

Busiris was the son of Poseidon and Epaphus's daughter Libya or Lysianassa (Isocrates). He was also one of the cruelest kings of Egypt. On the advice of the Cypriot seer Phrasius, he sacrificed all strangers to Zeus to placate the god and end a nine-year drought that plagued Memphis. Busiris's first sacrifice was the Cypriot seer and he continued offering strangers to Zeus until Heracles arrived to visit. The Greek hero killed Busiris, his son Iphidamon, the herald Chalios, and all of Busiris's servants, thus putting an end to the ritual sacrifices.

Amycus

Amycus was the king of the Bebryces. His name means "to mangle" or shred. According to mythology, he was the son of Poseidon and the nymph Melie. He was quite inhospitable and would forcibly challenge all strangers to a boxing match, when he would kill them. According to Apollonius Rhodius and Apollodorus, he was defeated and killed by the one of the Dioscuri, Polydeuces, when the Argonauts landed in Bebryces. According to Theocritus, the Dioscuri came upon Amycus while he was sleeping in the woods and forced him to swear on his father Poseidon that he would never box with a stranger again. According to one account, a laurel tree sprouted from his grave and would spew swearwords if its branches were disturbed.

A wall-painting of dolphins at the Queen's Palace in Knossos (1600 B.C., Archaeological Museum of Heraklion, Crete).

Cercyon

Cercyon, the mythical king of Eleusis, was another one of Poseidon's sons. He, too, forced strangers to wrestle with him, then killed them during their contest. Cercyon later suffered the same fate at the hands of Theseus. Cercyon fathered a daughter, Alope. She was seduced by her grandfather Poseidon and bore him a son, Hippothoon, the eponym of one of the ten tribes of Athens.

Sceiron – Sinis – Procrustes

Mythological accounts list Scieron among the cruel, bloodthirsty sons fathered by Poseidon and killed by Theseus en route from Troezen to Athens. Scieron was a warlord who lay in wait at the Sceironian Rocks (Kakia Skala) for travelers, forcing them to wash his feet. As soon they kneeled, he would toss them over the cliff into the sea, where a tortoise devoured them. Sceiron suffered a similar fate at the hands of Theseus.

Sinis, also known as *Pityocamptes* (Pinebender), was another outlaw killed by Theseus. Sinis staked out the entrance to the Corinth isthmus and killed travelers by tying their hands to two pines. He would then bend the pines and release them suddenly, thus tearing his victims in two.

Another criminal fathered by the sea-god was Procrustes (Stretcher), whose real name was either Polypemon or Damastes. Procrustes lived in the plain between Eleusis and Attica. He would capture travelers, then lay them on a bed. If they were taller than the bed, Procrustes would chop off their limbs so that they fit. If they were shorter than the bed, he would use a hammer to flatten and extend their limbs until they reached the edge of the bed.

Theseus killed Procrustes in the same way the robber had killed travelers.

Eryx

A Sicilian hero and king of the Elymians, Eryx was the son of Poseidon and Aphrodite, according to one account. (In other mythological accounts he was the son of the Argonaut Butes.) Eryx was also in the habit of challenging strangers to wrestling matches, then killing them. Heracles put an end to these murders when he happened to arrive in Sicily with the cattle of Geryon. Heracles defeated and killed Eryx, thus ridding his land of a tyrant.

Polyphemus

Polyphemus, a man-eating, one-eyed Cyclops, was the son of Poseidon and the nymph Thoosa. He lived in a semi-wild state with the other Cyclopes on an island, where he grazed sheep and goats, but did not farm or follow the rules of an organized society. Odysseus and his sailors landed on Polyphemus's island on their journey back from Troy. Polyphemus trapped them in his cave and ate several members of Odysseus's crew until the clever hero deceived the Cyclops. He got Polyphemus drunk, then blinded him, and smuggled his sailors out of the cave tied to the bellies of sheep and goats that Polyphemus had let out to graze. Odysseus's hubris angered Poseidon, who whipped up the seas, further delaying Odysseus's return to Ithaca.

Cycnus

Poseidon is also cited as the father of the Trojan hero Cycnus, who was the result of the sea-god's union with Skamandronice. Cycnus owes his name to the whiteness of his skin or, according to another account, to the fact that he was raised by a swan (*kiknos* is Greek for swan). From his first marriage, Cycnus had two children, Tenes and Hemithea. After their stepmother Philonome made accusations against them, Cycnus locked the children into a trunk and threw it into the sea. The trunk eventually reached an island, which was named Tenedos after Tenes. Their heartless father was later killed on the island in a duel with Achilles.

Orion

Orion appears in *The Odyssey* as a famous hunter who continued to indulge his sport in Hades even after his death. According to one account, Orion was the son of Poseidon and Euryale, the daughter of Minos whose father had given her the ability to walk on the waves. Orion's beauty caught the eye of Eos, who kidnapped him; Artemis was also attracted to the youth. Upset by his sister's love for Orion, Apollo challenged Artemis to hit a dark, barely visible object in the sea with her arrow. This object was Orion, who was thus killed by the arrows of his beloved. To console herself, she immortalized him as a constellation and placed him in the heavens next to the hound Sirius.

According to another myth, Orion was born from the hide of a bull that Poseidon, Apollo, and Hermes gave to Hyrieus – Poseidon's son by the Pleiade Alcyone. Hyrieus buried the hide in the ground and nine months later a child, Orion, grew from that spot. Artemis also figures in another account of Orion's death, in which she is disconcerted by his advances and kills him with the sting of a deadly scorpion. A slightly different account claims that she sent the scorpion to earth after Orion bragged that no animal could escape his arrows.

Mythology links Orion to the northeastern Aegean island of Chios. Orion visited the island to rid it of wild animals, then fell in love with and raped Merope, daughter of King Oenopion (the son of Dionysus and Ariadne). To avenge his daughter's rape, Oenopion blinded Orion. He regained his sight by carrying one of Hephaestus's workers on his shoulders as a guide to the east where Helius could be found. Cycnus later returned to Chios to seek revenge on Oenopion, but was not able to find the king as he had hidden in a basement.

In Boeotian myths, Orion fell in love and pursued the Pleiades for five years until Zeus turned them into a constellation.

Otus and Ephialtes

According to one tradition, the mythical giants Otus and Ephialtes were born to Poseidon and Iphimedeia, daughter of Triops (by another account, they are Poseidon's grandsons from Aloeus, while in Iphimedeia appears in some accounts as Poseidon's daughter). The giants grew so quickly that at the ages of nine they were nine *oryies* (about fifty feet) tall and nine *pychis* (about 27 feet) wide. Arrogant and confident of their strength, they wanted to change land into sea and sea into land, so they could climb up to the heavens and attack Zeus. Thus, they piled Mount Pelion on Mount Ossa and Mount Ossa on Mount Olympus. Their strength was so great that they captured and held the war-god Ares, who was freed with assistance from Hermes.

There are various accounts of how the two giants were punished by Zeus – Ephialtes for falling love with Hera and Otus for falling in love with Artemis. According to one account, the giants killed each other on the islands of Naxos while hunting a deer sent by Artemis as punishment for Otus's sacrilegious advances. After their death, the giants were tied back-to-back in Underworld, where snakes slithered over their bodies and a crow continuously cawed in their ears.

The cult of Poseidon

As the god of the sea, Poseidon was worshipped in all coastal settlements and on all islands, while sanctuaries dedicated to the god were usually found on capes –such as the famed Temple of Poseidon at Cape Sounion– or near springs, rivers, lakes, or caves. Numerous cities bore his name. These cities include Troezen, which was originally called Posidonia, Posidonia in Lower Italy, and Posidonia on the island of Syros (which has since be renamed Dellagrazia).

Elaborate celebrations were staged in Poseidon's honor that featured the sacrifice of horses or bulls that were then thrown into the sea. Fish, pigs, and wild boar were also sacrificed to the sea-god.

The cult of Poseidon seems to have begun in Thessaly, where the earliest myths about the sea-god originated. From Thessaly, the worship of Poseidon spread to Boeotia, where one of his sons –Minyas– became king of Orchomenus. The only known oracle devoted to Poseidon was located at Ogchistos.

Poseidon was worshipped at Delphi before the sanctuary was dedicated to Apollo. The sea-god was the father of the hero Delphius as well as of Parnassus.

The cult of the sea-god was widespread in the Peloponnese, where temples dedicated to the god existed at Patras, Rio, Aegeio, Helike, Aegae,

Pellini, Genesio in the Argolid, in Arcadian Mantineia, in Sparta, at Cape Tainaron, in Elis, and at Olympia.

But the most famous temple dedicated to Poseidon in the Peloponnese was at the Corinth isthmus. Panhellenic athletic competitions known as the *Isthmia* were held near the Temple of Poseidon. These games were originally linked to the chthonic worship of the hero Melicertes-Palaemon. According to tradition, Theseus founded the games after he rid the area of the sea-god's bandit sons.

The *Isthmian Games* were held every three years at the end of April, between the second and third years of each Olympiad. They were known as *stephanites* (*stephani* is Greek for wreath) competitions as the winner received as a prize a wreath made of dried celery, which was later replaced by a wreath made from the branches of the sacred pine that grew near the Temple of Poseidon. Contests were held in riding, music, sailing, and gymnastics in three categories of competition: men, youths (who had not yet grown beards) and children. A horse race was also held where competitors raced a distance equal to the length of four stadia.

Of course, temples dedicated to Poseidon are also found on islands like Evia (Euboea) and Skyros in the Northern Sporades, and Syros and Tinos in the Cyclades. On Naxos, Dionysus supplanted Poseidon. He was also worshipped in Greek colonies, especially at Syvari and Taranta in Sicily, while there were also impressive temples dedicated to Poseidon at Syracuse and Selinounda.

Poseidon crushes Polybotes in the battle against the Giants. Polybotes has been associated with the birth of the Dodecanese island of Nisyros. According to mythology, the island was formed when Poseidon used his trident to break off a piece of the island of Kos that he then used to crush the giant, thus creating a new island (Rhodian mosaic).

ATHENA

The virgin goddess of war Athena was one of the most important deities among the twelve gods of Mount Olympus. She was loved throughout the Greek world and accorded various characteristics. The epic poets Homer and Hesiod refer to Athena as the favorite daughter of Zeus and call her *omvrimopatri*, that is, the daughter of a powerful father. Both narrate the tale of her unusual birth, which today is considered a metaphor for meteorological phenomena such as clouds, thunder, lightning, storms, and rain.

In *Theogony*, Hesiod describes how Uranus and Gaea persuaded Zeus to swallow his pregnant wife Metis, who was wiser than gods and human, so he would not risk losing his power. When Metis reached term, Hephaestus (or, by some accounts, Prometheus) split open Zeus's skull and out sprung Athena, fully formed and dressed in armor. At the exact moment of her birth, the sky was torn and a loud noise echoed across the earth, while enormous waves whipped the sea, and the sun stopped moving across the sky until Athena removed her armor.

There are several versions of Athena's birth. According to one, she emerged on Crete from a cloud that Zeus struck with his thunderbolt. In another version, Zeus fought with her so she would emerge from his head. In yet another, she appears as the daughter of Pallas, a winged Giant, whom she later killed because he tried to seduce her. Athena is sometimes mentioned as the daughter or Itonos, or Hephaestus, or Poseidon, or Triton, who disowned her father after an argument and was later adopted by Zeus.

Athena's epithet *Tritogeneia* is also related to her origin as it links her with Triton, the trumpeter of the sea. Yet the

Athena Varvakeios. A Roman copy of the chryselephantine (gold and ivory) statue of the goddess by Pheidias that was located inside the Parthenon (National Archaeological Museum).

most widespread interpretation of this epithet links the name to Athena's birthplace near the Tritonis spring. Depending on local variations, the spring was located in Thessaly, Arcadia, Boeotia, or on Crete, while by some accounts the Tritonis was located in Libya or at the far end of the earth.

The Palladium

Several myths relate how the epithet "*Pallas*" came to be attached to the goddess Athena. By one account, it was inspired by the vibrating spear in Athena's hand when she was born (from the Greek verb *pallo*, which means vibrate or brandish). According to the other accounts, the epithet's origin is Pallas, the sea-god Triton's daughter with whom Athena was raised. One day, as the two girls quarreled while playing. Zeus, who had been observing them, feared that Pallas might strike Athena so he placed his shield, or *aegis*, in front of her. Athena took advantage of this and struck back at her playmate, who died from the blow. Grief-stricken at the loss of her friend, Athena made a statue of Pallas and dressed it with the shield that had frightened the young girl. She placed the statue next to Zeus, who later flung it towards Helius as Atlas's daughter Electra –who bore Zeus two children, Iasion and Dardanus– dangled from it. According to one version, Zeus gave the Palladium to Dardanus, king of Troy, who kept the statue hidden in the innermost recesses of Troy's temple because the city's fortune depended on the statue's safety.

Athena and the other Olympian gods

Athena and Zeus

Athena was Zeus's favorite child and fought valiantly at his side in the battle against the Giants, which is why she is also sometimes called *Gigantoleteira, Gigantoletis,* or *Gigantofontis* (giant slayer). But according to Homer, Athena conspired with Hera and Poseidon to bind Zeus when his authoritarianism became unbearable, but this quarrel did not affect their relationship.

Athena and Hephaestus

In Greek mythology, Athena personified virginity, but one myth from Attica relates how Hephaestus tried to rape her. The goddess fought back, but some of Hephaestus's semen dribbled on her leg. She wiped it off with a bit of wool and flung it on the ground. Erichthonius, an early king of Athens, was born on the spot where Hephaestus's sperm fell.

Athena and Poseidon

One ancient myth held that Athena was the daughter of Poseidon with the oceanid Coryphe. But the most interesting story linking Athena and Poseidon concerns their competition to become patron of Attica. Several versions of this battle have come to light, but two are most prevalent:
- Poseidon struck his trident against the rock of the Acropolis, causing either a saline spring or a horse –which symbolized potable water– emerged from the crack, signaling the god's intention to either turn the inhabitants of Attica towards the sea or enrich their land with plenty of water. Athena

then struck the rock with her spear, and an olive tree sprouted in the crevice. The Olympian gods judged Athena to be the winner of the contest and she became the protectress of the Athens. She taught the Athenians how to cultivate the olive tree and produce olive oil, but the city-state suffered from severe drought.

- The citizens of Athens were called on to choose which of the two gods they wanted as their patron. The men voted for Poseidon and the women, who had the right to vote, cast their ballots for Athena who won because the women outnumbered the men. Poseidon then flooded the country; its inhabitants sought to mollify the sea-god by stripping women of the right to vote, the right to give their name to their children, and the right to call themselves Athenians.

Athena and Aphrodite

Athena considered her boyish, virgin looks to be superior to those of Aphrodite so she vied against the goddess of love for the apple of Eris, goddess of discord. Athena never forgave either Paris or the Trojans for choosing Aphrodite over her. The antagonistic relationship between Athena and the goddess of beauty and love comes across quite clearly in *The Iliad*, as Athena protects the Achaeans, advising and assisting Diomedes to strike the Trojans' protectress, Aphrodite.

Athena and Apollo

According to some accounts, Athena vied against Apollo for his prophetic powers as well as the fortune-telling skills he had learned from the Thriae, winged nymphs of Mount Parnassus who could divine the future by reading pebbles on the beds of torrents. But Zeus favored Apollo in this instance. Angered, Athena tossed a handful of pebbles down on one of the plains of Attica, which has since been known as the Thriaecian plain.

Relief of the goddess Athena, protectress of Athens, 460 B.C. (Acropolis Museum). As the city of Athens grew, the goddess was not only worshipped as the protectress of home and family in the broader sense of these terms and was thus also worshipped as the protectress of the city's residents and their peaceful occupations.

Athena and the Greek heroes

Athena and Heracles

Athena repeatedly favored Heracles, for instance by helping him kill the Stymphalian birds. He, in turn, gave her the golden apples from the garden of the Hesperides, which Athena returned to the garden.

Athena and Perseus

According to an Argive myth, Athena helped Perseus slay Gorgon, a monster so hideous that anyone who looked at it would be turned to stone. Euripides, however, attributes the Gorgon's death to the goddess herself, which may explain the poets' use of the epithet *Gorgofonos*, *Gorgopis*, and *Gorgo* for Athena.

In either case, the Gorgon's head was placed on Athena's shield where it retained its power to turn those who looked at it to stone. Athena's shield or *aegis* was a basic component of the suit of armor she had been given by Zeus and which was made either from the hide of the goat Amaltheia or from the hide of the Aigis (goat), a horrid Phrygian monster that Athena killed.

Athena and Bellerophon

When the Gorgon was beheaded, the winged horse Pegasus sprung from the wound. Athena helped the Corinthian hero Bellerophon tame the horse by appearing to Bellerophon in his dream and giving him a magic golden bridle.

The many guises of Athena

The ancient Greeks recognized several traits in Athena, including the powers of war, peace, protection, and healing. She thus had many epithets. She was a goddess who loved battle and her fighting powers that were superior to those possessed by the war-god Ares. She inspired courage, prudence, and valor, guaranteeing victory to those whose side she took in battle. For this reason, she was worshipped as *Athena Nike*, as well as *Akraia*, since the sanctuaries dedicated to Athena in the

Bronze gorgon from the Acropolis, early fifth century B.C. (National Archaeological Museum).

THE OLYMPIAN GODS

Athena. Detail from the metope, or square panel of frieze, of the Temple of Zeus at Olympia, 460 B.C. (Olympia Archaeological Museum).

acropolis of a city-state were usually the last refuge during an enemy attack.

Athena is also credited as a trainer of warhorses, and is therefore worshipped as *Damasippos* (horse tamer) as well as *Hippia* (horse rider). She was also credited with inventing the *pyrichios*, or war dance, that was performed with great energy during the *Panathenaic Festival*. She instructed Danaus on how to build the first warship, the *pentikondoro*, which was a trireme with fifty oars – a figure inspired by the number of daughters Danaus had. A trireme always brought the mantle to the Acropolis during the *Panathenaic Festival*.

As a protectress of cities, Athena is known by the epithets *Erysiptolis*, *Poliouchos*, *Polias*, *Poliatis*, or *Poliarchos*. She was the head of the *ekklesia* (assembly) of the *demos* (administrative district of Athens) and is acknowledged as the founder of the *Areopagus*, or Supreme Court, from which she also earned the epithet *Areia*.

Athena was the goddess of peaceful works, prudence, intellect, and political alliances. She is the *mother-god* because protects women from infertility, but is also known as *Hygieia* (health) for showing Pericles how to cure a worker who was severely injured during the reconstruction of the Propylaia on the Acropolis.

Protectress of music

The ancient Greeks believed that it was Athena who taught mortals about the arts such as music, and that she first invented both the war bugle and the flute.

When Perseus beheaded the Gorgon, mortal cries were heard emitted by the monster's sisters Stheno and Euryale. These sounds came from the snakes that emerged from their heads. To imitate these sounds, Athena made holes in the bone of a deer and played the new instrument she had invented on Mount Olympus. But Hera and Aphrodite made fun of Athena because her face became distorted when she blew into the flute. Angry, Athena went to a river to observe her reflection in the water as she played the instrument. Seeing that Hera and Aphrodite had been right in ridiculing her, she threw the instrument away and cursed anyone who dared pick it up.

Patron of the arts

Homer writes that Athena wove her own mantle as well as Hera's clothes, and taught women to spin yarn from wool, weave, and embroider. She is thus worshipped as *Ergani*, or industrious; her symbol is the shuttle, which she is depicted as holding on the Palladium. The myth of Arachne, the famed weaver of Lydia, is linked to these skills.

Arachne competed against Athena in a weaving contest, then tried to hang herself after losing to the goddess. Athena then turned the girl into a spider (or *arachne* in Greek), an insect that is condemned to weaving beautiful, yet ephemeral works.

Athena also taught men the art of agriculture and is worshipped as *Agriska* or *Agrypha*. She also taught them how to yoke oxen to plows and carts, for which she earned the epithet *Boudeia* or *Boarmeia* in Thessaly and Boeotia.

Athena also invented the arts and crafts of pottery, shoe-making, goldsmithery, etching, pyrography, sculpture, architecture, construction, and metalworking –and is thus worshipped as *Machanitis*– as well as navigation. She is also known as *Anemotis*, or protectress of the winds, and *Aithnia*, protectress of swimming.

Athena of Piraeus.
Work by Kiphisidotus or Ephranoros,
fourth century B.C.
(Piraeus Archaeological Museum).

DEMETER

Demeter, the goddess of agriculture, was the daughter of Cronus and Rhea, so she shared the fate of her siblings Poseidon, Hades, Hera, and Hestia until Zeus deposed her father. It is widely believed that her name is derived from the words *da* or *di*, which meant earth, and *mitir*, which means mother – hence, *Dimitra*. It is also widely held that Demeter was a new name for Gaea, who embraced seeds with her mysterious forces and made them grow and flourish, producing rich harvests. (in Greek, cereals are called *dimitriaka*).

Contrary to those who consider Demeter as a Greek goddess, identifying her as the evolution of the Great Mother Goddess, Rhea, Cybele, or the Creto-Mycenaean matriarchal deity, Herodotus claims that Demeter is the Egyptian goddess Isis, whose worship was introduced into the Peloponnese by the Pelasgians and then spread by the Arcadians. The most important sanctuaries dedicated to Demeter were found in Thessaly, Arcadia, Attica, and Boeotia.

Demeter's loves

Homer (*The Odyssey*) and other ancient writers mention the myth of Demeter's love for the hero Iasion, a son of Minos and the nymph Phronia or, alternatively, the child of Coroebus and Electra who united in a thrice-plowed field. Indeed, Hesiod mentions that their holy marriage –a centerpiece of the Eleusinian mysteries– took place on Crete (*Theogony*). According to several versions, Iasion was struck by a thunderbolt thrown by Zeus, who had changed into a bull to woo Demeter; Persephone was born from their union.

But Poseidon also desired his sister. To escape his advances, she changed into a mare and hid herself among the horses of Ogygus, son of Apollo. But the sea-god changed himself into a stallion and forced himself on her. Two children were born from their union: a daughter whose name no one dared utter and the horse Areion.

Demeter seated on a throne as she greets Kore, who is carrying torches. (Relief, 480 B.C., Elefsina Archaeological Museum).

The myth of Erysichthon

Erysichthon or Aethon was a Thessalian hero and son of either Triopas or Myrmidon and a grandson of Poseidon. Demeter considered Erysichthon to be the most hateful creature in the world, so she punished him by cursing him with an insatiable hunger. Callimachus related this legend in his hymn to Demeter, as well as by the writers Lycophron, Nicander, and Ovid.

According to these accounts, there was a sacred grove dedicated to the goddess at Dotios in Thessaly. An enormous oak grew in the middle of this grove. The oak's tip touched the heavens, and locals had decorated the tree with ribbons and dedications. But Erysichthon –who was arrogant, disrespectful, and greedy– decided to destroy the sacred woods and chop the oak to use its timber to build a hall for symposia. Because none of his slaves dared fell the tree, he cut it himself.

Demeter punished his sacrilegious act with the curse of bulimia. After eating everything in his house, Erysichthon wandered out on the streets, eating the food worshippers left for Hecate, but without being able to satisfy his hunger. To get money to buy more food, he sold his beloved daughter Mestra, who was Poseidon's lover. But the sea-god gave her the power to change form, so she kept returning to her father, who would then sell her again. After many long, tormenting years, Erysichthon died by devouring himself.

Persephone. Detail from wall painting known as the "Burial of Persephone" (Vergina).

Demeter and Kore

The primary myth centered on Demeter involves the abduction of her beloved daughter Persephone. (The ancient Greeks had a hard time pronouncing her pre-Hellenic name, which was given in the Eleusinian worship and spread through the Homeric hymn to Demeter). According to this myth, Hades –with the consent of Zeus– snatched Demeter's daughter as she was gathering flowers and led her to his dark kingdom. Demeter heard the cries of *Kore* (literally, daughter) and ran to her assistance, but was too late: the young woman had disappeared from the face of the earth. Grief-stricken, the goddess wandered around the land for nine days without washing or eating, carrying lit brands, mourning for her daughter completely.

On the tenth day, Demeter encountered Hecate and went with her to

see Helius, who told her what had happened to her daughter. Filled with rage at Zeus and the other gods for looking the other way, she left Mount Olympus and, disguised as an old woman, arrived at Eleusis. There she met the daughters of King Celeus, whom she begged to take her into her home where she would willingly work as a nurse for any infants in the household. Queen Metaneira took her in and employed her as the nurse of her young son Demophoon.

At the palace of Celeus, Demeter took the seat she was offered by the slave Iambe – or Baubo, according to the Orphic version. Iambe realized the old woman was troubled and tried to cheer her up by telling her jokes to make her laugh. She also prepared a special drink, *kykeon*, made from barley, water, and mint. (Kykeon was usually made with wine, which Demeter refused to drink).

The goddess, still disguised as an old woman, assumed the care of Demophoon; to make him immortal, she anointed him with ambrosia in the morning and laid him on embers to sleep at night. But the process of making him immortal was never completed as Metaneira saw the infant laying on the embers and rushed in to save him. Demeter then revealed her identity and asked Celeus to build a sanctuary and altar dedicated to her by the well where she had met his daughters when she had arrived at Eleusis.

The king willingly responded to her request and the goddess confined herself to the temple, where in her loneliness she cursed the heavens and the earth, which became infertile. Famine gripped the land and people began to starve.

In vain, the emissaries sent by Zeus asked her to soften her rage. She sent back the message that she would not return to Mount Olympus or allow the earth grow any vegetation unless she saw her beloved daughter. Zeus was forced to give in and sent Hermes to ask Hades to let Persephone ascend to the earth to see her mother. The god of the Underworld agreed, but fed Persephone with pomegranate seeds –symbols of marriage and fertility– before she left.

Mother and daughter had an emotional reunion, but having eaten the pomegranate fruit Persephone was obliged to return to Hades. Thus Demeter was forced to accept Zeus's suggest-

Pluto and Persephone, 460 B.C. (Reggio Museum, Italy).

ion –conveyed by Rhea at the Rarion plain– that Persephone spends one-third of the year with her husband and the other two-thirds of the year with her mother and the other Olympian gods. Demeter's rage subsided. She blessed the earth, which gave an abundant harvest. She also showed her gratitude to the Eleusinians for their hospitality by inducting the four kings of Eleusis –Triptopolemus, Diocleus, Eumolpus, and Celeus– into its mysteries.

The Eleusinian Mysteries

The Eleusinian Mysteries were the most respected of the sacred mysteries of the ancient Greeks and revealed to the initiated the great secret of life and death, as well as what happens to the soul after death. These mysteries were likely part of the worship rituals of the Pelasgians and were conducted by the royal families of Eleusis. These rituals gained fame in the seventh century B.C., when the kingdom of Eleusis was occupied by Athens and became a *demos*, or administrative district, of the city-state.

There were two Eleusinian mysteries: the great and the lesser mysteries. The lesser Eleusinian mysteries were held during the month of Anthesterion (February). This was a preparatory ritual and participation was mandatory for the initiated that submitted to cleansing and fasting under the guidance of the priest.

The grand Eleusinian mysteries were held during the month of Boedromion (September) and probably lasted for nine days – the number of days Demeter wandered the earth seeking her daughter. Athenians dispatched heralds, or *spondophorous*, throughout Greece to declare a two-month holy truce and invite observers, that is, official representatives to the mysteries.

The priests and priestesses of Eleusis carried the secret altars to Athens in a basket brightly decorated with red ribbons. After they arrived, the mass purification in the sea would commence, followed by sacrifices and the procession of the priests and priestesses back to Eleusis. Along the Sacred Way, the priests would show the *xoana*, or

The so-called "Scene of Ninnius", an old Eleusinian deity, depicts the initiation ritual of the Eleusinian Mysteries. In the upper segment, Demeter is shown with Kore in front of her, while the goddess is shown greeting Iacchus on the bottom right (first half of the fourth century B.C., Elefsina Archaeological Museum).

wooden figures, of Iacchus, conduct sacrifices, and chant hymns to Demeter and Kore. They were received back at Eleusis with a great fanfare.

After cleansing and fasting the mysteries would be held at the Telesterion. There is hardly any information about these rituals as revealing anything about them was an offence punishable by death. The scant information provided by Apollodorus the Athenian, the neo-Platonic Proclus, and the cristian authors, mention a dramatic recreation of the myth of Demeter and Kore known as the *dromena*. In complete darkness, the initiated saw Pluto seize Kore, their sacred wedding, Demeter's search for her daughter, and finally, the liberating light when the goddess and her daughter were reunited and the goddess then taught agriculture to Triptopolemus.

The *dromena* were not the only part of the ritual, which included the *epopteia*, that is, the display of sacred items, which were believed to be the wheat chaff and a replica of genitals symbolizing fertility and life.

The Eleusinian mysteries offered the initiated the prospect of a better earthly life but the hope and expectation of divine eternity after death as the mysteries preached the immortality of the soul. The mysteries were held until 395, when the Goth Alaric who set fire to the Eleusis sanctuary dealt the final blow.

Demeter Thesmophorus

The womb resembles the earth, which embraces the seed, nurtures it for a period, and then allows it to emerge into the light. Thus Demeter became the goddess of marriage who blessed children. At weddings, prayers were offered to Demeter for eugony and fertility. The goddess thus also became the protectress of women and was known as *Demeter Thesmophorus*, or she who protects laws and institutions, women's lives, and marriage. Every year, Athenian women celebrated Demeter and Kore at the *Thesmophoria*, a three-day festival dedicated to the fertility of nature and humankind.

Only married women took part in the *Thesmophoria*; female slaves and

Demeter presenting wheat to the Eleusinian hero Triptolemus, her herald and son of the King Celeus of Eleusis and Metaneira. Triptolemus became the symbol of the transition from shepherding to farming, while his name is linked to the thrice-sown field where Demeter lay with Iasion and later gave birth to Pluto.

Sitos, the fire of the ancient Greeks, symbolized life after death and was born from the earth-mother Demeter. The cycle and symbolism of life, death, and resurrection can be found in most religions. (Relief, circa 440-430 B.C., National Archaeological Museum).

institutions, of which the most important was marriage.

Because human bodies returned to the earth once their life cycle had been completed, in Attica the dead were known as *Demetrians*, that is, those who are returned to the earth. Souls, meantime, descend to Hades, where they are greeted by the breath of the dead and Persephone, Demeter's daughter. In this way, the goddess who gives life –the Mother– and the goddess who takes life but is also the protectress of the fields, Kore, are inextricably bound.

women of loose morals were banned from the celebration. During the festival, which included a procession and fasting, women abstained from all physical contact, wore white dresses, and exchanged vulgar expressions – presumably a part of the ritual that memorialized Iambe's jokes.

But Demeter was also the protectress of society, since people formed permanent settlements around agriculture and created common laws or

Depiction of Demeter in a thick veil with a scepter in her right hand as she offers wheat (not shown) to Triptolemus so he can give it to mortals to sow. On the right is Persephone, who is dressed in an Ionian-style robe and holds a lit torch. (Relief, circa 440-430 B.C., National Archaeological Museum).

APHRODITE

Aphrodite was the Olympian god who represented beauty and love. She inspired love and lust among the gods, mortals, and all the creatures that live on land or in the sea (Homer, *Hymn to Aphrodite*). Although Homer describes her as the daughter of Zeus and the Titan or oceanid Dione (*The Iliad, Hymn To Aphrodite*), it is certain that the cult of Aphrodite arrived in Greece from the east, via Phoenicia, Cyprus, and Cythera – all places where Aphrodite was worshipped under several names. The epithet *Ourania* (heavenly) and the freedom with which Aphrodite and the Phoenician goddess Astarte, queen of the heavens, were worshipped as the goddess of love and carnal desire reveal the lively influence of the Phoenician deity.

Ancient sources provide quite different versions of Aphrodite's birth. In *Theogony*, Hesiod writes that the goddess from the foam that formed in the sea around Uranus's genitals, which his son Cronus had cut off and tossed away. She is thus known as *Aphrodite Urania* as well as by the epithet *Aphrogeneia* (born of the foam). In the Homeric hymns, the Horae, or Seasons, welcome the foam-born Aphrodite in Cyprus and dress her before Hermes and Himeros (desire) escort her to Mount Olympus.

According to a different account, Aphrodite emerged from a conch in which she was taken to Cythera. Plato

Aphrodite of Milos, 150-125 B.C. (Louvre Museum, Paris).

writes that *Pandemos Aphrodite* is the daughter of Zeus and Dione but is the moral opposite of *Urania*. Although no references to Aphrodite have been found in texts written in Linear Script B, the goddess is generally associated with the Great Goddess of the Mediterranean's prehistoric civilizations. She is also the divine companion of the king of gods, the goddess of the heavens, as well as an *hetaira*, or courtesan, and goddess of vegetation and fertility.

Aphrodite and the other Olympian gods

Zeus could not help being affected by Aphrodite's charms and beauty. Whenever the goddess of love lured him into some erotic adventure, she took care to conceal it from his legal bride. Yet Aphrodite also helped Hera rein in her errant husband by giving her a belt that made her sexually irresistible.

In mythology, Aphrodite is sometimes described as being married to the lame fire-god Hephaestus and sometimes to the war-god Ares, with whom she had Eros, Harmonia (who married Cadmus), Deimus (Fear), and Phobus (Panic). According to Homer, Aphrodite was the legal bride of Hephaestus, but was unfaithful to him with Ares.

Aphrodite's mortal lovers

Anchises

Aphrodite did not limit her dalliances to the gods. In retaliation for the lust for mortals that she inspired in the gods, Zeus made the desire to unite with mortals enter her soul, too. The Homeric hymn to the goddess describes how she fell in love with the handsome Anchises as he was tending her herds on the slopes of Mount Ida. After getting ready at her perfumed temple at Paphos, she rushed to meet him, accompanied by panthers, wolves, bears, and lions. Stunned by her beauty, Anchises asked her whether she was an Olympian goddess. Aphrodite lied, telling him that she was the daughter of the Phrygian king Otreus who had come to marry him on the orders of Hermes. Anchises was unable to control his lust and after removing her sparkling jewels

Birth of Aphrodite. According to one tradition, Aphrodite was born from a conch in which she was taken to Cythera.

and beautiful dress, lay with her without knowing that she was an immortal.

When Anchises awoke and saw the goddess dressed in her fine jewels, he asked her to show him mercy as any mortal who united with a goddess could lose his youthful vigor. Aphrodite assured him that he would not be saved from aging, but in exchange she would bear him a son, Aeneas, who would be like a god and who would be raised by the Idaean nymphs.

Aphrodite's benevolence towards Anchistes became a source of bitterness for the goddess because it humbled her in the eyes of her fellow Olympians who, before then, had feared her power to lure them into entanglements with mortals. She advised Anchistes not to reveal the true identity of his son's mother, but to say that he fathered it with some nymph or he would be stricken by one of Zeus's thunderbolts.

Adonis

The myth of Adonis, which originated from the East, presents Aphrodite in two forms. The goddess was enraged by Myrrha or Smyrna, daughter of the Assyrian king Theias for refusing to worship her, so she took her revenge by inspiring in the girl an insatiable lust for her father. Thanks to the collusion of her nurse, Myrrha managed to sate her lust for twelve nights but when Theias realized he had unknowingly committed adultery, he lunged at his daughter in a murderous rage. Frightened, she begged the gods to save her. Her prayer was heard and she was turned into a myrrh tree. Ten months later, the tree's trunk split halfway; a handsome young man emerged. Aphrodite was thoroughly charmed by him and shut him in a trunk that she entrusted to Persephone,

Aphrodite of Rhodes (first century B.C.). Harmonia, who was born from Aphrodite's union with Ares, symbolizes the idea that harmony is a fusion of harsh and tender or wild and tame characteristics. Harmonia is also a somewhat archetypal concept of the coexistence of hate and love or disaster and creation as the dominant elements of life.

Aphrodite (100 B.C.). Detail from group sculpture depicting the goddess with Eros and Pan (National Archaelogical Museum).

asking her to hide him from gods and mortals.

But Persephone fell in love with the handsome Adonis and refused to return him to Aphrodite. The two goddesses asked Zeus to resolve their dispute. According to Apollodorus the Athenian, Zeus divided the year into three periods: Adonis would spend the first period as he pleased, the second period with Persephone, and the third period with Aphrodite. But Adonis chose to spend his free time with Aphrodite.

Raised by nymphs, the handsome youth was a skillful hunter. During one hunt in the forest, Adonis suddenly found himself facing an enormous wild boar and was fatally injured. Observing the scene from afar, Aphrodite rushed to his aid. But in her haste, she forgot to wear her sandals and a rose thorn pricked her foot. Blood from the prick trickled onto the white roses, turning them red. Aphrodite took Adonis's dead body and laid it on a bed of lettuce plants, which the ancients believed to be aphrodisiac. The wild anemone was also said to have grown from the tears Aphrodite shed for her dead lover.

Adonis's death was attributed to the envy of Ares, who changed into a wild boar to kill the goddess's favorite. Another version attributes Adonis's death to Apollo who sought to avenge the son of Erymanthus, whom Aphrodite blinded because he saw her bathing after a tryst with Adonis. Like Ares, Apollo changed into a wild boar to kill her beloved.

Apollodorus the Athenian links the myth to Adonis to the myth of Hyacinth. Cleio, daughter of Mnemosyne and Zeus, had been accused by Aphrodite of being in love with Adonis. To retaliate, the goddess made Cleio fall in love with Pierus, son of Magnes. Hyacinth was born from the union of Cleio and Pierus.

In Greece, Adonis was the object of true worship. The focus of his cult was the mysteries known as *Adoneia* in which mostly women took part. Plutarch describes how Athenian women sought to pay tribute to the dead youth by carrying idols of the dead, beating their breasts, and mourning as at funerals, but then continued by celebrating his resurrection. This was also the practice in Syria and Egypt.

Cinyras, the first king of Cyprus, was the poet who composed the celebratory songs and funerary elegies for Adonis's death. The king, who had been given the gifts of music and song by Apollo, introduced the cult of Aphrodite to Cyprus. Cinyras was believed to have arrived on Cyprus from Byblos in Syria, where Adonis had been worshipped. Cinyras became the first priest on the island and passed along the vocation to his family. He had three daughters with Metharme and, for unknown reasons, this enraged Aphrodite; the girls were seized by frenzy and lay with anyone who alighted on Cyprus. Later, they died in Egypt.

Helen and Paris

One of Aphrodite's most famous victims was Helen, the beauty over whom the Trojan War was fought. To win a beauty contest with Hera and Athena, Aphrodite charmed Paris and promised hum that he could have the daughter of Zeus and Leda if he chose her as the most beautiful of the three goddesses. Paris gave the prize to Aphrodite, who traveled to Sparta and abducted Helen, wife of Menelaus, as she had promised. Aphrodite's protection of Paris was quite effective. In *The Iliad's* third rhapsody, Homer writes that the Greeks and Trojans were determined to seek an end to the war with a duel between the cuckolded husband Menelaus and Helen's kidnapper, Paris. Aphrodite rushed to the aid of her defeated protege, covering him with a thick cloud, then snatched him, and delivered him to his scented marital bed.

Observing the duel between her husband and her lover from behind the walls of Troy, Helen felt a surge of admiration for the husband she had deserted. Sensing this, Aphrodite changed into an old servant who doted on Helen and had followed her from Lacedaemoneia, then tried to lead her to her lover's bed. Helen recognized the goddess; complaining about the censure she had suffered, Helen tells Aphrodite that she no longer wants to live with Paris. Aphrodite then threatens to abandon her, escalate the war, and destroy her. Thus Helen is persuaded by the goddess to remain at the side of a man who cannot stand up to comparison with her deserted, legal husband.

Medea

Aphrodite played an especially important role in the expedition of the Argonauts as Jason took advantage of the passion for him she inflamed in Medea's heart to steal the golden fleece and escape from Colchis.

Zephyrus and Hyacinth (Attic kylix, 490 B.C.). Hyacinth was a pre-hellenic god of vegetation and counterpart to Adonis. The cult of Hyacinth was replaced by the cult of Apollo. At Amyclae in Lacedaemonia, Hyacinth was worshipped as a hero and the large festival held in his honor, the Hyacinthia, subsequently evolved into a festival celebrating the god Apollo.

Aphrodite, goddess of love and nature's fertile powers, rules the birth and death of every living creature. Her cult commonly featured the "sacred prostitution" that was typical of the worship of many of Eastern fertility deities.

Pasiphae – Ariadne – Phaedra

The bride and daughters of Minos became tragic victims of the passions that Aphrodite ignited in their souls. Initially, the goddess turned against Pasiphae, wife of Minos and daughter of Helius. Helius had had tipped off Hephaestus to the goddess's extramarital affair with Ares, and because Aphrodite could not seek revenge against him, turned instead against his daughter, instilling in her a deep lust for a bull. Pasiphae managed to fulfill her passion; as a result of this union, she gave birth to the Minotaur.

When Theseus traveled to Crete to kill the Minotaur and rid Athens of the blood-tax imposed on it by Minos, he was successful thanks to the help he received from Ariadne, in whom Aphrodite had instilled a lust for the handsome foreigner. Like Medea, Ariadne betrayed her father's interests for the sake of her lover – and she, too, was deserted by the faithless man. Aphrodite consoled her by predicting her marriage to Dionysus and giving her a gold wreath.

Ariadne's sister Phaedra was also a victim of the lust inspired by Aphrodite. Angered by the fact that Hippolytus, son of Theseus and the Amazon Hippolyte, was ignoring her, the goddess pierced the heart of Theseus's second wife, Phaedra, with an illicit lust for her stepson. From Euripides to Racine, the poets speak of her futile attempts to rid herself of the lust that tormented her. Even Hippolytus's death does not free her from her desire, so she decides to end her life: *"If Aphrodite so desires, I will die too, last and bitter."*

Hippodameia

There is a tragic similarity in the stories of Phaedra and Hippodameia, daughter of Oenomaus, king of Pisa. With the help of Myrtilus, Oenomaus's charioteer, Pelops manages to defeat Oenomaus in a chariot race and win the hand of Hippodameia. But she was in love with Myrtilus, so she pretended to be thirsty and sent Pelops to fetch her some water from a nearby well. During his absence, Hippodameia confessed her love to Myrtilus, but he rejected her not wishing to insult Pelops. Afraid that Myrtilus would expose her to Pelops, Hippodameia decided to beat him to it. The moment Pelops returned, she told him that the charioteer had tried to rape her. Pelops was so outraged that he tossed Myrtilus into the sea.

The daughters of Proetus

Some writers attribute the madness that seized the daughters of King Proetus to Aphrodite's rage, although they do not explain what provoked the goddess. It is said that the goddess either freed them of their inhibitions or took their beauty. According to another account, Aphrodite punished them by giving them leprosy.

Aegeus

Aphrodite also figures in the myth of Aegeus, who attributed his lack of favor to the sterility of his first two wives. He consulted the Oracle of Delphi, but did not understand its divination so he turned to Pittheus, son of Pelops. Pittheus got Aegeus drunk and led him to the bed of his daughter, Aethra, whom Poseidon visited that same night. Aegeus appears to have introduced the cult of Aphrodite to Athens.

Atalante

Atalante abhorred the idea of marriage so she submitted all those who sought her hand to a test that ended in their deaths. The test was a foot race. The virgin would have the young men set out first; she would then race behind them, overtake them, and kill them. Although the maiden's habit was well-known, Melanippus (or Melanion) did not hesitate to accept her challenge after seeking Aphrodite's assistance. The goddess have him several of the golden apples from the garden of the Hesperides. During the race, when Melanippus saw Atalante draw near, he would drop one of the apples. The maiden would stoop to pick the apple up, allowing the youth to widen the distance between them. He was thus able to run the entire course without being overtaken by Atalante. Naturally, the two were married.

The myth does end there: one day when the couple was hunting, they wandered into an area consecrated to Zeus where they succumbed to the joys of love. Angered at their act, Zeus turned them both into lions.

Selemnus

In some myths, Aphrodite is shown helping mortals who had fallen victim to an unfortunate lust or who had simply won her sympathy. One example is the shepherd Selemnus, who fell in love with the nymph Argyra. When he lost his looks, she deserted him. Selemnus died from his grief. Aphrodite was moved by his deep love and changed him into a river. Yet even in his new form, Selemnus remained grief-stricken. Aphrodite came to his aid a second time and gave him the ability to forget all unlucky love affairs. The ancient Greeks' belief that the Selemnus River would erase the sorrows of all those who bathed in its waters is rooted in this myth.

Phaon

According to a myth from the island of Lesbos, the ferryman Phaon agreed to carry an old woman to the opposite shore for free. The passenger was actually Aphrodite, who rewarded his generosity by giving him a magic ointment. Phaon used the ointment; within a few days he had become the most handsome man on Lesbos. Every woman on the island fell in love with him, including the famed poet Sappho. In a different version, Aphrodite fell in love with Phaon and hid him from her female rivals in a wheat field.

Dexicreon

A Samian merchant, Dexicreon is said to have accepted Aphrodite's generous protection and favor. One day as he was loading his ship with merchandise, the goddess advised him to only load potable water and set sail as quickly as possible. Dexicreon followed her advice. When his ship had traveled a slight distance from the shore, the wind turned completely calm, immobilizing all the boats anchored there. The crews soon became thirsty, and Dexicreon became rich selling them the water he had stocked. He expressed his gratitude to Aphrodite by dedicating a statue to the goddess on the island.

Butes

One of Jason's companions during the expedition of the Argonauts, Butes was the son of either Teleon or Poseidon. He was exceptionally brave and daring. When the *Argo* sailed by the island of the Sirens, Orpheus blocked the Argonauts' ears so they could not hear the Sirens' melodious harp and submit to their calling. Only Butes was unable to resist, so he dove into the sea and swam ashore. But Aphrodite intervened and carried him off to her cave at Lilybaeum in Sicily. There she lay with Butes and bore him a son, Eryx.

The cult of Aphrodite

Several ancient writers confirm the eastern origin of the worship of Aphrodite. Pausanias writes that the Assyrians were the first to worship Ourania, and her cult then spread to Paphos on Cyprus, the Phoenicians at Askalona in Syria, and then to Cythera. Herodotus writes that the Assyrians called the goddess Mylitta, the Arabs called her Alilat, the Scythians called her Argimpasa, and the Persians called her Mitra. According to Cypriot tradition, the followers of Aphrodite would prove their devotion by laying with strangers – something that was particularly widespread in the East. Indeed, Strabo notes the existence of over a thousand *hetairae,* or courtesans, at her sanctuary at Acrocorinth. In Thebes, Aphrodite Urania is also linked to the Phoenician ruler Cadmus, who married Aphrodite's daughter Harmonia.

Aphrodite's links to Cyprus and Cythera are evident from the Homeric epithets of *Cypris*, *Cythereia*, and *Papheia* and the most important sanctuaries dedicated to the goddess have been found at Paphos, Idalios, and Amathounda.

In the Mediterranean, important sanctuaries dedicated to Aphrodite have been found at Cnidos, Halicarnassus, Ephesus, and Abidos.

The cult of Aphrodite was especially widespread on Cos and Rhodes, while on Delos it was believed that a *xoano*, or wooden idol, of the goddess had been

Aphrodite from Solous, first century B.C. (Cyprus Archaeological Museum).

brought to the island by Theseus.

The myth of Aphrodite as being born from the surf and her direct link to Cyprus and Cythera quite naturally created an association between the goddess and the sea.

Thus, many temples dedicated to Aphrodite are located along the coast or in harbors or capes, such as the temples at Aegeio, Patras, Cnidos, Attica (*Aphrodite Coleias*), Troezen (*Aphrodite Akraia*), and Hermione, where she was known as *Ponteia* (from *pontus* or ocean) and *Limeneia* (from *limenas* or port); she was also considered a patron of sailors, who called her *Ponteia*, *Pelayeia* or *Euploieia* because they believed she sent them good winds.

Aphrodite was worshipped at Knossos as the goddess of fertility and vegetation, and as a symbol of blooming and withering and of life and of death.

Thus, one of her epithets was *Antheia*, from *anthos* or flower. In Athens, a temple and statue on the northern section of the Acropolis were dedicated to *Aphrodite en kipois*, which reflected local Cypriot epithets of *Hierokipois* or *Hierokipeia*, both references to her sacred gardens.

Vegetation gods are often associated with the Underworld, thus Aphrodite had the characteristics of a chthonic deity: at Delphi, there was a statue of Aphrodite *Epitymbeia*; temples dedicated to Aphrodite *Melainidos* existed at Thespies, Corinth, and Mantineia; and, in Argos she was known by the curious epithet *Tymboruchus*.

Although Aphrodite is the love-goddess, she is also honored as a war-goddess next to Ares.

Pausanias mentions statues of *Oplismenis Aphrodites* (Armed Aphrodite) at Sparta and Cythera, while the epithet *Hetaira*, with which she was worshipped in Athens, may be unrelated to her erotic identity.

The name *Pandimos* is also unrelated to the Pandimos Aphrodite who appears in Plato's *Symposium* as the symbol of carnal love, but is an expression of her role as protectress of the civil society and a symbol of the goddess's presence at every level of the class structure. Typically, her sanctuary in Athens is found near the Agora, which was were citizens assembled.

Aphrodite's symbols

Aphrodite's most important symbol is the breastplate and belt, which contains her entire erotic power. According to Homer, Aphrodite gave this belt to Hera so she could charm Zeus. The wreath she is shown wearing in an illustration with Pan also has similar powers. Objects of beauty such as the perfumed clothing that she wore when she appeared before Paris and her sparkling jewels are typical accessories. As the goddess of beauty, Aphrodite holds a mirror but is also reflected in it. As a symbol of lust, she was associated with the ankles, and the luckiest throw of the dice bore her name.

Plants sacred to Aphrodite are the rose, myrtle, anemone, pomegranate, poppy, and apple. The dove, swan, and goose are birds sacred to the goddess. The lion is a symbol of her eastern provenance, but in Greece she was mostly associated with small animals that symbolized love – the rabbit, the tortoise (on which Aphrodite Ourania stands), and the ram or goat. The dolphin symbolizes her origins from the sea.

Aphrodite in art

Archaeologists have unearthed prehistoric idols of a naked fertility goddess, shown either pressing her breasts or holding a dove. There is no evidence suggesting a link between these idols and the Olympian goddess Aphrodite. The first depictions of Aphrodite are in the form of a *xoano* (primitive wooden figure). After the fifth century B.C., she is depicted in a form that is quite close to the form of this idol. She is also depicted this way on red-figure amphorae of the Late Classical period.

The earliest verified depictions of Aphrodite are found on Archaiac pottery, where her identity is confirmed by an inscription. On a fragment of a seventh century B.C. amphora from Naxos, as well as on the *Francois pot*, she is shown at Ares's side. The *Lyon kore*, dated to the sixth century B.C., shows a helmeted goddess dressed in an Ionic tunic and holding a dove. The statue has been widely interpreted as depicting Aphrodite. This form was quite common, although a controversy has emerged over whether these idols are depictions of female deities. In the Cypriot idols of the

Statues of Eros (Archaeological Museum of Heraklion, Crete).

seventh and sixth centuries B.C., Aphrodite is distinguished by her jewelry.

As early as the seventh century B.C., Aphrodite was a popular motif on hand-mirrors. She is often shown wearing a wreath, or holding an apple or a dove, and is framed by Sphinx or Eros. At Delphi, she is depicted on the frieze of the Siphnian Treasury standing next to Ares at an assembly of gods. In the Classical period, Aphrodite appears on virtually every form of art, including pottery, sculpture, and miniatures. In the early fifth century B.C., many artists depict her on pottery in scenes known as the *"crisis of Paris"*. In some scenes, the winged Hermes accompanies Aphrodite, while in others she is placing adornments on Helen, bathing, participating in an assembly of gods, or simply appears in scenes from the Trojan War and the Argonauts' expedition.

After the fifth century B.C., Aphrodite is depicted on red-figure pottery as the goddess of love. Eros often –but not always– accompanies her. There are numerous scenes on pots by Meidias in which the lavishly dressed and bejeweled Aphrodite is depicted with a passionate, lustful look. Throughout the fourth century B.C., Aphrodite is one of the most common motifs on mirrors, where she is usually shown with a swan, goose, or ram, as well as with Pan and Eros, or Hermes, or Adonis and Eros. In large sculptures, she is depicted as early as the mid-fifth century B.C. dressed in all her Olympian finery. Callias was said to have donated to the Acropolis a statue of Aphrodite by the sculptor Calamis; it has been identified as the *Aspasia-Cassandra* statue, a copy of which is displayed at the Naples Museum (Italy).

On the Parthenon, Aphrodite is depicted on two pediments and the eastern frieze among other gods. There is a clear resemblance between her form on the frieze and the limited number of copies of *Aphrodite Doria-Pamphili*, which marks the passage of the goddess into monumental art. The statue is believed to be the work of either Agorocritus or his workshop. *Aphrodite Ourania* only appears in the fifth century B.C. as a motif. A Pheidian chryselephantine statue of the goddess is presented at Elis, and a marble statue is donated to Melite.

The style of these statues is reflected in the copies displayed in Berlin, in which the goddess is dressed in a robe and rests her left foot on a tortoise (symbol of Aphrodite Ourania), while touching a bench with her left hand; in other statues, the object her hand touched was either a tree trunk or a the capital of a column. The goddess appears in this form, with slight variations, through the Hellenistic era.

Another Pheidian style depicts Aphrodite in the garden and may have been the work of Alcamenes. Again, Aphrodite is shown supporting herself with left hand touching a tree, while her left foot is crossed over her right foot. The statue of Aphrodite from Dafni on display at the National Archaeological Museum in Athens is believed to be a loose copy of this style. The *Aphrodite of Frejus-Naples* is believed to be the work of Callimachus, another student of Pheidias. The statue shows the goddess dressed in a robe, which has gracefully slipped off her shoulder exposing her right breast. The dress only covers her back; its folds are draped over her right arm as she gently lifts the fabric. This is the most popular Classical depiction of Aphrodite and remained prevalent, with some variations, through late antiquity.

The earliest known depiction of Aphrodite armed is a Classical-era statue found at Epidaurus and displayed at the National Archaeological Museum in Athens. The goddess is fully robed and holds a Telamon.

Aphrodite is the main subject in the art of Praxiteles. The statue displayed at the Louvre Museum in Paris is believed to date from his early years; the goddess is depicted half-naked, with her robe tied around her hips. In the fourth century B.C., Praxiteles's *Aphrodite Cnidia* ushers in a new era in the depiction of Aphrodite. It is believed to portray the sacred bath of the goddess, a celebration of *Aphrodite Pandimos* and *Aphrodite Peithous* during which cult idols were baptized in the sea.

This would explain the presence of the amphora and the fabric, which can be seen in the copy of the statue in the Capitol building in Rome.

There are several copies of this style in which Aphrodite is shown naked, covering her breast with her right hand and her pubis with her left hand.

Statue of Aphrodite found near the altar of the Temple of Isis Lochias, second century B.C. (Dion Museum).

This is one of the most popular subjects in Greek art and persisted through Roman times. The statue of *Aphrodite Pandimos* found in Elis, in which the naked goddess is depicted with a ram, is the work of Scopas. The sculptor also shows *Aphrodite with Lust* in a statue at Samothrace.

At the end of the third century B.C., images of Aphrodite untying (or tying) her sandal are also quite popular in the bathing genre. *Aphrodite Anadyomene* (Rising), an image of the goddess wringing water from her hair with her two arms raised over her head, is also considered part of the sacred bathing theme. Other images include Aphrodite *Pselioumeni* in which the goddess is bedecked in jewels or shown gazing at her reflection in the mirror. In the fifth century B.C., we find another variation on the bathing theme in *Oclazoussa Aphrodite* in drawings on clay pots. A similar theme was depicted in the third-century-B.C. sculpture of Doidalsas, whose work was taken to Rome, where copies became popular decorations in spas and gardens. The best copies are on display in Rome and at the Louvre in Paris. One variation on this theme can be seen in a Rhodian statuette that depicts *Aphrodite Rising* is in a sitting position. This statue is believed to date from the first century B.C. – the same period as the group of *Aphrodite holding her sandal and Pan* that is on display at the National Archaeological Museum in Athens.

Aphrodite threatens Pan with her sandal, while being helped by Eros (first century B.C., National Archaeological Museum).

HEPHAESTUS

Hephaestus created heavenly and earthly fire, including the fire of thunder and the flames of the volcanoes. Homer informs that he was the legal son of Hera and Zeus, but according to Hesiod, Hera gave birth to him by herself because she had quarreled with Zeus – the reason why Zeus threw him out of Olympus. According to one account, Hephaestus was born a gimp; unable to cope with his handicap, his mother tossed the infant into the sea, where Thetis and Eurynome raised him. Thus hidden, the lame god secretly practiced the art of metalworking and made Achilles's shield at the request of Thetis. There are other accounts of the god's deformity. In one version, Zeus became angered with Hephaestus for taking Hera's side in a quarrel, so he grabbed Hephaestus by the foot and flung him off Mount Olympus.

Hephaestus landed on Lemnos, whose inhabitants, the Sintians (or Sinties), took care of Hephaestus and built a large temple dedicated to the god on the island. Hephaestus was maimed during this fall.

It is obvious that the ancient Greeks sought to interpret the volcanic origins of the Aegean islands and volcanic activity in general by creating a god of fire as they initially believed that volcanic eruptions were caused by something that had fallen from the sky. Since all volcanoes have periods of inactivity, they conceived the idea that Hephaestus did not always live in exile, but occasionally returned to Mount Olympus.

Hephaestus, drunk and supported by a satyr, ascends to Mount Olympus to release the bonds of his mother Hera. (Detail from red-figure pelike, 435-430 B.C., Munich Archaeological Museum).

THE ESSENTIAL GREEK MYTHOLOGY

A popular subject on decorated pottery was the scene of Hephaestus's return to Mount Olympus after the intervention of Dionysus. Satyrs and maenads accompany the god of earthly fire and volcanic activity to the gods' residence, 545 B.C. (Metropolitan Museum).

Hephaestus and the other Olympian gods

Hephaestus and Hera

The relationship between Hephaestus and his mother Hera is at times contradictory. He is sometimes seen as consoling her or rushing to her aid – as in the case of her quarrel with Zeus or when she asked him to help Achilles in his fight with the river Xanthus – while other times he is seen as exacting his revenge on her. One myth relates how Hephaestus built Hera a wonderful throne, but when Hera sat on it, she was immobilized by invisible bonds that no one could untie. Despite the gods' pleas and Ares's threats, Hephaestus left for Lemnos. Dionysus finally succeeded in luring him back to Mount Olympus by getting him drunk on sweet wine. Hephaestus, however, asked to be rewarded for untying Hera, whom he released after Zeus promised to grant him whatever he asked. Hephaestus then demanded to be married to the goddess of beauty, Aphrodite.

Hephaestus and Athena

In a different version, Hephaestus is said to have demanded to marry Athena in return for releasing Hera's bonds. But when he entered her room, the virgin goddess was armed and fought him off. Other myths mention his repeated, unsuccessful attempts to rape Athena. One time, his sperm dribbled on her leg; disgusted, the goddess wiped it off with wool (*erion*) that she then tossed to the ground (*chthona*). The sperm fertilized the soil and Erichthonius was born on that spot.

Hephaestus and Zeus

The relationship between Hephaestus and Zeus is distinguished by submission and respect, which may have been inspired by Hephaestus's injury. In the battle against the Giants, Hephaestus helped the king of the gods –who may have been his father– by throwing lit brands at the rebels. He is also said to have made Zeus's shield, or *aegis*. Hephaestus also helped Zeus give birth to Athena by splitting his head open with an axe. On Zeus's orders, Hephaestus created Pandora, bride of Epimetheus.

Hephaestus and Aphrodite

Although Homer mentions the beautiful Charita as Hephaestus's wife, it was widely accepted that he married Aphrodite, as promised by Zeus in exchange for releasing Hera from her bonds. Their marriage was not sound, as Aphrodite cheated on Hephaestus with Ares. Rather provocatively, she even lay with her lover in the marital bed when her husband was at work. Helius told Hephaestus about Aphrodite's infidelities. Hephaestus made invisible bonds, which immobilized the two lovers as soon as they lay together. He then invited all the other gods to witness the sight and, having completely embarrassed the couple, released them.

The children of Hephaestus

Hephaestus did not have many romantic adventures, thus he did not father many children. According to some ancient writers, Eros was the son of Hephaestus and Aphrodite, although most texts claim Eros was the son of Zeus or Hermes or Ares. The Cabeiri of Samothrace are believed to be Hephaestus's children or grandchildren from the nymph Cabeiro.

The following are believed to be sons of Hephaestus:
- Periphetes, a fierce outlaw who killed travelers in the Epidaurus region with his club. He was killed by Theseus.
- Pylius, who healed Philoctetes's wound on Lemnos.
- Ardalus of Troezen.
- Palaemon or Palaemonius, who was also lame.

The cult of Hephaestus

As fire-god, Hephaestus was also considered the great metalworker who built grand and impressive objects like Helius's chariot, Heracles's golden breastplate, Diomedes's breastplate, Achilles's armor and shield, Zeus's scepter and throne, the arrows of Artemis and Apollo, and the gold chalices of Helius, Dionysus, and other gods. He built a bronze palace on Mount Olympus for the gods, while for himself he made gold robot-statues that could speak and think to serve him. He also made two silver hounds to guard the home of Alcinous, and two wild bulls with bronze legs that spewed fire from their nostrils that he gave to Medea's father Aeetes. Hephaestus also built Talus, a giant robot that he gave Minos to patrol the shores of Crete.

Later myths claim Hephaestus's workshop was on Lemnos, where the island's volcano, Moschylos, was active in antiquity. His friend Cedalion also lived on Lemnos. Several writers claim Cedalion was Hephaestus's son, while others say he was just an apprentice.

The Temple of Hephaestus on Lemnos was believed to have been built on the exact spot where a lightning bolt first struck the earth. The *Hephaesteia* were celebrated on the island every year: for nine days, all the fires on the island were put on and lit with the new flame brought by boat from the sanctuary of Delos.

As colonies expanded the reach of the Greek world, mythology was enriched with new accounts. Thus, Hephaestus is said to have established a second workshop at Mount Aetna in Sicily. Typhoeus had been trapped under the volcano during the battle against the Giants; Hephaestus kept him immobilized by forcing Typhoeus to balance an anvil on his head. Hephaestus's assistants in Sicily were the Cyclopes. According to one myth, this is where Hephaestus was united with the oceanid Aetna, with whom he fathered the two fire-spirits or Palikoi.

Outside Lemnos and Sicily, Hephaestus was also worshipped in Athens. In his temple, the Hephaesteion, there were statues of both him and Athena. Athenians held torch races known as the *Hephaesteia* or *Chalkeia* in honor of the two gods.

The shrine of the Cabeiri on Cape Chloe near Hephaesteia on the island of Limnos, the "most-beloved of all lands" of Hephaestus. Ousted from Mount Olympus, the god of earthly fire found refuge on the island, where he set up his underground workshops.

HESTIA

As the hearth-goddess, Hestia, first-born daughter of Cronus and Rhea, was the most ancient fire deity. She thus occupied a position of honor in the Olympian pantheon. Greeks' offerings to the goddess included their first harvests and first libations they distilled.

Hestia's importance is rooted in the importance of the hearth in ancient Greek society, as well as in several other ancient societies. The hearth was not only vital to daily activities and needs, but was also equally vital to each household that built a small altar for worshipping the gods which protected their home. Thus, the hearth was transformed into a goddess of fire, which was necessary for civilization that sheltered family life and offered refuge to suppliants.

Hestia, however, was not only the protectress of the limited family circle, but of the entire city as each settlement –the extended family– had a common hearth, the Prytaneio, where a fire burned continually in honor of the goddess. This is where foreign emissaries, distinguished visitors, and benefactors were received and fed. When a city founded a colony, the settlers took with them a torch lit from the sacred flame with which to light the hearth in their new homeland.

Myths and symbols

Hestia's dominance of the center of the earth symbolizes the fire at its center as well as the belief that the earth marked the center of the universe, and other planets revolved around it. This belief provides an interpretation of the myth in which Poseidon and Apollo sought to unite with Hestia. The goddess rejected their request, having vowed to protect her virginity. Zeus rewarded her by installing her in the center of the home, that is, by giving her the most prominent place in the home. Indeed, the sun (Apollo) sees Gaea (Hestia) but does unite with her; the sea (Poseidon) embraces her, but does not cover her. Thus Hestia remains a virgin because fire is the ultimate purifier, but Gaea (Hestia) remains motionless and thus cannot give birth.

Hestia in art

The ancient writers provide little information about how the goddess was portrayed in art, and archaeologists have yet to unearth some find that would overturn the prevalent theory that Hestia's rather vague personality did not inspire many of the ancient Greek artists. There are, however, some unconfirmed references to a statue by Glaucus (fifth century B.C.), a work by Scopas (fourth century B.C.) as well as the existence of statues of Hestia in the antechamber of the Temple of Zeus at Olympia, at Pherae in Achaia, and at the Prytaneion in Athens.

The famous relief of the goddess dressed in a simple garment and her right hand raised towards the sky –from where fire was brought down to mortals– has been dated to Roman times and is often attributed to either Demeter or Kore. Nonetheless, the Romans made special honor to Hestia, whom they called *Vesta*.

Hestia and the Hestiades

The *"inextinguishable flame"* burned at an altar in the Temple of Hestia in Rome. Three priestesses and six virgins known as the Hestiades tended the flame. Only the Hestiades were allowed in the innermost recess of the temple where the Palladium and other sacred relics were kept. The Hestiades remained in the service of Hestia for thirty years, were chosen from the daughters of free families who had two living parents.

The Hestiades enjoyed many privileges: they were provided with free food, were not required to take an oath before offering testimony, were transported everywhere by vehicle, and were not placed under guardianship. On the other hand, those who violated rules and lost their virginity while serving as Hestiades were buried with criminals.

Hestia, goddess of the family hearth and the sacred flame of the altar, depicted with a flower in one hand and a branch heavy with fruit in the other. (Detail from red-figure kylix, 520 B.C., National Archaeological Museum of Tarkynia.)

ARES

The war-god Ares is the most hated of all the Olympian gods, and described *"as a bloodthirsty killer and conqueror of castles"*. He was the only legal son of Zeus and Hera, although Ovid claims Ares was born as a result of Hera's simple contact with a flower in the Oleanus plain.

The Iliad mentions Thrace as Ares's birthplace. His son Phobus was also born in Thrace. Herodotus writes that Ares is only included among the gods who are only respected by the Thracians. The myths of the Amazons, who are considered his daughters, also suggest he was born in Thrace. For this reason, in Greece he was only worshipped in Boeotia and Attica, where Thracian tribes had settled. It is also possible that Ares is an exclusively Greek deity who was identified with a similar Thracian deity.

Ares and the other gods of Olympus

Ares and Zeus

Ares's relationships with the other Olympian gods were not friendly because of his mean character and his penchant for wars, discord, and fights. Even his father, Zeus, expressed his dislike for Ares.

Ares personified the forces of violence, destruction, and the irrational fury of war that blinds the warrior. He is depicted in full armor on this fifth century pottery (Vatican Museum).

Ares and Athena

Ares was especially hostile towards Athena, who was also a war deity. During the Trojan War, Ares fought on the side of the Trojans even though he had promised his mother, Hera, that he would help the Greeks. He was wounded by Diomedes, whose hand had been guided by Athena (Homer, *The Iliad*). The two gods faced off against each other in the final battle that would determine the fate of Troy; Ares was defeated once again by Athena, who wounded him.

In another account, Ares was enraged by the death of his son

Ascalaphus, so he turned against the gods and ordered his sons Deimus and Phobus to harness their horses. Athena then assumed the defense of their home on Olympus. She descended to its doorstep where she disarmed Ares and took his armor. Finally, she persuaded him to abandon his murderous plans. Despite his considerable strength, Ares did not play a particularly important role in the battle against the Giants and only took part in killing Mimas.

Ares and Aphrodite

Ares is mentioned alternately as husband and lover of Aphrodite. Homer writes that Aphrodite was the legal bride of Hephaestus, but took Ares as her lover. Helius tipped off Hephaestus about their illicit affair and the fire-god got even: he built invisible, indestructible nets which he suspended over the marital bed he shared with Aphrodite and announced that he was leaving for Lemnos. Carefree, the two lovers lay together and were caught in the nets. Hephaestus returned and caught his bride with Ares. He then called the other gods to come see the two lovers, and after thoroughly embarrassing them agreed to free them in exchange for reparations from Ares for committing adultery (*The Odyssey*).

Whether husband or lover, Ares was extremely jealous of Aphrodite. Unable to bear her lust for the beautiful young Adonis, he changed into a wild boar and killed the youth.

Ares and the Aloeuids

Ares was captured three times by the hideous giants Otus and Ephialtes, sons or grandsons of Poseidon and Iphimedeia (who was married to Aloeus). The first time, the giants were trying to scale Mount Olympus and attack Zeus by stacking Mount Ossa atop Mount Olympus and Mount Pelion atop Mount Ossa. Ares escaped thirteen months later with help from Hermes, who had heard about the war-god's capture from the Aloeuids' stepmother, the beautiful Eeriboea.

Later, when Ephialtes was trying to seduce Hera and Otus was trying to seduce Artemis, the two giants instead captured Ares a second time. Hermes freed him again. Embarrassed, Ares hid on Naxos. The Aloeuids captured Ares a third time and shut him in a bronze prison for thirteen months to punish him for killing Adonis.

Ares and the heroes

Ares and Heracles

Ares was defeated every time he or his sons, Cycnus and the Thracian king Diomedes, fought against Heracles, who was the favorite hero of the goddess Athena.

The wild Cycnus, son of Ares and Pelopia, would kill anyone traveling from Thermopylae to Tempe, and planned to build a temple to his father with their skulls. With Ares's help, Cycnus attacked Heracles. The hero initially retreated until he saw Ares withdraw, then moved in again, and killed Cycnus.

Hesiod presents a different version of the myth, in which Heracles –who was riding a chariot driven by Iolaus– killed Cycnus and wounded Ares, who attacked him to avenge the death of his son. In this version, Athena saved Heracles. Apollodorus the Athenian writes that Cycnus challenged Heracles to a contest. Ares wanted to help his son and was about to burn him, when Zeus threw a thunderbolt between Cycnus and Heracles to separate them.

Heracles defeated another son of Ares in Thrace: Diomedes, a king of the Bistones who fed his mares on human flesh. The Stymphalian birds raised by Ares were also flesh-eating; Heracles killed them with his arrows with some help from Athena.

Ares and Cadmus

Cadmus, the legendary founder of Thebes, provoked the anger of the god of war by killing a dragon that had been born from the union of Ares with the nymph Telphusa. To purify himself from the murder, Cadmus served as Ares's servant as a year. The two were then reconciled and Ares consented to Cadmus's marriage with Harmonia, a daughter Ares had fathered with Aphrodite.

The children of Ares

Ares and the Areopagus

With Alcippe, daughter of the Athenian king Cecrops, Ares fathered a daughter, Alcippe. She was raped by Poseidon's son Halirrhothius. Ares avenged his daughter by killing the rapist, but Poseidon appealed to the council of the gods seeking justice. The court convened on a hillock near the Acropolis of Athens. Ares was declared innocent, but to purify himself from the murder was forced to work as a slave for a year.

The hillock where the court convened was named the *Areopagus* (rock of Ares), and criminal cases were tried there. According to another myth, the *Areopagus* (or Areios Pagus) took its name from the war-god's daughters, the Amazons, who set up camp on the hillock and made sacrifices to their father when they mounted a campaign to remove Athena from the Acropolis.

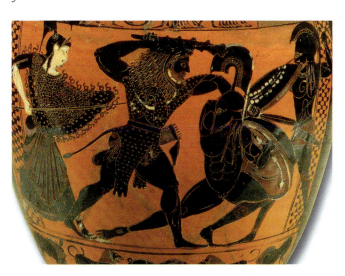

Heracles, aided by Athena, kills Cycnus, son of Ares, who is depicted on the right comforting his son (fifth century B.C., Vatican Museum).

The myth of Oenomaus

Oenomaus was the son of Ares and Harpina, daughter of the river Asopus. He became king of Pisa, in Elis. Because he was in love with his daughter Hippodameia —or because of a prophecy that his son-in-law would kill him— he invited all of her suitors to a chariot race from the Temple of Zeus in Olympia to the Temple of Poseidon at Corinth. The suitors would set off first while Oenomaus made a sacrifice to Hephaestus.

The king always caught up with the suitors because his horses Psylla and Harpina were gifts from Ares. Oenomaus's charioteer Myrtilus, a son of Hermes, would kill the suitors and nail their heads either to the palace entrance or to the columns of the temple of Ares or temple of Poseidon.

Thirteen suitors for Hippodameia had already met their death when Pelops showed up to court her. He managed to finish and win the race, thanks to help from Poseidon and Myrtilus. Poseidon had given Pelops a golden chariot drawn by winged horses. Myrtilus agreed to help Pelops in exchange for a night with Hippodameia, if Pelops won.

Thus, Myrtilus removed the nails from the wheels of the king's chariot, which veered off course. Oenomaus was toppled from his seat, tangled in the reins, and dragged to his death by his horses. With his dying breath, he cursed his charioteer to die by the hand of the race's winner. Oenomaus's curse came true, but the murder of Myrtilus brought a series of disasters on the descendants of Pelops.

Meleager and Atalante

Ares fathered another son, Meleager, with Althaea, the legal wife of the king of Calydon, Oeneus. Meleager died tragically. Seven days after the child was born, the Moerae told Althaea that her son would die the moment a magic brand was tossed into the hearth. Frightened, she immediately put out the fire and hid the torch in a box to save her infant son's life.

Artemis was angered when Oeneus neglected her at a sacrifice, so she sent a wild boar to Calydonia to wreak havoc. To rid his land of the beast, Oeneus organized a large hunt in which Meleager took part, along with Althaea's brothers, and Atalante. She wounded the boar, and then Meleager finished it off. The young man fell in love with the brave Atalante and offered her the boar. But Althaea's brothers also wanted the prize. A fight broke out, and Meleager killed his uncles. Furious at her son, Althaea tossed the brand into the fire, causing Meleager's death.

The Iliad offers a different version of the myth of Meleager. After the killing of the Caledonian boar, Artemis fomented a war between the Aetolians and Curetes for the boar's head. Althaea's brothers led the Curetes. Meleager killed his uncles, but withdrew from the battle after being cursed by his mother. But the Curetes torched the city, prompting him to join in its defense after the pleas of his wife, Cleopatra.

Homer does not mention the hero's death, but according to other writers the arrows of Achilles, who fought on the side of the Curetes, killed him. After his death, Meleager's mother

THE OLYMPIAN GODS

Fully armed, Ares on the Francois *crater (570 B.C., Florence Archaeological Museum).*

Deimus and Phobus (Hesiod, *Theogony*), although some writers also list Eros and Priapus as their children. Deimus and Phobus always appeared together and represented fear and panic, respectively. They accompanied their father everywhere and fought by his side. Their demonic forms also decorated the shields of Agamemnon (Homer, *The Iliad*), Heracles (Hesiod), and Achilles.

The Spartans founded a temple in honor of Phobus, who they considered to be a harmful deity yet also believed that he was one of the firmest foundations of the state and called on him to protect Spartan soldiers by sowing panic in their enemies. For the same reason, Theseus offered a sacrifice to Deimus and Phobus before doing battle with the Amazons.

and wife hung themselves, while Artemis took pity on his inconsolable sisters and turned them into birds – the *meleagrides,* or guineafowl, who continue to mourn the loss of their brother.

Deimus and Phobus

In addition to Harmonia, Ares fathered two sons with Aphrodite –

Other sons of Ares

Ares had other children, too. With Aerope, daughter of Cepheus, he fathered Aeropus who survived by sucking his dead mother's breast even though she died during childbirth (Pausanias). He lay with Philonome, who bore the Arcadian king Lycastus, while Phlegyas was born from his union with Dotis or Chryse.

Ares was said to have fathered a

son in Libya. His name was also Lycastus and he had the habit of killing strangers and sacrificing them to his father. He captured Diomedes, who landed in Libya after the fall of Troy. Lycastus's daughter Callirrhoe fell in love with the prisoner and persuaded her father to free him. But Diomedes did not reciprocate her affection, so the girl killed herself.

The cult of Ares

The oldest sanctuary of Ares was in Thebes, where inhabitants believed they were descended from the Spartans, who grew from the teeth of Ares's monster-son slain by Cadmus. The city's fortifications were dedicated to Ares and known as the Areion.

The oath taken by the Athenian youths and the naming of the Athenian criminal court as the Areopagus (or Areios Pagus) illustrates how deep-rooted the cult of Ares was in Athens. Pausanias also mentions a temple dedicated to the war-god.

The existence of a double altar featuring statues of Ares and Aphrodite on the road between Argos and Mantineia –dedicated by Polyneices– suggests that the cult of Ares spread from Boeotia to the Peloponnese. Pausanias describes temples dedicated to Ares at Hermioni, Troezen, Megalopolis, Tegea, and Laconia.

The Spartans sacrificed roosters, oxen, and dogs to the ancient statue of the *Enyalios Ares*. Isolated, local accounts mention celebrations on Lemnos and in Sparta known as the *Hecatomphonia*, where a human

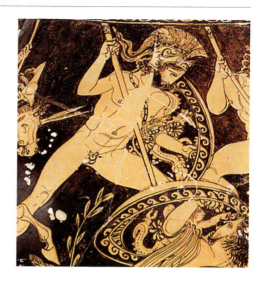

sacrifice was made to the god to memorialize the annihilation of 100 enemies in some battle. Yet while Ares is presented as a god who enjoyed bloody sacrifices, he was originally a vegetation deity.

Ares fought on foot or in his chariot, drawn by his horses Phobus, Aethon, Phlogius, Conabus, all sons of Erinya and Boreas.

In addition to his sons Deimus and Phobus, he was accompanied into battle by Eris (Discord) and the fast hounds of the Hades, the Keres, who scattered disaster (the Keres later joined the Moerae).

Ares's symbols were the spear and the brand that they threw down on enemy lines to signal the start of battle. The vulture and the hound were sacred to Ares, who changed into a hound to escape the monster Typhoeus.

APOLLO

God of fire, music, and divination, Apollo was also the god of illness and of healing, a legislator, eternal youth, and great kouros. Many scholars consider him the most Greek of all the Olympian gods as he belonged to an older generation of deities, as suggested by his maternal epithet *Letoieideis* or *Latoos*.

There are several myths that recount Apollo's birth. According to the most popular version, Apollo was the son of Zeus and Leto, daughter of the Titans Coeus and Phoebe. Zeus's jealous wife, Hera, persecuted Leto. Aware of Zeus's union with Leto, Hera knew that if Leto gave birth to a son, he could challenge her own son, Ares. She thus persuaded Gaea not to refuse to allow Leto refuge on earth so she could give birth.

The Homeric epic describes all the places where the pregnant Leto sought refuge until Poseidon raised the island of Delos from the sea and anchored it with four columns so Leto could alight on the island and give birth. But Hera managed to create more problems for Leto by preventing the birth-goddess Eileithyia from reaching her for nine days. The other gods finally intervened and

Apollo, from the "Battle of the Centaurs" on the western pediment of the Temple of Zeus at Olympia (470-456 B.C., Olympia Archaeological Museum).

Leto gave birth to Apollo and Artemis.

Other versions mention Ortygia, near Ephesus, as the island on which Apollo was born. Tegeira in Boeotia and Amphigeneia in Triphylia have also been mentioned as his birthplace. In another version, Leto, who was descended from the Hyperboreans, changed into a wolf to evade Hera and then sought refuge on Delos to give birth. By another account, Leto took her children to Lycia, where she stopped by a spring or a marsh to bathe, drink water, or bathe her newborn children but was chased away by local shepherds. They immediately changed into frogs and Leto, led by a pack of wolves, arrived at the river Xanthus, which she dedicated to Apollo. To show her gratitude to the wolves for saving her, she gave the name Lycia (*lycos* is Greek for wolf) to the land, although the most likely root of Lycia's name is *lux* or light.

Apollo and Python

Some myths mention that even before she became gave birth to Apollo and Artemis, Leto had been relentlessly pursued by the female snake-monster Python, who had been sent by Hera to kill her. Apollo shot his first enemy with his deadly arrows when he was just four months old. The battle was took place at Chrissa in Phocis, at the foothills of Mount Parnassus, where the Oracle of Delphi was founded later.

Following Python's death, Apollo purified himself by going into self-exile for either one or eight years. When his punishment ended, he returned to Delphi wearing a laurel wreath. Seeking to pay tribute to the god, Delphi's inhabitants established the *Septeria* festival, a re-enactment of Apollo's battle with Python that was held every nine years.

Apollo the slave

To take vengeance on the Cyclopes who made the lightning bolt that Zeus used to kill the son of Asclepius, Apollo killed all their sons since the Cyclopes themselves were immortal. To purify himself after the murders, he was forced by Zeus to become the slave of the king of Pherae, Admetus. Some writers claim that Apollo went to work for the handsome Admetus voluntarily because he had become smitten with the king.

Apollo was also forced to become the servant and shepherd of the Trojan king Laomedon because he took part in the gods' revolt against Zeus. Poseidon was punished the same way for the same reason. Pindar writes that both gods were charged with rebuilding the walls around Troy. But because Laomedon did not pay them the agreed upon fee, the two gods took their revenge: Apollo sent the plague to his land and Poseidon sent a sea monster to terrorize and seize his people.

Apollo and the Hyperboreans

Every winter, Apollo departed for his mother's homeland, the land of the Hyperboreans. The god would spend the three winter months with this legendary tribe that lived in a place that never existed and was *"east of the sun and west of the moon."* He would then return to Greece playing the lyre while riding in a chariot drawn by swans or a griffin.

Apollo's affair with Themisto, daughter of king Zavidios, with whom he fathered Galeus, founder of the famed dynasty of prophets.

Apollo and Heracles

The best-known myth about the relationship between Apollo and Heracles centers on the sacred tripod of Delphi. After the murder of Iphitus, Heracles fell sick. He decided to consult the Oracle of Delphi for a cure, but the Pythia refused to give the hero a prophecy. This angered Heracles, who left the sanctuary and took the tripod with him to found his own oracle. His actions angered Apollo, who rushed to confront him, but their father Zeus intervened and separated the two by throwing a thunderbolt between them. The two half-brothers bowed to Zeus's will and compromised. Heracles returned the sacred tripod to Pythia, who then answered his question with a prophecy.

When Heracles died, he became a god and Apollo accompanied him to his new, heavenly home while playing music on his lyre.

Apollo and Marsyas

According to another myth, Apollo invented the flute, which he gave to Athena as a present. But when she saw how her face was distorted while playing this wind instrument, she threw it on the ground and placed a curse on it. The satyr Marsyas picked up the flute, indifferent to Athena's curse. Marsyas became an accomplished player and was so proud of his skill that

Twins Artemis and Apollo with their parents Leto and Zeus, 410 B.C. (Brauron Museum).

he began to boast that he could play the flute better than Apollo played his lyre.

Marsyas then challenged Apollo to a contest. Teimolus, Midas, and the Muses or Cybele were appointed judges. Apollo beat Marsyas and was severely punished: he was hung and skinned alive by a Scythian slave. Midas, who had ruled in favor of Marsyas, was also punished: his ears were turned into the ears of a donkey.

Apollo's lovers

Apollo figures in numerous amorous adventures with young women and young me. Despite his good looks, he had many misadventures, perhaps because Hera took revenge on his mother Leto –Hera's rival– through Apollo. According to the Homer's hymn to Aphrodite, Apollo tried to unite with the virgin Hestia, who rejected him, as well as with his virgin sister Artemis. He lay with the muse Calliope, who bore him the poet Ialemus. Songs of mourning that grieve for the premature deaths of young people as well as for small animals are known as *ialemoi* in his honor.

Apollo and Daphne

Apollo fell deeply in love with the nymph Daphne (Laurel), who was the daughter of Gaea by either the

The musical contest between Apollo and Marsyas (relief, 330-320 B.C., National Archaeological Museum).

river-god Ladon, Amyclas, or the Thessalian river-god Peneius.

According to Arcadian and Eleian tradition, Leucippus, son of the Pisa's king Oenomaus, also fell in love with Daphne. To woo her, he disguised himself as a girl and then managed to slip into Daphne's circle of friends. Apollo sought to neutralize his rival, so he suggested to Daphne that she and her friends take a swim in the Ladon River. The other girls stripped Leucippus, then killed him when they saw he was actually a man.

Apollo now had a clear playing field, but Daphne rejected his advances and tried to run away. Apollo chased and caught her. But as he embraced her, Daphne prayed to Gaea for help. Hearing the girl's pleas, her mother caused the earth to part and swallow the girl. A laurel sprouted on the spot where Daphne disappeared into the earth. The tree was thus considered sacred to Apollo.

By one account, Daphne was swallowed by the earth in Syria, somewhere near the city of Antioch along the Orontis River. The city was subsequently renamed Antioch by Daphne.

Apollo and Coryceia

Apollo lay with the nymph Coryceia, who bore him a son, Lycoreas. He founded the most ancient city of Phocis, Lycoria on the northwestern foothills of Mount Parnassus, near the Coryceian Cave.

White kylix from the Delphi sanctuary depicting Apollo. The crow may represent the god's love for Coronis, who he shot with an arrow like Zeus shot Semele (490 B.C., Delphi Archaeological Museum).

Apollo and Ocyrrhoe

The nymph Ocyrrhoe, daughter of the Samian river Imbrasus tried to avoid Apollo's romantic overtures by boarding a ship. But the god turned the ship to stone and changed its sailors into fish.

Apollo and Coronis

Coronis was the daughter of the Lapith king Phlegyas. She lay with Apollo but as soon as she realized that she was pregnant agreed to marry Ischys to avoid provoking her father's anger. The god killed her for her infidelity; according to a different account, Apollo left Coronis's punishment to Artemis, but saved the child she was carrying. The child was the hero and god of healing Asclepius.

Apollo and Boline

The nymph Boline, eponym of the Achaean township of Boline by the Bolinaios river, threw herself into the sea to avoid Apollo's advances. But the god granted her immortality.

Apollo and Melia

Melia, a nymph and daughter of Oceanus, bore Apollo a son, the river Ismenus, father of Dirce.

Apollo and Marpessa

Apollo fell in love with Marpessa, a daughter of the Aetolian king Evenus and Demonice or Alcippe. Apollo's rival for Marpessa was Idas, who carried the girl off to Messenia on a winged chariot that was a gift from Poseidon. Marpessa's father chased Idas but drowned in the Aetolian river that spills into the Patras Gulf (the river was named Evenus after the king). Apollo continued the chase, and when he caught up with Idas and Marpessa began to fight with his rival. Zeus intervened, then ruled that Marpessa should choose between the two. Fearing that as she aged, she would no longer be attractive to Apollo, Marpessa chose Idas. Apollo respected her choice and stopped pursuing her.

Apollo and Cassandra

Cassandra, or Alexandra, was the

Poseidon, Apollo, Artemis (447-432 B.C., Acropolis Museum).

THE OLYMPIAN GODS

had taken refuge. When the spoils of war were divided, Cassandra was given to Agamemnon as a slave. She was taken back to Mycenae by the king and was murdered by Clytemnestra.

Apollo and Cyrene

According to Thessalian mythology, Cyrene was the daughter of Hypseus, king of the Lapiths, who lived on Mount Pelion where they hunted and tended their herds. Apollo fell in love with Cyrene when he saw her fighting a lion with her bare hands. He carried off her against her will in a chariot drawn by swans and took her to Libya, which he presented to her as a gift. There, Cyrene founded a city in her name. She bore Apollo a son, Aristaeus.

Apollo and Creusa

Apollo won the love of Creusa, daughter of the Athenian king Erechtheus and Praxithea. She bore him a son, Ion, eponym of the Ionians. According to Euripides's tragedy *Ion*, Creusa put the infant in a basket and exposed it at the cave where she lay with Apollo. Hermes carried the infant off to Delphi, where it was raised while respectfully serving at the temple.

Creusa later married Xuthus. Because their marriage was childless, they sought the help of the Oracle at Delphi. Apollo persuaded Xuthus that Ion was his son, but Creusa –who had lost her own child– rebelled when she saw Ion entering the palace and tried to poison him. Her attempt to kill him was unsuccessful, and her plot was exposed.

Head from gold and ivory statue of Apollo found at Delphi with a head of Artemis (550 B.C., Delphi Archaeological Museum).

prettiest of the daughters of the Trojan king Priam and Hecuba, but she had a tragic fate. Cassandra received the gift of prophecy by Apollo, who neutralized her powers of divination when she rejected him. Thus, no one believed Cassandra when she made her prophecies, even when she predicted the destruction that would befall Troy as a result of Paris's love for Helen or when she predicted the city's fall would be precipitated by the Trojan Horse.

When the Achaeans sacked Troy, the Locrian Ajax seized the princess from the altar of Athena, where she

Ion turned on his would-be murderer, who sought refuge in an altar where she prayed for help. Just then, Pythia arrived with various items such as the basket in which Ion had been exposed. Thus, with Athena's intervention, Creusa recognized her son.

Apollo and Rhoeo

Rhoeo was the daughter of Staphylus, who was the son of Dionysus and Chrysothemis. According to Attic tradition, the young woman bore Apollo a son, Sounios. But in other versions, her father locked her in a trunk and tossed it into the sea when he found out she was pregnant. Rhoeo washed up on the shores of Euboea, where she gave birth to Anius. His father, Apollo, carried Anius to Delos and gave him the gift of prophecy.

Apollo and Psamathe

Psamathe, daughter of the King Crotopus of Argos, was also Apollo's lover. She came to a tragic end by his hand because she exposed their child Linus, who was born in a forest and devoured by guard dogs. Apollo then sent Poene, a child-snatching monster with snakes for hair and iron talons, to terrorize the land. The monster was slain by Coroebus, a noble Argive youth. Apollo then sent the plague to Argos, prompting Coroebus to seek advice from the Oracle at Delphi, where he voluntarily offered himself as a sacrifice. Pythia imposed a light penalty: she told him to carry a sacred tripod for as long as he could, then build a temple to Apollo on the spot where he put the tripod down and make his home there. Thus, the myth explains the founding and name of the ancient city of Tripodiscus, which is located northwest of Megara at the foot of the Geraneia ridge.

Apollo and Castalia

The Castalian Spring that gushes in the gorge of the Phaedriades was named after a young Delphi woman, Castalia, who fell in the spring to avoid Apollo's advances.

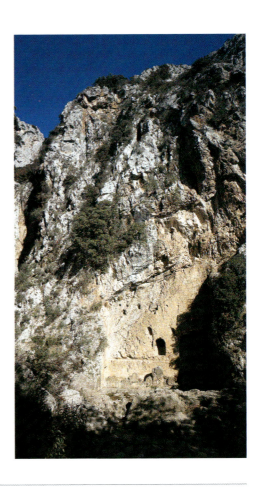

The Castalian Spring at Delphi.

Apollo and Chione

Chione was the daughter of the warrior Daedalion. She lay with Apollo and bore a son, Philammon. But she insulted Artemis by claiming to be more beautiful than the goddess, who shot and killed her with one of her arrows. Inconsolable, her father threw himself off Mount Parnassus, but was changed into a hawk by Apollo.

Apollo and Dryope

Dryope was the daughter of King Dryops or Eyrypylus or Eurytus of Oechalia. When Apollo say her playing with the hamadryads, he fell in love with her. To get close to the girl, he changed into a tortoise. But when Dryope picked the tortoise up, it changed into a snake and scared away the wood nymphs. Apollo lay with the girl, who bore him Amphissus, founder of the city of Oeti. The hamadryads later seized Dryope and made her a nymph. A poplar and spring appeared on the spot from which she was kidnapped.

Apollo and Thrya

From his union with Thrya, Apollo had a handsome son, Cycnus, who was the object of everyone's desire. To avoid the advances of the persistent Phylius, Cycnus assigned him three tasks to complete. Phylius complied and Cycnus was forced to submit to Phylius's advances. When Phylius deserted Cycnus, the youth and his mother fell into a mosquito-filled swamp. Apollo then changed them into birds (*kyknos* is Greek for swan.)

Apollo and Manto

When Thebes fell to the Epigoni (sons of the seven champions), Manto, the daughter of Teiresias, was devoted to the Oracle of Delphi as one of the spoils of war. There she became the new priestess of the oracle as well as Apollo's lover. She bore the god a son, Mopsus. Manto founded an oracle dedicated to Apollo at Clarus in Asia Minor. There, Mopsus became the cause for the death of the seer Calchas in accordance with a prophecy that Calchas would die when he met a seer with stronger powers.

Apollo and Leucatus

Leucatus was a handsome youth who threw himself into the sea from the southwestern-most point of the island of Leucas to avoid Apollo's advances. The island was named Leucada after the youth. To mollify Apollo, the island's inhabitants built a temple to the god *Apollo Leucatas* on the cape. Every year, they would tie feathers and raptors on a convict and toss him off the cliff.

Apollo and Cyparissus

According to mythology, Cyparissus was a very handsome youth who sought to escape Apollo's advances by fleeting to the banks of the Syrian river Orontis, where he was changed into a cypress tree. The Roman poet Ovid writes that the youth begged Apollo to turn him into a cypress tree because he was desolate at the death of his pet stag. Apollo answered his

Apollo with guitar on a shell pot found at the foothills of Mount Aegina.

prayer, and since then the cypress tree has been planted around graves and cemeteries as a symbol of mourning.

Apollo and Hyacinth

Hyacinth was the son of Amyclas, founder of the city of Amyclae in Laconia. Hyacinth returned Apollo's love, which provoked the jealousy of Zephyrus, as the handsome youth had not responded to his advances. Thus Zephyrus used the wind to blow the discus cast by Apollo off course, so it killed Hyacinth. Grief-stricken, Apollo turned Hyacinth into a flower whose blossoms formed the shape of their initials, YA. A three-day festival in Hyacinth's honor known as the *Hyacionthia* was held every year in Amyclae during the month of Hecatombaeon (July).

The cult of Apollo

Myths linking Apollo to Daphne and Hyacinth, the epithets *Phytalmios*, *Eriphylos*, *Enagros*, *Arotrios*, and *Sitalkas*, suggest a very old connection of the god to vegetation and agriculture. This suggestion is reinforced by the nature of the fertility cult of Hyacinth and the god's epithets that indicate he was worshipped as a patron of fertility, grains, (*Smintheas*, or pursuer of rodents, and *Parnopius*, or exterminator of locusts) and the harvest. Additional evidence is offered by the important Dorian celebration *Carneia* that was held in Sparta every four years. Another agricultural celebration in honor of Apollo as patron of fertile vegetation was the *Pyanopseia* held every autumn. During the festival, a child whose parents were still living would lead a procession to the god's sanctuary. The child would carry an olive branch, or *eiresione*, from which figs and small loaves of bread dangled during the procession, then enter the sanctuary and place the *eiresione* on the altar.

As a vegetation-god, Apollo was also the patron of sheep and herds. Several myths mention his service as a shepherd in the employ of Admetus, Eumelus, and Laodamas. There is also the myth of the theft of Hermes cattle, as well as the god's epithets as *Carneios* (from the ancient Greek for ram), *Arnocopis*, *Nomis*, *Opaon Melon*, *Arnocomas*, *Epimelios*, and *Poimnios* (from the Greek for flock). Mythological accounts of his mother's transformation into a wolf, his union with Cyrene in the form of a wolf, and the epithets *Lyceius*, *Lycoergus*, *Lycoctonus*, and *Lycegenis* (from the Greek root *lycos*, or wolf) further suggest that Apollo incorporated the ancient god Lycos, who was the enemy of flocks but was thus transformed into the protector of shepherds and an enemy of the wolf.

In *The Iliad*'s first rhapsody, Homer presents Apollo as spreading illness and death in the camp of the Achaeans. He thus appears as the god of destruction and death, but simultaneously as the god who has the power to prevent them and become, through worship, a healer *(Therapeutis)* who is able to ward off evil *(Alexikakos, Apotropaios)* and magically cure illness through these paeans. Apollo was worshipped as a healer at Epidaurus and in Laconia, where he was known as *Maleatas*, in Cynouria and in Piraeus as *Aceseios*, and in Elis as *Epicoureios*.

Throughout Greece, Apollo was considered as a great legislator, and until the fifth century B.C. lawmakers would have their laws ratified by the Oracle of Delphi, while the Spartans believed their laws were a gift from the god to Lycurgus.

The greatest contribution of the Apollonian spirit was the change in the social perception of homicide, as under the guiding influence of the Delphi oracle the chain of avenging murders, or vendetta, was broken and a cathartic ritual for the actual murderer or the instigator of a murder was introduced. Thus, after being purified through penitence, a murderer could be reintroduced into society. Delphi's influence

The cult of Apollo on the island of Delos, an important religious center and birthplace of the god, dates to the 10th century B.C., and the first Athenian alliance was forged at this temple. Pictured here is the famed "Terrace of Lions" (late seventh century B.C.), with the lion sculptures dedicated by the Naxians.

also ended human sacrifices and the horrid sacrificial rituals were replaced by more judicious offerings.

But Apollo's most important power, which overshadowed all the others, was prophecy. Oracles dedicated to the god were found throughout Greece and Asia Minor. One of the most important oracles was at Thebes. It is the Temple of Apollo Ismeneios, where a cedar *xoano*, or wooden idol, of the god made by the Sicyon sculptor Canachus was kept. This sacred oracle was located outside the walls of Thebes, near the son of Apollo and Ismenus River. The oracle's prophecies were divined from *empyromanteia* (ember divination) and later *klidonas* (water divination). The sanctuary reached its peak between 600 and 300 B.C., and worshippers would bring the oracle sacred tripods. The celebration of the *Daphnophories* was held in Apollo's honor during which a child was chosen to be oracle's priest or *Daphnophoros*.

The Oracle of Delph

While there were numerous important sanctuaries dedicated to Apollo in Asia Minor, on the islands of Lesbos and Chios, and in Boeotia and Thessaly on the Greek mainland, the most famous sanctuary was the Oracle of Delphi in Phocis, at the *omphalos*, or navel, of the earth. According to the ancient writers, Apollo arrived at Chrissa at the foot of the snow-covered Mount Parnassus to build his sanctuary after slaying the monster Python and supplanting the land's first seer, Gaea. In another version, Apollo's oracle was given to him as a birthday present from the Titan Phoebe, the third deity to rule the sanctuary after Gaea and Themis.

Apollo's prophecies were relayed through his high priestess at the Delphi oracle, Pythia – a woman over the age of fifty who had led a virtuous life. Unfortunately, there is no available

Delphi, Temple of Apollo (mid-fourth century B.C.). Peripteral structure in the Doric style, six columns wide and fifteen columns long. The temple was built under the supervision of the Corinthian architect Spintharos. The first temple was believed to have been made of bronze and built by the god Hephaestus. After its destruction by fire or an earthquake, a stone temple was built by the famed architects Trophonios and Agamedous, but was destroyed in 548 B.C. by fire. Another temple, known as the temple of the Alcmeonidae (506/5-373 B.C.), which was later replaced by the temple whose ruins have survived to the present.

information on how a simple mortal was chosen to be the god's priestess. However, at its peak, the sanctuary had three priestesses –two alternates and one substitute.

Plutarch writes that Pythia would deliver her prophecies only once a year, on the seven day of the Delphic month Bysios, which appears to have coincided with the beginning of spring and Apollo's birthday. In the sixth century B.C., the sanctuary switched from issuing prophecies once a year to issuing them once a month. The sanctuary was closed during the three winter months that Apollo spent with the Hyperboreans, although the oracle's seers overcame this by using different methods of divination such as *cleromanteia*.

To see whether Apollo was positively disposed towards a request for a prophecy, they sprinkled an ewe with cold water before sacrificing it. If the animal trembled, this was a good sign: the god was near and Pythia could sit on the sacred tripod, enter a trance, and communicate with him.

Before entering the temple, the petitioner would have to make an offering at the outer altar of a type of sacred pie, which was quite expensive. The petitioner would then cross the threshold and enter into the inner altar, where the eternal flame burned, and make a sacrificial offering of sheep or goats. The petitioner would then enter the sanctum, where he was instructed to think pure thoughts and speak auspicious words, but neither the petitioner nor the priest-seer would see Pythia as she muttered incoherently. Thus the seer would convey the prophecies she delivered in metered prose in the first person, as it was understood that these were the god's words and that Pythia was merely his conduit.

The Tholos. The Sanctuary of Athena Pronaia, which has been dated to the early fourth century B.C., had a peristyle of 20 Doric columns and featured Corinthian columns inside. The exterior metope was decorated with depictions of the battle of the Amazons. The structure's purpose is not known.

ARTEMIS

An important goddess of the Greek pantheon, Artemis was the proud god of nature and hunting. She was thus perceived as a young virgin who rules and protects wildlife, but also helps women with childbirth and cause sudden death.

Artemis is described in Homer's epics as being the daughter of Zeus and Leto – and Apollo's twin sister. This identity is prevalent through later art and literature, but the goddess appears in such a variety of forms and with such diverse symbols that the origin of her myths and cult differ throughout the Greek world, suggesting that Artemis was a pre-Hellenic deity.

The birth of Artemis

The myths surrounding the birth of the goddess reflect the diverse descriptions of her form and powers. Artemis is mentioned as being the daughter of Zeus and Demeter or Persephone, Demeter's daughter. The prevalent version of her birth is contained in Homer's hymns, in which Leto, Zeus's lover, gives birth to Artemis on the remote islet of Ogygia while being hounded by Hera (Ogygia is a name found in all lands where Artemis is worshipped). The following day, Artemis helps her mother give birth to Apollo on the island of Delos.

Apollo and Artemis

Apollo's twin sister, Artemis is linked to the both the cult of her brother and his adventures. She kills the nymph Coronis who rejected Apollo, and doesn't even abandon her brother even during his purification for the murder of Python. She also accompanies him to the land of the Hyperboreans and joins him in defending their mother Leto by killing Niobe's children after Niobe insulted Leto.

In the battle with the Giants, Artemis changed into a deer and used her arrows to shot dead Gaios or Raios. According to one account, when the Aloeuids –the giants Otus and Ephialtes– tried to scale Mount

Artemis. Chryselephantine statue (sixth century B.C., Delphi Museum, bronze collection).

THE OLYMPIAN GODS

Artemis on relief found at Brauron sanctuary (fourth century B.C., Brauron Museum).

In some accounts, Artemis sent the wild boar to kill Aphrodite's lover, Adonis. She also appears to be quite vengeful as she punishes Admetus and Oeneus for failing to honor her with a sacrifice.

Olympus to woo her and Hera, Artemis tossed a deer between them; the two giants killed each other while trying to kill the deer.

Artemis and mortals

According to one myth, Artemis killed Minos's daughter Ariadne on the request of Dionysus. Artemis was also indirectly responsible for the death of Ariadne's sister Phaedra who killed herself over Hippolytus. Phaedra was smitten with her virgin stepson, but he rejected her attempts to seduce him because he was dedicated to Artemis.

Bronze statue of Artemis (350 B.C., Piraeus Archaeological Museum).

HERMES

Hermes, the messenger and herald of the Olympian gods, was the son of Zeus and the pleiade Maia, daughter of Atlas. In his hymn to Hermes, Homer mentions that the god was born in a cave of Mount Cyllene, and while still an infant, went to Pieria, and stole Apollo's cattle. The infant god was so precocious that he covered the animals' hooves so they would not leave tracks, hid the cattle at Pylos, and then returned to Cyllene. Outside the cave he found a tortoise, which he killed. He then used her shell and the intestines he removed from the cattle to invent the lyre.

But Apollo, who had the power of prophecy, discovered the thief and went to Cyllene where Hermes was asleep in his crib. He snatched the infant and took him to Olympus. At first, Hermes denied he charges of theft, before being forced to confess and return the cattle. To pacify his brother, Hermes gave him the tortoise shell lyre; Apollo in turn gave Hermes a staff so he could graze his animals as well as the gift of prophecy by casting cubes. Their friendship was thus sealed and Apollo swore that Hermes would always be his favorite among gods and mortals.

Hermes by Praxiteles (circa 330 B.C., Olympia Archaeological Museum). The gods' herald carrying Dionysus's younger brother to the nymphs.

Hermes's relationships with gods and mortals

Hermes took part in the battle against the Giants and was able to kill Hippolytus thanks to a magic helmet Hermes had been given by Hades that made whoever wore it invisible.

Hermes served Zeus and executed his commands quite willingly. Because of Hermes's intelligence, Zeus would seek the herald's assistance in all difficult situations, especially in his illicit romances when Hermes would often help him evade Hera's jealousy and anger. Occasions when Hermes helped Zeus include the time when Typhoeus cut the sinews of Zeus's feet; when Hermes killed the hound Argus, which was guarding his father's lover Io on Hera's orders; by carrying the infant Dionysus first to Euboea and then to Mount Nysa; and Hermes accompanies Hephaestus to Caucasus where he chains Prometheus, all the whole mocking the Titan for going against the king of the gods.

But Hermes is also the willing herald and messenger of all the gods who seek his help. He freed Ares who had been locked in a bronze jail by the Aloeuids, Otus and Ephialtes. He also leads Athena, Hera, and Aphrodite to Paris to judge their beauty contest, and is present when Hades snatches Persephone as well as when she returns to the earth.

Hermes was also charged with selling Heracles as a slave, but stood by the hero at difficult moments such as when Heracles descended to the Underworld to steal the watchdog Cerberus and bring Alcestes back to life. Hermes also encouraged Perseus to kill the Medusa. As a token of his gratitude, Perseus gave the god a helmet he had been given by Hades, while Hermes gave the hero a silver scythe, which was the weapon Perseus used to Gorgon.

Hermes's lovers and children

Hermes is said to have had romances with several nymphs and fathered many children with them. His better-known children include the hooved Pan, who he fathered with Dryope; Priapus; and, Autolycus, the father of Laertes and grandfather of Odysseus. Hermes fathered Autolycus with Chione, and his son inherited the god's ability to disguise stolen bounty – a talent he used to steal Sisyphus's cattle.

Hermes also lay with Minos's daughter Acacallis, who bore him Kydon, founder of the Cretan city of Kydonia. From his union with Cecrops's daughter Herse, Hermes had Cephalus, and from his union with Polemele, he fathered Eudorus. Other children of Hermes include Samon or Saoon, the eponymous hero of Samothrace; Polybus, a king of Corinth and stepfather of Oedipus; Cyrikas, eponym of the Attic tribe of Kyrykon (Heralds); Daphnis, Hermaphroditus and many others.

Daphnis

Daphnis, a Sicilian hero who tended his herds on the slopes of Mount Aetna, invented bucolic poetry. He was the son of Hermes from the god's union with a nymph. Daphnis owes his name to his birth in a laurel wood, where he was also raised by nymphs. According to another version, he was exposed by his mother, but found and raised by a bucolic people. He was exceptionally handsome and his love songs, which he accompanied with a musical instrument, lured gods and mortals – especially the nymphs, muses, Apollo, Artemis, Priapus, and Pan, who taught him how to play music. Daphnis died in the prime of his life, and was mourned by nature, gods, and mortals.

The poet Stesichorus, who first recorded the myth of Daphnis in literature, says the Sicilian hero died after being blinded by one of the nymphs, Naias, because he betrayed her with the daughter of the Sicilian king. In other versions, Daphnis either fell off a rock or was turned into a rock or was carried to the heavens by Hermes, while Sicilians later made offerings on the spot from which he disappeared.

Other myths link Daphnis to Phrygia (which explains his epithet *Idaios*), where he went searching for the nymph Pibeleia or Thaleia, who had been snatched by pirates and sold as a slave to the king of the Lityerses. Daphnis was nearly killed by the savage king, but Heracles intervened to save him. Daphnis then taught Marsyas to play the flute. Another myth links the handsome shepherd to Euboea, while Loggos's bucolic tale relates the story of Daphnis and Chloe, two innocent youths initiated into the secrets of love.

Daphnis's special relationship with nature, his death at the prime of his life, and nature's grief at his passing suggest he was a vegetation-god who symbolized the wilting and death of nature in winter.

Hermaphroditus

Hermaphroditus was the very beautiful son of Hermes and Aphrodite who had the gender traits of both his parents. Once, as he was wandering through a forest of Halicarnassus, he stopped by a lake to see his reflection in its water. The lake's nymph Salmacis saw him and fell madly in love. To avoid her, he jumped into a river. The nymph followed him, then caught him in her embrace and began kissing him passionately while praying to the gods that she be eternally united with him. The gods heard her prayer and fused their bodies so that no one could tell whether the body belonged to a man or a woman. According to the myth, any man who bathed in that river's waters would become a hermaphrodite.

The ancient Greeks threw hermaphrodites into the sea, and it was not until the seventeenth century that their rights were respected by law, albeit with religious and political restrictions.

The powers of Hermes

Herald and messenger

Brave and fleet-footed, Hermes became the gods' messenger and herald, edging out Iris. His symbol was the *kerykeion*, a gold herald's wand or caduceus that was first depicted as being branched and later as having either two snakes or two feathers wrapped around its ends. His other symbol was a pair of winged sandals.

As herald, Hermes was gifted with an exceptional memory and strong voice. The myth of the Stentorian, a herald whose voice is as loud as the voices of fifty people, has been associated with these traits. Stentorian was killed by Hermes, whom he had challenged to a contest of voices.

Patron of youth

Hermes is the most youthful and flexible of the Olympians gods, in short, the ideal of the Greek youth or *ephebus*. He was thus honored by Greek youths as *enagonios* and *agonios*. Like Apollo and Heracles, Hermes was the patron of the *gymnasium* and *palaistra*, buildings used for athletic and educational activities. Athletic contests were held throughout Greece in Hermes's honor. These competitions were known as *Hermaia*, and the best known was a boys' torch race held at Delos, where youths were under the protection of Hermes and Heracles.

Patron of herds

The agricultural nature of the patron-god of herds is evident from epithets such as *Milosoos, Nomios, Epimilios,* and *Agrotir* as well as localized versions of myths in areas where Hermes was worshipped, especially in the grazing lands of Arcadia where the god's birthplace, Mount Cyllene, is located. Hermes is often depicted as wearing a shepherd's cap known as *petasos* or seated on a ram or carrying a kid (thus the epithet *Kriophorus*).

In Homer's hymn to the god, Hermes is not only

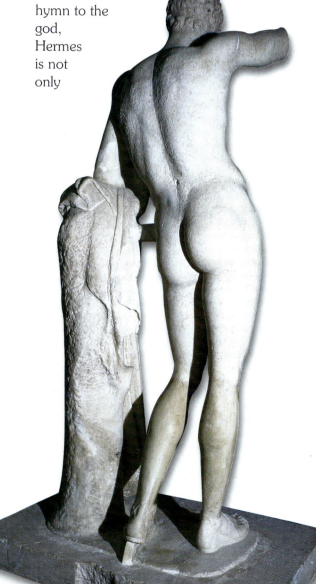

Rear view of the famed statue of Hermes with the Dionysian infant by Praxiteles (fourth century B.C., Olympia Archaeological Museum).

portrayed as the protector of sheep, oxen, horses, and mules but of hounds, lions, and wild beasts as well.

Patron of roads

Hermes was considered the patron and savior of travelers, who called him *Odeios, Enodeios, Hegemoneios,* and *Agetor*. Proof of this ancient cult are the stone-heaps known as *hermaia* (also *hermaioi lophoi* and *hermakes*) that travelers erected as markers along paths to guide fellow travelers where there were no roads. These piles of stones were later replaced by *Hermai*, which Athenians were credited with invented and which they built along paths and roads, next to the *palaistra*, the gymnasium, the stadium, at the agora, at sanctuaries, but also by the entrance to dwellings. The *Hermai* were a type of statue with a god's head (Hermes or Dionysus), and were often two-headed. The torso was a square column, from which the god's genital organs protruded. The *Hermai* were crafted with simple techniques. The importance of these figures was illustrated by the famous trial of Alcebiades and his friends, who chopped the members off the *Hermai* in a drunken spree.

Patron of trade and thefts

Merchants also considered Hermes their patron and called him *Kerdoos* (from the Greek *kerdos*, or profit). He was credited with invented weights and measures. This explains why statues of Hermes in the agora depicted the god holding a pouch full of coins. Because fraud and theft also marked trade, Hermes also became the patron of thieves, since as an infant he had displayed a talent for thievery by stealing the cattle of his brother, Apollo.

Patron of scholars

Hermes was an intelligent god who used his intellect and powers of persuasion. He was known as *logios* (scholar) and was considered the patron of orators and philosophers. The ancient Greeks credited Hermes with the invention of writing, while the Alexandrians identified him with the Egyptian god Thoth. As the son of Maia, one of the Pleiades who had become a constellation, they also considered him the father of astronomy and, by extension, the father of mathematics.

Patron of health, sleep, and dreams

Although Hermes was not a god of medicine, he helped people who were ill. In Tanagra, inhabitants would tell the story of how Hermes saved the city from the plague by parading a ram outside Tanagra's walls. The event was commemorated every year in a celebration in which the most beautiful youth represented the god and walked around the city's walls carrying a ram.

Hermes was also knowledgeable about the medicinal herbs that grew on the slopes of Mount Cyllene, where he was born. He used this knowledge to give Odysseus a moly, a small white flower with a black root, to protect him from Circe's sorcery.

Hermes was also known as *hypnodotis*, or sleep-giver; he brought sleep and wakefulness, and was also the sender of dreams. Before retiring at night, the ancient Greeks would offer him the last drops of their libation. Once in bed, they would lay facing the god's image so he would protect them while they slept.

Companion of the dead

Hermes did not abandon people even when they departed for their eternal resting-place, but accompanied their souls to the Underworld. He was thus known as *psychopombos, psychagogos, necropombos, pombos,* and *tamias ton nekron* –or treasurer of the dead. The snakes –chthonic symbols– on his *kerykeion*, or caduceus, likely symbolized this trait.

God of fertility

Hermes was worshipped as an ithyphallitic god – that is, having an erect phallus. Herodotus writes that the Athenians received their trait from the Pelasgians, who founded the Cabeirian mysteries practiced in Samothrace, where Hermes was worshipped as *Kadmilos* or *Kasmilos*. On Imvros, an island consecrated to Hermes, the ithyphallitic god was worshipped as *Imvramus*.

Later writers mention that the ithyphallitic Hermes was the son of Uranos and Hemera, or from the chthonic Artemis or Aphrodite. In several local myths, Hermes was worshipped as a fertility god and a god of fertile land. In Cyllene, a statue in the shape of a phallus represented him. The god's genitals were also highlighted in the *Hermai* while the ram, a domestic animal identified with reproduction, was one of Hermes's primary symbols.

Hermes, as an usher of souls, leads the young Myrrhina to Underworld. On the left, grieving relatives bid their final farewell. (Marble flask, circa 430-420 B.C., National Archaeological Museum).

HADES

Pluto and Persephone (440 B.C., British Museum).

The ancient Greeks believed Hades was the son of Cronus and Rhea who was given the Underworld to rule as his share of Cronus's domain. (Homer, *The Iliad*). His name is believed to derive from Aidoneus, or unseen one, from the ancient root *Fid* or *idein* (see). Alternately, his name derived from the words *ao* or *pneo* (breath), *ido* (thanks), although more recent linguistic studies see a link between his name and the Sanskrit word *asu* (soul), *asFoFis* (land where souls go), *aisFa* (fate), and *aiFon* (duration of life).

In *The Iliad*, Homer mentions that Hades had a magic helmet or *kyne* made from the hide of a dog (*kyn*), a gift from the Cyclopes. Whoever wore the helmet became invisible; Hades wore it during the battle against the Giants. Homer also mentions that he was wounded by Heracles and ascended to Mount Olympus, where Paean or Paeeon healed him.

Hades figures in one of the most widely known myths: the abduction of Persephone with Zeus's consent, as mentioned by Homer in his hymn to Demeter. According to Homer, Kore was picking flowers in a field at Nysa and she leaned over to cut a narcissus –a flower which Gaea grew as tribute to the youth Narcissus– the earth parted and Hades emerged on his chariot and grabbed Kore, who barely had time to let out a cry. The

Pluto and Persephone (Apulian crater, 360-350 B.C., British Museum). The "most despised god" and Kore are depicting on a four-horse chariot as they travel to the dark kingdom of the dead accompanied by Hermes while the goddess Hecate lights their way with a torch.

THE OLYMPIAN GODS

abduction provoked Demeter's rage and sent her on a search for her missing daughter. The issue was settled with a compromise, according to which Persephone would spend eight months in the light on the surface of the earth and four months in the darkness of the Underworld.

Persephone did not have many rivals. Mythology only mentions one dalliance with the nymph Menthe who Persephone or Demeter relentlessly pursued and dismembered; afterwards, Hades turned her into a plant, the mint. Leuce, Oceanus's daughter, is sometimes mentioned as his lover.

When she died, she grew into the silver-leafed poplar – the tree that grew in the Elysian Fields. Heracles made a wreath from the poplar's branches that he wore when he returned from the land of the dead.

The ancient Greeks did not build temples to the heartless Hades. As Pausanias writes, only the Eleians founded a sanctuary in his honor. The temple was only open once a year and sacrifices of animals with black fur were made there.

Merciless, touch, untamed, unemotional, hated, but rich and powerful from the souls of the dead, Hades was the great judge of mortals and their common fate. He was often honored with Dionysus, which is why he is sometimes called *Zagreus*. In *The Iliad*, he lives beneath the earth, while in *The Odyssey* he lives beyond Oceanus in the land of the Cimmerions which is bounded by the rivers Acheron, Pyriphlegethon, Cocytus, and Styx. The gates of Hades were guarded by monstrous dog Cerberus, who had three (or, by some accounts, fifty) heads with which he devoured whoever dared approach his master's palace. Hades's satellites included the Erinyes (Furies), the Ceres, Ate, Nemesis, and the Moerae (Fates), while his roommate was Dike (Justice).

The ancient Greeks identified several sites with the entrance to the kingdom of the dead. These places usually featured openings in the earth and included Taenarum in the southern Peloponnese, Lake Acherousia, Kymi, or Hippios Colonus in Athens.

Demeter, holding a plough, watches Hades-Pluto sow seeds from the Horn of Amaltheia onto the sown field. (Red-figure pelike, 430-420 B.C., National Archaeological Museum.)

111

Dionysus and the Dionysian Gods

DIONYSUS

A bon vivant, Dionysus was the most loved of the ancient Greek gods. His cult was had the most complex history as it arrived in Greece from Phrygia, Thrace, or Egypt. Originally a fertility god, he was identified with the patron-god of winemaking and was later transformed into a mysterious god whose passions –including his death and resurrection– symbolize the natural cycle of life and the perpetual story of life and rebirth.

The introduction, spread, and acceptance of the orgiastic, Dionysian cult –which ran counter to the Greek spirit– did not happen smoothly in every part of the Greek world. This is reflected in the various myths of Lycurgus or Pentheus, as well as in Euripides's tragedy *The Bacchae*. The Oracle of Delphi facilitated the introduction of the Dionysus into the ancient Greek pantheon, but it is doubtful that this was due to the god's original identification with prophecy, although Dionysus's effusive character was added to Apollo's divinatory activity. In any case, the Delphic year was divided equally between the cult of Apollo and the cult of Dionysus. Thus, from the sixth century B.C., his cult was practiced in every Greek city.

Bronze statue of Dionysus depicting deities of three different origins (150 B.C., National Archaeological Museum).

Mosaic floor depicting Dionysus seated on a panther. The god is shown wearing a wreath of ivy and holding a thyrsos and tambourine (second half of second century B.C., House of Masks, Delos).

The birth of Dionysus

Although there are many myths that center on the birth of Dionysus –and a number of sites that claim to be his birthplace– in the most prevalent version Dionysus was born in Thebes. His mother was Semele, a daughter of Cadmus and Harmonia.

Zeus fell in love with Semele and lay with her at her father's palace. But Zeus's jealous wife Hera decided to take revenge on the god for his infidelity. She appeared before Semele in the form of her nurse, Beroe, and persuaded Semele to demand that Zeus appear before her as he did before his wife, in his full Olympian glory, to prove his love. Zeus objected, but Semele was insistent so he gave in: he was framed by thunder and lightning, which struck Semele and burned her. To save the child she was carrying, Zeus took it from her womb and sewed it inside his thigh where it remained until reaching term. Thus Dionysus, son of Zeus (from the Greek for Zeus, *Dias*), was born *dithyrambos*, or from two "doors" – his mother's womb and his father's thigh.

According to a different version, Dionysus was saved from the flames by Gaea, who wrapped him in the ivy that covered the walls of Cadmus's palace. Dionysus thus acquired the epithet *Pyrigenis*, or born of fire.

After his birth, Dionysus was given to the nymphs to be raised. There are many local variations of the myth of his upbringing:

- Apollo gave the infant Dionysus to Semele's sister, Ino, to raise at Orchomenus with her husband Athamas. To punish them, Hera drove both of them mad. As a result, Athamas killed Learchus and Ino threw herself into the sea with her son Melicertes. Hermes then rushed to save the infant, which he gave to the nymphs to raise at Nysa. (Nysa was identified with several cities in Greece, Asia, and North America.)
- Diodorus Sikeliotis writes that Dionysus was raised on the island of Naxos by the nymphs Coronis, Philia, and Cleiade.
- On Euboea, it was believed that Dionysus was raised by the nymph Macris, who fed the infant honey and was forced to seek refuge from Hera's wrath on the island of the Phaeacians.
- In Lydia, it was believed that the god was raised on Mount Timolos by the nymph Ipta or with the satyrs, the maenads, and seileni.

The god's birth in the Orphic tradition

Dionysus Zagreus, the great god of the Orphic cult, was the son of Zeus and Persephone, a horned four-eyed monster who was born from the union of Zeus and Rhea who changed into a snake during delivery. Fearing Hera might kill the child out of jealousy, Zeus entrusted it to the Curetes to guard and raise. But Hera learned the infant's whereabouts and sent the Titans to kidnap it. In vain, Zagreus tried to escape by successively changing into a lion, tiger, horse, and dragon. But the Titans caught and dismembered him. Furious, Zeus struck the Titans with thunderbolts.

Apollo, on his father's orders, collected the piece of his brother Zagreus and buried them near the sacred tripod of the Delphi oracle. Athena, meantime, took Zagreus's heart and gave it to Zeus who swallowed it and then gave birth to the second Zagreus-Dionysus, who was destined to share his father's glory and power.

Thus, in the Orphic myth, Zagreus-Dionysus symbolizes the eternal source of life (that he received from his father Zeus) and its union with chthonian gods (through his mother Persephone). He is the ultimate ruler of the underworld – indeed, he is sometimes considered to be the son of Hades or Hades himself – but also is the ruler of the immortals (since he has a place on the throne of Zeus) and the immortal soul, which eternally dies and is resurrected in the natural and moral world.

Dionysus, the vineyard, and wine

The ancient Greeks attributed the introduction vine cultivation and winemaking. Of course, several places seek to claim the honor of being the first to produce wine. For example, in the myth of Icarius, grapes are cultivated first in Attica.

The king Icarius extended his hospitality to Dionysus who reciprocated by teaching the king culture of the vine and the art of winemaking, but cautioned him to hide the flasks of wine because it would lead to disaster. Icarius ignored Dionysus's advice and offered some wine to a group of passing shepherds who got drunk, beat him to death, then tossed his body into the Anygro well, and covered it with rocks. With help from her dog Maera, Icarius's daughter Erigone eventually found his body.

Dionysus and Lycurgus

The myth of the king of the Edonians reflects the obstacles to the introduction of the Dionysian cult in some places. Homer writes how while hunting in the mountains of Thrace, Lycurgus, a son of Dryas, hit the nymphs raising Dionysus. Frightened, the young god jumped into the sea and found refuge in the arms of Thetis. The gods blinded Lycurgus, who died a short while later.

According to a different version, while Dionysus and his train were wandering through Thrace, Lycurgus, who also captured the maenads and satyrs, drove them out. Dionysus, in turn, drove Lycurgus to madness; in a frenzy, he killed his own son, thinking he was tearing up a vineyard. After this, the earth stopped bearing fruit. The Edonians sought advice from Dionysus through an oracle on how to end the famine. Learning that it would not end as long as the king lived, they captured him and chained him to Mount Pangaeus, where horses

Dionysus (fifth century B.C. kylix, Berlin Archaeological Museum).

dismembered him. But there are variations on this myth.

- Furious at Dionysus, Lycurgus tried to rape Semele and uproot all the vines from the land of the Edonians. To punish the king, Dionysus drove him mad so that he killed his mother and his son, and cut off his own leg thinking it was a vine. He then jumped off Mount Rhodope and was devoured by panthers.
- Lycurgus planned to strangle Dionysus, who had just returned from India. The god escaped, crossed the Hellespont, where he gathered his troupe, marched against Lycurgus, defeated, and killed him.

Dionysus and the Minyans

Dionysus also ran into resistance at Orchomenus, where the daughters of king Minyas –Leucippe, Arsippe, and Alcathoe– refused to take part in the orgiastic cult with the other women. The god tried to persuade them by changing into a girl. He also tried to frighten them by changing into a lion, a bull, and a panther. But the Minyans would not give in, so he drove them mad and made Leucippe kill her son Hippasus.

Dionysus and Pentheus

The greatest resistance to the Dionysian cult was mounted by the god's cousin, Pentheus, a king of

Dionysus (western frieze of Temple of Apollo, Delphi, fourth century B.C., Delphi Museum).

Thebes and son of Agave (his mother's sister) and Echion. Dionysus appeared at the palace where his mother had been struck by a thunderbolt and drove the Theban women wild with the frenzied rites of the Dionysian cult and they rushed to the mountains to join in. Returning from a journey abroad, Pentheus was infuriated by Dionysus so he captured the god and some of the maenads and locked them up. Dionysus was freed. Pentheus disguised himself as a maenad and followed Dionysus up Mount Cithaeron, where he was torn to be pieces by the maenads, while his mother Agave, who mistook him for a lion, nailed his head to an ivy-covered club used in bacchic rituals.

Dionysus on the interior of a black-figure kylix by Exekias (sixth century B.C.). The dolphins represent pirates who, frightened, jumped into the sea when they realized that the god was on board their ship (Munich Archaeological Museum).

Dionysus on Naxos

In antiquity, Naxos was also named Dionysiada. The island is inextricably linked to Dionysian mythology. Its first recorded inhabitants, the Thracians, introduced the cult of Dionysus to the island, but the myth of Dionysus continues to live on through the island's folk traditions and culture.

According to the most prevalent myth surrounding the birth of Dionysus, the god was raised on Naxos by the nymphs Philia, Cleiade, and Coronis. To show his gratitude to the island's inhabitants, Dionysus blessed the island with happiness and abundance. Indeed, the land was so fertile that the ancient writers claimed that its rivers flowed with sweet, fragrant wine.

On Naxos, Dionysus married Minos's daughter Ariadne, whom Theseus had abandoned on the island. They had three children: Staphylus, Oenopion, and Euadne.

The island also served as the backdrop for many of the god's adventures, including his agreement with Hephaestus on the apple of discord and his kidnapping by Tyrrhenian (Etruscan) pirates.

This is how the abduction is described in an Homeric hymn: On trip to Naxos, the pirates grabbed Dionysus and chained him, but the chains fell away from his divine body. Sweet wine also trickled from the ship and a vine entwined with sacred ivy covered its mast. The god changed into a lion and then a bear, frightening the crewmembers so much that they jumped overboard and were turned into dolphins.

Dionysus in India

According to Pausanias, Dionysus went on an expedition to India. He built a bridge over the Euphrates River and crossed the Tigris River riding on a lion's back. Arriving in India, the god and his strange train were greeted with hostility by the Indians. After warring against him for three or five years, the Indians submitted to the god who taught gave them the vine as a present and taught them how to cultivate land.

DIONYSUS AND THE DIONYSIAN GODS

Dionysus and the other gods

Irresistible, Dionysus ruled over both land and sea. He took part in the battle against the Giants, who were frightened into fleeing by the braying of the donkeys ridden by him and his company.

Dionysus was the only god who managed to get Hephaestus drunk and thus coax him back to Mount Olympus to release the invisible bonds with which he had tied Hera up.

Dionysus also descended to the Underworld, fought him, and returned to earth with his mother Semele who took the name Thyone and became his inseparable companion.

Hellenistic era mosaic floor (Galilee, Israel).

The Dionysian cult and celebrations

Wilted and withered in winter, nature is reborn every spring, then begins to shed its leaves again in autumn as its cycle slowly turned towards natural death. The ancients would observe these changes in the weather cycle with admiration and awe as these changes were directly linked to the planting of seeds and agricultural production. Thus, ancient beings quickly embraced the celebratory cult of the patron-god of nature.

Dionysian rituals had elements of ecstasy and mysticism. Through an intoxication of the senses, worshippers would cleanse their souls and purify their lives. The bacchants, as they were called, would dance around beating drums and playing flutes, shouting and making animal cries, carried phalluses, which were symbols of fertility. The Dionysian cult liberated women, who carrying brands and ivy-covered clubs, roamed through the woods at nights in a frenzied state, calling to the god using various epithets.

Farmers were the first to worship Dionysus. Watching this god of poverty freeing the poor from their daily toil, the wealthy classes believed Dionysus was dangerous and banned his cult.

But with the passage of time and the spread of vine cultivation, his cult also spread. Some clever tyrants who sought to win popular support allowed Dionysus to be worshipped freely; indeed, Periander in Corinth, Cleisthenes in Syceon, and Peisistratus in Athens made the impressive gesture of officially adopted his cult.

At all Dionysian cult centers, bacchants worshipped their god through the haze of inebriation. Wearing goat hides and ivy wreaths, they rubbed their bodies with must residue and changed into satyrs as they used song and dance to re-enact the god's adventures. Their choral lyric was known as the dithyramb, in honor of Dionysus's double birth. The genre

The phallus, symbol of Dionysus and nature's fertility, was proudly carried in procession during feasts honoring the god thus trumpeting the ancient Greeks' belief in the hideous powers of the "indecent."
(House of Dionysus, 300 B.C., Delos.)

marks the creation of one of the brightest creations of the human mind, ancient drama, which gained great glory during the fifth century B.C. in Athens.

The most important Dionysian celebrations were:

- The *Grand Dionysia* held every year during the month of Elaphebolianos (end March-early April) in Athens in honor of *Dionysus Eleutheraea* whose *xoana*, or small wooden figures, were brought to Athens from Eleutherae, a small village on the border between Attica and Boeotia. Before and after the Peloponnesian Wars, the festival lasted five days, while during the war it only lasted three. Ambassadors from all the Greek city-states took part in the festival. Athens would use the opportunity to show off its wealth and power. The public ceremony culminated with sacrifices, torch races, phallus processions, dithyramb competitions, and the teaching of the incomparable works of Attic drama at the Theater of Dionysus at the foot of the Acropolis.

- The *Kat' Agrous Dionysia* was celebrated during the month of Poseideona (end December-early January) in every *demos*, or administrative area. The centerpiece of the celebration was the *komos*, or procession, in which the phallus was led around the settlement by worshippers chanting to Phallus, Dionysus, or one of his companions.

- The *Lynaea* was the Dionysian celebration of the Ionians held in the Ionian month of Lynaeonas, which corresponded to the Attic month Gamiliona (end January-early February). Month and festival were named after the *linos*, or winepress. The celebration featured a procession and competition of lyric poems and plays, especially comedies. After 432 B.C. a tragedy competition was added to the official events, although it was limited to two tragedies without satirical drama.

- The *Anthesteria*, or celebration of spring, was held on the 11th, 12th, and 13th days of the Attic month

Dionysus (detail from bronze, gold-plated crater of Derveni, 330-320 B.C., Thessaloniki Archaeological Museum).

Anthesteriona (end February-early March) and lasted for three days. On the first day, which was called *Pithoyeia*, clay storage jars called *pitharia* were opened so the new wine could be tasted, after offering some at the altar of Dionysus on the southern slope of the Acropolis. On the second day, *Choes*, wine-drinking contests were held – a ritual attributed to Orestes when he arrived in Athens after committing matricide. Contest participants were given jugs called *choes* that were filled with wine to drink as fast as they could. The contest was followed by a ritual known as *hierogameia*, which was a re-enactment of Dionysus's marriage to the wife of the ruler-king. The third day, *Chytroi*, was dedicated to the souls of the dead, who were invited to take part in a meal prepared in large pots or *chytres*. The meal was prepared from various seeds and was also offered to the chthonic *Psychopombos Hermes* and to the souls of the deceased.

The mystic cult of Dionysus

The Orphic cult of mysticism centers on the liberator god Dionysus-Zagreus, the supreme ruler of the universe, the world's soul. The god's battle against the Titans, his death and resurrection, symbolize the Orphics' secret teaching of the adventures of life in the natural and moral world. In the Orphic view, human beings have a dual nature. Good and evil coexist inside people: Zeus created human beings form the ashes of the evil Titans who had fed on the parts of Dionysus's body, so they also contained the Dionysian soul, the immortal divine and incorruptible element. Thus Dionysus's adventures symbolized the passions and adventures of human existence, which were the result of sin and ancestral carnage. The purpose of these mystic rituals was to release these sins and cleanse the soul.

Because the Titans dismembered Dionysus, human beings became the reason that the divine essence in the multiplicity of the infinite cosmic forms and expressions, that are linked. The Orphic principle is, therefore, described through faith: Hades, Zeus, Helius, and Dionysus are one.

The mystery unfolded in the form of a performance in which the lead role was the enactment of the *Hierogameia* that symbolized the spiritual marriage of the ritualistic Dionysus-Father and Mother-Earth with the purpose of the rebirth of Dionysus-infant.

In the same spirit, some scholars identify Dionysus with Iacchus, the secret god of Eleusis, son of Demeter and son or fiancé of Kore.

DIONYSUS AND THE DIONYSIAN GODS

SATYRS AND SEILENI

Companions of Dionysus, the satyrs —or Tityroi, as the Dorians called them— were half human, half animal and considered minor demons of forests and mountains. Hesiod writes that they were born to the five daughters of Phoroneus, who also fathered the nymphs and the Curetes. But other writers describe the satyrs as children of Hermes and Iptheme or of the naiads and Seilenus.

The satyrs looked like goats, and had horns, long tails, and hooved feet. They were cheerful, playful, and frisky creatures who frequently made advances to the nymphs and the

Seilenus (tomb of Philip at Vergina, Thessaloniki Museum).

maenads; even today, men who display a lustful, somewhat crude behavior are called satyrs.

The satyrs were often linked, and sometimes even confused, with the seileni. The seileni were originally believed to be demons of flowing waters and fertility of the land. Like the satyrs, they were men with some animal features. But instead of resembling goats like the satyrs, the seileni had some of the physical traits of horses like the half-horse, half-man creatures known as centaurs. The best known of the seileni was Seilenus, Diony-

Bronze Seilenus (530-520 B.C., Olympia Archaeological Museum). The seileni were phallic demons with horse traits (ears, tails, hooves) and from the mid-sixth century B.C. were described as companions of Dionysus. A typical feature used to depict the seileni was the wine cup.

sus's tutor who was born from the blood that dripped from the Uranus's wound when his genitals were cut off. In art, Seilenus is depicted as a bald old man with a thick nose, large stomach and hog's ears. Like all satyrs and seileni, he loved drinking wine and when drunk had the gift of prophecy. Mortals who sought to learn the future thus frequently captured him.

Over time, the way both satyrs and seileni was depicted was softened. Gradually, they took the form of humans who disguised themselves by wearing goat hides and smearing themselves with must residue. They took part in the Dionysian celebrations, from which ancient drama emerged.

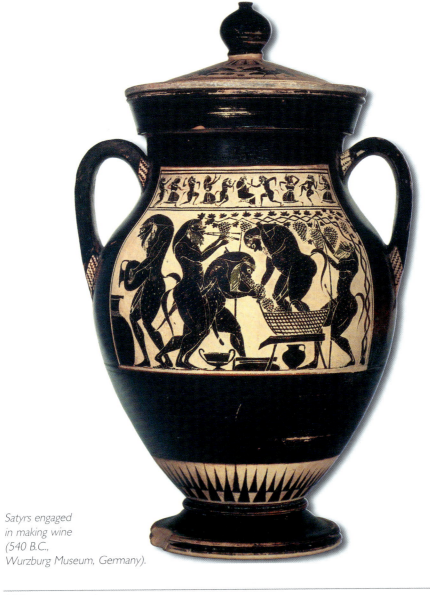

Satyrs engaged in making wine (540 B.C., Wurzburg Museum, Germany).

MAENADS

Also known as *Bacchae*, *Lynaes*, or *Thyes*, the maenads were female votaries of Dionysus who formed part of his train. They were originally lesser deities whom the ancient Greeks identified with the nymphs who raised Dionysus and symbolized the divine natural powers of fertility and reproduction.

Homer described the maenads as women who danced themselves delirious ecstasy as they accompanied Dionysus, who they called despot.

As eastern elements —especially from Lydia, Phrygia, and Thrace— were assimilated into Greek culture, followers of Dionysus began wearing animal hides and waving *thyrsi* (ivy-covered clubs decorated with ribbons) or lit torches as they expressed their worship by beating cymbals, drums, and playing flutes in orgiastic rites held in the mountains during which they devoured raw animal flesh. This sacred meal was their ultimate rite, during which the bacchants identified themselves with Dionysus and assumed his power. Phallic rituals were an inextricable part of the cult.

The maenads' Dionysian worship rituals held day and night during the celebrations of the *Epiphaneia* and the *Parousia* (presence) of Dionysus are described vividly in Euripides's tragedy *The Bacchae*, which was written after 410 B.C. in the court of the Macedonian king Archelaus. From this account, the ritual culminates with the ultimate exultation that is nothing but frenzied violence and, in this case, the murder of the god.

Sleeping maenad
(detail from Derveni crater, 300-320 B.C., Thessaloniki Archaeological Museum).

PAN

God of forests and mountains and patron of herds, Pan was the son of Hermes and the nymph Dryope, according to Homer. By another account, he was the son of either Zeus or Apollo and Callisto or Oenoe or the Arcadian nymph Penelope.

According to Homer's hymn, when Pan was born his mother looked down on her sweetly smiling infant and saw he had goat's feet and horns. Frightened by his hairy face, she abandoned the infant, but Hermes wrapped the baby in a rabbit skin and took it up to Mount Olympus. The gods were charmed by the odd looks of Hermes's son; Dionysus, who took a special liking to the child, named him Pan (or all) because everyone loved him.

Carefree, cheerful, playful, and frisky, Pan became a member of Dionysus's entourage. He pranced through woods and over mountains, stopping to rest in caves, chases nymphs, and played his beloved pipes. Pan also frequently amused himself by creeping up on flocks of sheep and emitting loud cries that startled the sheep, causing them to panic – a word inspired by the god's name.

Shepherds' habit of bringing their

Statuette of Pan (National Archaeological Museum).

flocks down to the sea to wash the sheep as well as shepherds' fondness for the sport of hunting earned Pan the name of *actius*, or protector of fishermen and hunters.

Pan is a Greek god and his cult was founded in Arcadia, which was also known as Pania. The Arcadians worshipped Pan as the highest god who was above, or at least equal, to Zeus. Arcadian coins depicted a deity with the inscription "Diopan". Sanctuaries dedicated to Pan were found on the Mount Lycaeon, at Mainalos, and other Arcadian peaks such as Nomio and Parthenio, in the ancient city of Lycosura, and all agricultural and shepherd centers of the Peloponnese, from where his cult gradual spread to the rest of Greece.

The cult of Pan was introduced to Athens in the fifth century B.C. and its establishment coincided with the Battle of Marathon (490 B.C.). Herodotus writes that the goat-footed god appeared before the herald Pheidippides, who was on his way to Sparta to seek help – to complain about the fact that Athenians did not worship him, but promising to help them if they did. After defeating the Medons, the Athenians dedicated a marble statue to Pan that they placed in a cave in the rock of the Acropolis. They paid tribute to Pan along with Hermes, Achelous, and the nymphs three times a year by offering pandemic sacrifices.

The Greeks spread the cult of Pan to Cyrene, Libya, Egypt, and Italy. In neo-Platonic cultures he was elevated to the pantheon of greater gods that represents all the forces of nature and

Seilenus (detail from Derveni crater, 330-320 B.C., Thessaloniki Archaeological Museum).

was called *Great Pan*, a dominating god and father of the universe.

Syrinx – Echo – Pitys

The myths concerning the nymphs Syrinx, Echo, and Pitys are linked to Pan, as the god frequently fell in love with and pursued the young wood spirits that accompanied him in dance and in song.

Syrinx was a nymph of Orestiada who, will trying to escape Pan's amorous advances, and ran to the Ladon River. Just as Pan reached out to touch her, she prayed to the river to transform her. Thus when Pan's fingers closed around her, they closed around a reed, which he then used to craft his favorite pipes. The instrument became his most widely recognized symbol and the ancient Greeks would often say they could hear the sound of Pan playing the pipes echoing on Mount Mainalos as well as on the Acropolis in Athens.

Pan's romantic adventures with Echo came to a similar end. The nymph was famed for her song and her musical accomplishments as she played both the flute and Pan's pipes. Furious at the nymph for rejecting his advances, Pan urged the shepherds to fall on her and tear her to pieces. Gaea, who felt sympathy for the nymph, picked up her pieces and buried them in the ground. Since then Echo, repeats the sounds she hears.

According to another myth, Hera punished Echo because the young nymph would distract Hera with endless chatter to cover up his dalliances. Hera thus punished her by condemning the nymph to only be able to repeat others' words.

There is another myth about Echo. In this version, the nymph hid in a cave and pined for her unrequited love for the youth Narcissus. In the cave, Echo faded and was turned into a rock that echoes the voices of those calling her.

Pan is unlucky in love even when his advances are not rejected. This was the case with the nymph Pitys, who rejected the rather brutal Boreas in favor of Pan. But Boreas, the Thracian god of the north wind, took his revenge on Pitys, blowing her off a cliff. Gaea again took pity on the nymph and changed her into a tree, the *pitys* or pine.

Relief depicting Pan, Apollo, Hermes, and three dancing nymphs. (Second half of the second century B.C., National Archaeological Museum).

PRIAPUS

Priapus was another member of Dionysus's entourage. He was believed to be the son of Dionysus and Aphrodite or the nymph Chione, or the son of Hermes or Adonis or Zeus with Aphrodite. A symbol of nature's powers of fertility, he was a patron of gardens, vines, meadows, and the herds that grazed in them. Priapus is depicted with Asiatic garb and enormous genitals that is adorned with a wreath of seeds and grapes. He also wears a turban decorated with vine leaves on his head.

One of the most widely-known myths about Priapus concern his romantic adventures with the nymph Lotis who is transformed into a lotus tree to escape his advances. The donkey figures prominently in this myth, as it was the animal's braying that woke the nymph and startled her into flight.

There is another myth that is related to the argument between man and beast over the size of their phalluses.

The center of the cult of Priapus was Lampsacus on the Hellespont, from where the cult spread to Propontis, as the Sea of Marmara was known in Roman times, and then to Greece and Italy. As the god of reproduction and the patron of stockbreeders, fishermen, sailors, and travelers, Priapus was worshipped as a catholic principal of the universe, a creator-god and provider of all goods.

Bronze Seilenus from Dodona (550-530 B.C., National Archaeological Museum). The exaggerated penis was characteristic of Priamus and did not represent only carnal love and fertility but also protected humans, animals, and plants from the "evil eye."

THE CENTAURS THE LAPITHS

According to Pindaros, the first centaur was born from the union of Ixion and Nephele, a cloud, who Zeus had changed into the form of Hera. The Charites, or Graces, were not present at the birth of this hybrid creature, which later bred with the Magnesian mares. The mares, in turn, gave birth to an entire tribe of mythical creatures who were human from the waist up and horse from the waist down.

In a different version, Nephele gave birth to many centaurs who had human form, but who united with the mares of Pelion to give birth to the half-human, half-horse creatures. By another account, the centaurs were born to the nymph Dia who lay with both Ixion and the winged-horse Pegasus on the same night.

Nonetheless, the Alexandrian poet Nonnos writes in his poem *Dionysias,* that the centaurs were born to Gaea, who was fertilized by the sperm of Zeus in the god's unsuccessful attempt to rape Aphrodite on Cyprus.

Homer describes the centaurs as a wild species of Thessalian horses that lived Mount Pelion and Mount Ossa

Lapith wrestling a centaur (detail from the battle of the centaurs, western frieze of Temple of Zeus at Olympia, 460 B.C., Olympia Archaeological Museum).

and was wiped out by the Lapiths as a result of the inappropriate behavior of the centaur Eurytus or Eurytion at the wedding of the Lapith king Peirithous and Hippodameia. In this poetic narrative, Homer describes the war between the civilized Lapiths and the uncivilized centaurs:

It was wine that inflamed the Centaur Eurytion when he was staying with Peirithous among the Lapithae. When the wine had got into his head, he went mad and did ill deeds about the house of Peirithous; this angered the heroes who were there assembled so they rushed at him and cut off his ears and nostrils; they dragged him through the doorway out of the house so he went away crazed and bore the burden of his crime, bereft of understanding. There was war between mankind and the centaurs, but he brought it upon himself through his own drunkenness.

According to a different version, the centaurs abducted the Lapith women; Theseus is said to have joined Peirithous in the war against the centaurs.

The centaurs' fondness of wine and drunkenness is seen in the myth about Heracles and the centaur Pholus. But Heracles was not the only figure in mythology to become embroiled in a fight with a centaur; Alcmene's son killed the centaur Eurytion when he forced King Dexamenus to give him his daughter Deianeira as his bride. The centaur Nessus was responsible for the death of Heracles.

Lust was another centaur characteristic. Mythology contains frequent references about their amorous attacks on nymphs and mortal women. Atalante killed the centaurs Hylaios and Rhoecus when, wearing pine wreaths and carrying lit trees, they lunged to rape her.

The most famous centaur was the sage Cheiron. He was the son of

"Battle of the Centaurs" (western frieze of Temple of Zeus at Olympia, 460 B.C., Olympia Archaeological

Cronus, who disguised himself as a horse to lay with the oceanid Philyra. Knowledgeable in medicine, he lived in Mount Pelion –the centaurs' home– and cured wounded animals using mountain herbs. Apollo entrusted the upbringing of Asclepius to Cheiron, who taught the boy medicine. Cheiron also raised other heroes, including the Dioscuri, Jason, and Achilles – who was his grandson from Endeis, mother of Peleus. Even though Cheiron was immortal, he gave up his immortality for Prometheus. He was killed by one of Heracles's arrows that had been dipped in the poison of the Lerna Hydra. He was later turned into the constellation Sagittarius.

Cheiron's wife was the naiad Chariclo, daughter of Apollo, Perseus, or Oceanus. Their daughter Ocyrrhoe was transformed into a horse name Hippe or Hippo because she went against the gods' will revealed their fates to her father and Asclepius.

Pholus is another well-known centaur. He was the son of Seilenus and a nymph who had extended her hospitality to Heracles at Pholoe in Arcadia. Seeking to please him, she opened a vat of wine that she had been given by Dionysus. The wine's smell attracted the centaurs who fought Heracles. During the battle, the hero inadvertently killed Pholus's friend.

The centaurs are a mythological representation of the equestrian arts and were depicted in the scenes on the metopes of the Theseio or Hephaesteion in Athens and the Parthenon, as well as on the frieze of the Temple of Apollo Epicoureios in the Arcadian city of Phigaleia.

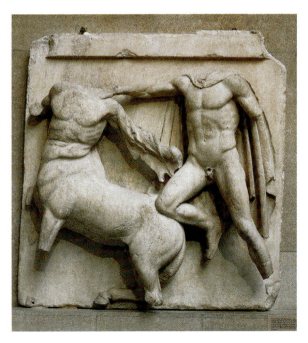

Lapith attacking a centaur (northern metope from the Parthenon, Elgin Marbles, British Museum).

The Lesser Gods

LESSER GODS OF URANUS

Iris

Iris, possibly the personification of the rainbow, was the gods' fleet-footed messenger. She was the daughter of Thaumas and the oceanid Electra, and granddaughter of Gaea and Poseidon. Most writers describe her as a virgin, although according to one myth she lay with Zephyrus and gave birth to Eros.

Iris carried the water of the river Styx on which the immortals took oaths. She also conveyed Zeus's orders to the other gods and changed into human form to convey the will of the gods to mortals.

In Homer's hymn to Apollo, Iris helps Leto give birth by summoning the goddess of childbirth Eileithyia without Hera's knowledge, even though she often performed errands for Hera. In Alexandrian times, the poet Callimachus had described Iris as seated like a dog at Hera's feet, ready at any moment of the day or night to do her bidding.

Iris is the only deity that Homer describes as having wings. Thus in artistic performances where she is shown without feathers, she is depicted holding a herald's symbol. The ancient writers only mention one place where Iris was worshipped: the islet of Hecate near Delos.

Winged, fleet-footed, dressed in a short robe and golden winged sandals, Iris moves between heaven and earth but also travels to the depths of the sea and the Underworld to announce the imminent arrival or presence of the gods.

Charites (Graces)

The Graces personified attraction, charm, and desire, and symbolize graces and happiness in nature and in the lives of mortals. There are several myths surrounding their number, names, and parents. Hesiod mentions three Charites –Euphrosyne, Aglaea, and Thaleia– who were the daughters of Zeus and the oceanid Eurynome. Other writers mention Hera as their mother, while some mention Eunomia, Harmonia, or Lythe. Some claim their father was Uranus. The ancient traveler Pausanias writes that their parents were Helius and Aegle, and that two Charites –Cleta and Phaenna– were worshipped in Sparta, while Athenians also worshipped two Charites – Auxo and Hegemone. But it seems that three Charites were worshipped in Attica– Thallo, Auxo, and Carpe –where they were often confused with the Horae. Hegemone was a name of Hecate, who was also worshipped with the Graces.

The Charites were givers of all goods. They used flowers and fruits as symbols to civilize mortals' lives and the arts draw their charm from the Graces. They were invited to all the celebrations on Mount Olympus. The Charites had an especially close relationship to Aphrodite, whom they bathed, perfumed, and dressed when she fled to Paphos after being humiliated by her husband Hephaestus when he caught her in their bed with her lover Ares.

The Charites are the enemies of exaggeration. They are also the goddesses of gratitude, a characteristic of their cult that was widespread in Boeotia, Athens, the Peloponnese, the Cyclades, and Asia Minor.

Horae

The Horae guarded the gates of the heavens and Olympus, or alternately were believed to be in the service of Hera. Through the centuries, the Horae came to symbolize the seasons and, later, the subdivisions of the day or hours. They were daughters of Zeus and Themis. According to Hesiod, their names were Eunomia (Order), Dike (Justice), and Eirene (Peace).

The Horae were deities of both nature and moral order; inseparable, they gave mortals the gifts of justice, equality before the law, and a peaceful life.

Their worship was quite ancient in many parts of Greece, especially Corinth. In Athens, they were celebrated during the festival of the *Esodeia*, during which crowds carried *eiresiones*, or olive branches wrapped in wool on which they hung fruit that they offered the Horae. In Pallantium, the Horae –who were confused with the Charites and worshipped as Carpo and Thallo– were offered the first fruit of the harvest; when meat was offered in sacrifices, it was not roasted, but was boiled instead.

Muses

The Muses were goddesses of music and intellectual creation. Their origin is one of the most complex issues in Greek mythology. Homer mentions just one, whom he called on for inspiration to chant Achilles's anger in *The Iliad* and the adventures and achievements of the ingenious, or *polymichanos*, Odysseus in *The Odyssey*.

The cult of the Muses appears to have come from Thrace, but altered in Boeotia by the epic poets. Hesiod, the most distinguished of these poets, writes that the there were nine Muses who were born in Pieria and were the daughters of Zeus and Mnemosyne; their names were Cleio, Euterpe, Thaleia, Melpomene, Terpsichore, Erato, Polyhymnia, Urania, and Calliope.

The Muses' favorite place of residence was Mount Helicon, from which they would descend wrapped in a cloud to chant the events – past, present, and future.

The oldest sanctuary dedicated to the Muses was at Levithrios on the eastern slopes of Mount Olympus, from where their cult spread to Boeotia. As one account claims Apollo as their father, the Muses were also worshipped at Delphi. They were also honored on all islands settled by the Dorians and in the cities of Greater Greece. The *Mouseion*, an educational and scientific foundation established in Alexandria by the Ptolemies, included the famed Alexandrian Library that was destroyed by fire during the reign of Julius Caesar.

Animals were never sacrificed to the Muses, nor were wine libations prepa-

The Muses (Apollonian group, 330-320 B.C. relief, National Archaeological Museum).

The nine Muses (late Hellenistic mosaic floor from Cos, Rhodes Museum).

red for them. However, their altars were covered with olive branches on which incense and wheat seeds mixed with honey were burned. Their favorite plants were roses and ivy.

Helius

Helius (Sun) was the son of the Titan Hyperion and Theia, who was also sometimes called Euryphaessa. He was the brother of Eos (Dawn) and Selene (Moon), and according to the Homeric texts would tirelessly cross the sky on a chariot that was drawn by horses with breaths of flame, thus bringing light to gods and mortals. At night, he rested in a boat or a chalice in Oceanus, from where he rose every morning.

Omniscient, proud, and ruthless, the god severely punished anyone who crossed him. He was a witness and avenger, a god of truth and cohesion, with the power to cure but also blind those who gazed upon him. Once, when a son of Nereus bragged that he was faster than Helius, the god turned him into a mollusk.

Helius also blinded Phineus, either because he was a better seer than the god was or for showing Phrixus and Helle the way to Colchis.

Helius's herds

According to several myths, Helius had several wonderful herds on the island Thrinacia, present-day Sicily. Two nymphs, Phaethusa and Lampeto, daughters of Helius and Neaera, tended his strong, immortal animals. On his journey home to Ithaca, Odysseus landed on the island with his sailors; at the urging of Eurylochus, and despite having sworn to respect the god's herds, some of his sailors slaughtered and ate some of the cattle. Infuriated, Helius threatened to stop lighting the earth unless the gods punished the culprits.

Ancient texts contain many references to Helius's unions with goddesses and mortal women, with whom he fathered several of Greece's heroes. Best-known among his mistresses was Rhode, after whom the Dodecanese island of Rhodes is named. Helius and Rhode had seven sons and through them the grandchildren Lindos, Ialyssos, and Cameiros, who each founded one of the island's ancient cities.

Clytie was also a mistress of Helius. The god betrayed her for the love of the young Leucothoe, daughter of King Orchamus and Eurynome. To win him back, Clytie revealed the god's relationship with Leucothoe to Orchamus, who buried the girl alive. Helius tried to revive Leucothoe in vain. Filled with grief and rage, he never went near Clytie again; she refused to take food or water, and lay down on the earth crying as she watched her beloved cross the sky until she was eventually transformed into a violet.

Helius also lay with his sister Selene, who gave birth to the Horae, the Charites, and Aegle.

Helius. The basic narrative elements of myths in all Indo-European cultures contain references to the sun-god.

Phaethon

According to the most prevalent account, Phaethon was the son of Helius and Clyemene, daughter of Oceanus. Epaphus, son of Inachus, insulted Phaethon by telling him that his mother had lied when she claimed Phaethon was the son of Helius. He thus asked his mother, Clymene, for proof. So she took him to Helius, who assured Phaethon that he was his father and promised to fulfill an request he might have. Phaethon thus asked to be allowed to drive his father's chariot for a day. Helius was forced to acquiesce and handed over the chariot to the Phaethon, advising the boy to use the reins to guide it rather than resort to the whip.

Phaethon was an inexperienced rider. The horses, which realized the change in driver, became agitated and began to gallop wildly. Phaethon was frightened. The chariot veered dangerously close to the earth and scorched it, then would careen off course, becoming so remote that the earth became encrusted with ice. At one point, everything went up in flames: Phaethon lost control the reins, the stars fled and Gaea begged Zeus to help save the world. Zeus was then forced to strike Phaethon with a lightning bolt; the boy's body fell to the Eridanus River.

Imaginary recreation of the Colossus of Rhodes, a third century B.C. statue by the sculptor Chares of Lindos. The statue was 34 meters high and depicted the sun-god Helius, protector of the island which was the largest –if not only– center of his cult in all Greece and which survived until the very end of ancient Greek civilization.

Eos

Daughter of the Titan Hyperion and Theia and sister of Helius (Sun) and Selene (Moon), Eos was the eternally-young goddess of the dawn.

According to Homer, she would rise from her bed each morning, leaving her handsome husband Tithonus to bring light to gods and mortals.

In his hymn to Aphrodite, Homer writes that Tithonus, son of the Trojan Laomedon, was mortal. Eos fell in love with him and asked Zeus to grant him immortality. The father of gods and mortals granted her wish, but as Eos had not asked for eternal youth for her husband, Tithonus began to age. In the beginning Eos took care of him, but as he aged, she shut him in one of the rooms of her palace at the edge of Oceanus and earth. Only his voice could be heard coming out of the room, which buzzed and echoed until he became transformed into a cicada.

Eos and Cephalus

Apollodorus the Athenian narrates the tale of Cephalus, a famed hunter and son of Hermes and Herse, daughter of Cecrops. Eos abducted Cephalus just two months after his marriage to Procris, daughter of Erechtheus.

According to the Roman poet Ovid, Eos soon tired of hearing Cephalus talk about his love for Procris so she sent him back, yet first sowed some doubt in his mind about his wife's fidelity. Cephalus disguised

himself, then approached Procris as a stranger and wooed her with fancy presents. Believing that she his marital honor was in danger of being shaken, he revealed himself to Procris and sent her away. The young woman roamed forests and woods until Cephalus, realizing his mistake, asked her forgiveness.

In another version of the myth, Procris went to Crete, where Minos gave her a dog and a spear that never missed her target – both presents from Artemis. She returned home, chopped off her hair and disguised herself as a boy, who became Cephalus's hunting companion. Seeing how effective the boy's dog and spear were, Cephalus asked for them as presents. The boy agreed, on condition that Cephalus would lay with him. When Cephalus accepted, Procris became livid with envy and revealed herself to her husband. Eventually, the two made up and Procris gave Cephalus the gifts he desired. But because she no longer trusted him, she spied on Cephalus from behind a bush. Mistaking her for prey, he shot her. When he realized his tragic mistake, he was inconsolable and threw himself off Leucas, a cape on the island of Lefkada.

Eos also had other lovers, among them the handsome Orion and Cleitus.

Selene

Selene, daughter of Hyperion or Pallantas or Helius, was the personification of the moon. She was also known as Mene. Selene lay with Zeus and bore him the renowned beauty Pandia, Nemea, and Herse (the personification of dew). The poet Mousaios is also mentioned as her son. She is also considered mother of the Horae, who were born from her union with Helius.

Selene's greatest love was the handsome Endymion, king of Elis. By one account, the goddess spotted him as he slept in a cave on Mount Latmos in Caria. In another myth, Endymion was received on Mount Olympus, but later ejected by Zeus for daring to fall in love with Hera. In a different account, Zeus granted him the wish to choose any form he desired. Endymion chose eternal youth, but at the cost of eternal sleep. Thus Selene, who was in love with him, would visit and caress him every day as he slumbered.

An Arcadian myth recorded by Vergil in his poem *Agrotica* mentions that Selene fell in love with Pan, who lay with her in a clearing deep in the forest.

The cult of Selene was widespread in the Peloponnese, and the Spartans would not embark on any military campaign in an unfavorable lunar phase. In Nemea, a city of the Argolid, it was believed that the Nemean lion killed by Heracles was the son of Selene. In Athens, she was offered libations with wine or round wafers. The moon goddess was also considered the patron of menstrual flow, childbirth, and fertility of animals and humans. Her union with Helius was considered the ideal marriage.

Because the moon's crescent resembles a bull's horns, the goddess was depicted seated on a bull or a cow or on a chariot drawn by these horned beasts.

The cult of the moon-goddess Selene in ancient Greece was limited because the Greeks believed the worship of heavenly bodies to be a barbarian trait. But in post-Classical times, Selene was again associated with Artemis, Hecate, and other goddesses and honored as the most exalted ruler of the sky, stars, and harmony.

LESSER GODS OF THE SEA

Nereus and the Nereids

Nereus, the kindly old man of the sea in Greek mythology belonged to a generation that preceded the Olympian gods and, according to Hesiod, was the eldest son of Pontus and Gaea and brother of Thaumas, Phorcys, Ceto, and Eurybia. He lived at the bottom of the Aegean Sea. Nereus had the gift of prophecy and the ability to change into different forms. After wrestling with him, Heracles formed Nereus to tell him the way to the Hesperides.

Nereus lay with Doris, daughter of Oceanus. She bore him the nereids, who according to Hesiod were fifty sea nymphs, while other writers claimed their number was 100. The nereids lived with their father at the bottom of the sea and helped sailors.

Amphitrite and Thetis were the most widely-known among the nereids. Amphitrite was married to Poseidon and considered the queen of the sea. Thetis was married to Peleus, and was the mother of Achilles. Another well-known nereid was Galatea, who fell in love with the Cyclops Polyphemus, who crushed his rival for her affections Acis under a rock in Sicily. The river that sprung beneath the spot where he was crushed bears his name to this day.

Three-bodied demon (560-550 B.C., Acropolis Museum).

Proteus

The sea god Proteus was of Egyptian origin, according to the oldest mythological account. From Egypt, he went to Thrace, where he married the nymph Coronis and fathered two sons. His sons harassed travelers by challenging them to fights, then killing them. This boorish behavior prompted Proteus to ask Poseidon if he could move back to Egypt.

According to Homer, Proteus lived on the island of Pharos near the Egyptian city of Alexandria. He knew every sea, from surface to seabed. When the sun is at its peak, the old sea deity would become a sea cave in which seals slept.

Proteus had the ability to transform himself as well as the ability of prophecy. Herodotus mentions an Egyptian tradition, according to which Proteus was king of Egypt during the time of the Trojan War and gave shelter to Paris and Helen. In this version, Proteus kept Helen, whom he then returned to her husband Menelaus.

Glaucus

Glaucus was one of the most popular deities of sailors and fishermen. He was the son of Anthedon, the hero who gave his name to the Boeotian city, and Alcyone; by other accounts, he was the son of Polybus and Euboea, or alternately of Poseidon and a nymph.

By one account, Glaucus was a fisherman who seeing a dead fish brought back to life after touching a magic herb, decided to taste the herb. He did, and became immortal; he entered the sea, where he was welcomed by Oceanus and Tithys, who changed him into a sea deity. Another myth relates how Glaucus achieved immortality but not eternal youth; having made this bitter discovery, he threw himself into the sea. In another account, he is linked to the Argonauts' expedition.

During the clash with the Tyrrhenian (Etruscan) pirates, he was the only one who survived, thus Zeus threw him into the sea where he was transformed into a sea god. A different myth attributes Glaucus's plunge into the sea to his unrequited love for Melicertes or his desperate attempt to prove to his companions that he had attained immortality by drinking water with magic properties.

Glaucus's loves usually came to a sad end. One popular myth concerns his love for Scylla, a beautiful sea maiden to whom Glaucus offered shells and feather-less sea birds. But instead of responding to his advances, Scylla felt sorry for these birds and broke into tears. Jealous, Circe poisoned her bath and changed the girl into a horrible monster that lived on a rocky outcrop off the Sicilian coast.

His love for Symi, daughter of Ialyssus and Dotis, had a happier end. Glaucus carried her off a remote island, which now bears her name.

Glaucus is also mentioned in connection with Ariadne, who he fell in love with when Theseus abandoned the girl on the island of Naxos. But he was forced by Dionysus to abandon his pursuit of the girl.

Like all sea deities, Glaucus had the gift of prophecy. He was the father of Sybille of Kymi. At night, the mortal fisherman who became an immortal changed into an old man who wandered along coasts and islands lamenting his lost youth. Sailors who would heard his prophecies of disasters would try to avert them through prayers and fasts.

Some sailors imagined this sea deity as woman in teal, Glauce, who calls them into the spray. When the sea is rough, she is imagined as a three-headed woman. Glaucus was sometimes said to appear in sailors' dreams as a lamia or as a hawk diving to grab whatever it desires. Dreams, melancholic daydreams, worry, and a sense of foreboding in the constant fight against the waves are symbolically expressed in the myth of Glaucus that the ancient seafarers conjured as they traveled to the far ends of the sea.

Phorcus

In the *Theogony*, Phorcys appears as the brother of Nereus, while in other myths he is mentioned as the son of Oceanus and Tithys or as the brother of Cronus and Rhea or even as a Titan to whom Gaea secretly gave birth.

Hesiod writes that Phorcys lay with his sister Ceto, who bore him several children, including the Graeae, the Gorgons, the Hesperides, and the dragon that guarded the golden apples. He is also mentioned as the father of Echidna, Thoosa –who symbolizes the stormy sea– and Scylla.

The myth of Phorcys was widespread in Achaea and spread to Cephallonia and Ithaca.

Triton

The son of Poseidon and Amphitrite, Triton had a divine appearance although his body below the waist tapered into a long fish's tail. In the battle against the Giants, he fought at his father's side and used his conch-trumpet to scare off the Giants, as Hesiod notes in the *Theogony*. Ovid writes that Triton siphoned off the water that had covered the earth in the deluge. The messenger of Poseidon and Amphitrite, Triton had three symbols: a conch, whose sound was irresistible; a trident; and an oar.

Triton is linked to the myth of Heracles, according to which the hero had to fight Triton to find out where the Hesperides kept their golden apples. Like Nereus, Triton had the gift of prophecy. It was thanks to this gift that Jason was able to steer his ship, the *Argo*, out of Lake Tritonida and sail into open sea.

Although Triton was initially depicted as a deity in ancient Greek

Triton (pottery detail, 540 B.C.).
A sea-demon, Triton was a primitive force
of nature that could whip up the seas,
move islands, and seize youths
and maidens.

literature and art, he was later depicted with horns and pointy ears like those of the satyrs. He was also attributed the satyrs' lustful character and believed to have had many amorous affairs with the sea nymphs.

Sirens

The Sirens or Seirenes were believed to be the daughters of Phorcys or had been born from the blood of the horn of the river-god Achelous. Either Gaea or one of the Muses (Terpsichore, Melpomene, or Calliope) was believed to be the mother of these sweet-voiced women, who had human heads and bird bodies. Their voices enticed any man who heard their song; they then kept the man prisoner and remained with them forever, forsaking homeland and family.

The Sirens were man-eaters who lived on the sailors who made the mistake of sailing too close to the islands they inhabited.

According to some writers, these islands were located in the Tyrrhenian Sea (Licosa, San Pietro, and Galleta). But the Sirens were condemned to crash into the sea and drown if a sailor did not succumb to the charm of their song.

According to one myth, the Sirens competed against the Muses in song at Aptera on Crete. The Muses won; fuming, the Sirens snatched the Muses's feathered crowns and retreated to the sharp rocks at the entrance to the Messene strait, a deadly passage for sailors.

The ancient writers note that there were three Sirens. Parthenope, Leucosia, and Legeia are mentioned as daughters of Terpsichore; Thelxipeia, Aglaope, and Pecinoe are mentioned as daughters of Melpomene.

Odysseus managed to hear their song by not give in to it by ordering his crew to time him to the ship's mast. The Argonauts were ably to navigate safely past them thanks to the aid of Orpheus whose music kept them from responding to the Sirens' song.

In one myth, the Sirens were changed into birds for helping Demeter find Persephone. In another account, they were changed into birds because they did not stop Hades from snatching Kore or because they shunned love and thus earned the wrath of Aphrodite.

Mortals believed that the Sirens were responsible for the nightmares that plagued them at night, yet they were also believed to be beneficial deities for those who managed to appease them.

Heads of Siren idols (seventh century B.C., Hephaestia, Limnos, Limnos Museum).

Scylla and Charybdis

Scylla was a monstrous creature with twelve legs, six necks, six horrible heads each with three rows of strong teeth. She was so horrid looking that she even frightened the gods. Scylla lived atop a high cliff in Lower Italy, near Reggio, and ate marine creatures and unsuspecting travelers.

Scylla, once a beautiful sea nymph, was the daughter of Phorbas and Hecate or Typhoeus and Echidna or Phorcys. Amphitrite or Circe transformed her into a hideous monster in a jealous rage over Scylla's love for either Glaucus or Poseidon.

Charybdis, another sea monster, lived across sea from Scylla in Sicily. She personified whirlpools. Charybdis was the daughter of Poseidon and Gaea, but she was struck by Zeus's thunderbolt for stealing some of Heracles's cattle. She was flung into the Messene strait by the thunderbolt's force. Half-woman, half-fish, Charybdis would suck down the waters of the sea three times a day, then belch them back up, sucking sailors and their ships into the vortex.

Both monsters symbolized the dangers of the open sea and the difficulties faced by ancient mariners.

Scylla, the female sea-monster, represented the ultimate danger faced by sailors crossing the Messenian straits.

Oceanus

The ancient Greeks considered Oceanus to be a large river that circled the earth, and that the sun, moon, and stars rose from its far end. They also believed Oceanus was the source of all rivers and springs. Homer describes Oceanus as the father of all the gods. According to Hesiod, Oceanus was a Titan and the eldest son of Uranus and Gaea; he married Tethys, with whom he fathered 3,000 rivers and 3,000 oceanids.

In art, Oceanus is depicted like all rivers – with bull's horns on his head or with crab claws. His symbols are the jug, the horn, marine animals, the reed, and the scepter.

Oceanids

Oceanus and Tethys's 3,000 daughters were known as Oceanids, or Oceanidae. Homer only mentions two of them: Eurynome and Persa, wife of Helius and mother of the sorceress Circe and Aeetes, king of Colchis.

Aeschylus uses the Oceanids as the chorus in his tragedy *Prometheus Bound*. He also mentions Hesione as the wife of this suffering Titan. Aristophanes also presents *The Nephelai* (Clouds) in his comedy as Oceanids.

Nymphs

The nymphs were deities who protected springs, forests, meadows, trees, and caves. They were the personification of the beautiful, fertile forces of nature and were especially honored by young women preparing to wed. The cult of nymphs is rooted in Mycenaean civilization; they were considered benign and benevolent spirits who brought joy and were thus honored at altars with libations from honey, milk, and wine or with the sacrifices of small animals.

Depending on their origin and object they protected, nymphs were either Naiads (protectors of rivers and wells), Orestiades (protectors of forests), Dryads or Hamadryads (protectors of trees), and Agronome (protectors of meadows).

According to Homer, the nymphs were daughters of Zeus. Hesiod writes that some of them –the meliae– had been born from the blood spilled by Uranus or were the daughters of various rivers, such as the Achelous, the Cephisus, the Ismenus, or the Asopus.

The nymphs' amorous adventures with mortals, gods, and demons provided plenty of inspiration for mythologists, writers, and artists who depict this spirits as living in caves where they weave, but coming out to rest, sing, and dance.

Nymphs dancing to the tunes of Pan's flute (Attic relief, fourth century B.C., National Archaeological Museum).

GODS OF LOVE

Eros

Eros, the *"invincible god"*, is the personification of the mutual attraction and union of men and women. He is not mentioned in any of the Homeric texts, although in the *Theogony* Hesiod lists Eros among the primary god-creators of the world who appeared with Gaea and whose power was used to create life.

The handsomest of all the gods, the gold-winged Eros is unbeatable in battle and a source of creation. In orphic myths, he emerged from the egg that Chronus (Time) had given birth to in the arms of Chaos. According to Pherecydes, Eros brought Harmony to the primeval universe. In *Birds*, Aristophanes narrates how Eros was born from the egg that the black-winged Nyx placed in the arms of Erebus, then uniting with Chaos first gave birth to the birds and later created the ocean, the earth, and the immortal gods.

In Plato's *Symposium*, Diotima mentions that Eros is not a god but a demon –in other words, a lesser deity– who is the son of Poros (Wealth) and Penia (Poverty), thus symbolizing the human tendency towards and desire to attain and keep eternal happiness. In classical mythology, Eros is a secondary god, the son of Eileithyia or Iris and Zephyrus; in other myths he is considered the son of Aphrodite and Zeus, Ares, or Hermes.

Eros, the inseparable companion of his mother Aphrodite, was a beautiful, winged cherub with a bow and arrow that carried the sweet passion that torments mortals and immortals. With Pothus, Hemeros, and Peitho he is active in spring, when nature is reborn, and comes out to play with the Muses and the Charites. Eros is not only the god of love; he is also the protector of friendship and harmony. The Cretans and Lacedaemonians would make sacrifices to Eros before going to battle. The Thebans' Sacred Company was dedicated to Eros.

The cult of Eros

The ancient Greeks worshipped Eros from the earliest times. The Thracians who settled Helicaon and Mount Cithaeron introduced his cult into Boeotia. At Thespiae, which was a cult center of the god, there was a very

THE LESSER GODS

old stone statue of the god as well as the famed Hermes by Praxiteles. The Thespians also held festivals known as the *Eroteia* or *Erotidia* in his honor every five years featuring music as well as gymnastics and equestrian competitions.

In Athens, an altar to Eros was dedicated during the rule of Peisistratis at the entrance of the Academy, and Athenians lit their torches carried in the torch-races of the *Hephaesteia* from its fire. Statues and altars dedicated to Eros also existed in other parts of Greece, such as Megara, Elis, the island of Samos, Epidaurus, and Cyprus.

Idol of Eros (Museum of Ancient Corinth).

GODS OF THE UNDERWORLD

Dike

Roommate of the underworld gods, Dike personified the justice through retribution. There are many myths surrounding her parentage. Hesiod presents Dike as one of the three Charites (Eunomia, Eirene, and Dike), and a daughter of Zeus and Themis. Later writers present her as a daughter of Chronus or Cronus and Anange.

Her name is derived from the root *dik*, which is related to the verb "persecute." Thus, Dike is linked to the ancient custom of the persecution of the guilty by either the community or the victim's family. Dike's assistants were the Erinyes (Furies), who hound criminals.

Ate

Ate personified mental and emotional confusion and, according to Homer in *The Iliad*, led people to irrational and incomprehensible actions. She is considered a daughter of Zeus. Although both gods and demons are blamed for the fact that mortals are afflicted with the presence of Ate, blame is usually associated with the Erinyes.

Nemesis

Nemesis metes out retribution to the sacrilegious, disrespectful, and arrogant. The ancient writers considered her a goddess and she personifies the gods' frustration at the acts of mortals that lack moderation – even extreme success. Hesiod writes that Nemesis was born to Nyx without a father, while Cypriot epics claim that Helen was the daughter of Nemesis and Zeus, who was breast-fed by Leda.

Excavations at Rhamnous, a settlement in Attica, have unearthed ruins of a temple dedicated to Nemesis, while among the statues found at the site was a work of Agorocritus, a student of Pheidias. This statue, whose head is in the collection of the British Museum in London, was made of Paros marble brought by the Persians to Marathon where they intended to build a monument to what they had considered their certain victory. After their defeat, on the suggestion of Pheidias, the marble was used to sculpt a statue in honor of Nemesis, who had punished the arrogant Medous.

The cult of Nemesis was quite widespread in Asia Minor and the coins of ancient Smyrna were minted with Nemesis. Two very ancient *xoana* of Nemesis are considered sacred. Nemesis was depicted in statues at Olympia and reliefs in Thessaloniki and on the island of Thassos.

In Alexandrian times, Nemesis was linked to Eros, which may explains why she was depicted as having wings. Plato and Callimachus associate her to justice, while the goddess was later associated with Tyche and Adrasteia.

The Titan Themis, personification of the law and justice. Themis was the mother of the Horae and the Charites (Graces). She tended to the moral order and justice among gods and mortals, oversaw the ideal of hospitality, and protected the weak. She also had the gift of prophecy. Pictured is a statue by Chairestratus from the sanctuary of Rhamnous in Attica (280 B.C., National Archaeological Museum).

THE LESSER GODS

Keres

Ker, or the *"lady of death"* as Homer described her, was a goddess of destruction, violent death, and vengeance who wandered around battle fields with Eris (Discord) and Kydoemus, a war demon who is the personification of the noise of battle. Ker wore a garment that was dyed red by human blood that had been spilled.

In other accounts, the Keres were two demons who were blood-soaked, black, winged figures with human form. The hounds and daughters of Hades were also named Keres because they rabidly tracked their victims and circled the, while a swarm of Harpies and Erinyes fell on them, sinking their claws into their flesh, then leading them to Tartarus in Hades's kingdom.

Ker is linked to the fate of death. The ancient Greeks believed that the Keres followed anyone who was destined to die a violent death from the day he or she was born until the day he or she died. Thus, in *The Iliad* Achilles was called on to chose between two goddesses: one goddess promised he would live a long life as long as he did not abandon Phthia, but would die an unknown; the other goddess offered him fame and glory, but a short life provided he fought at Troy.

Also in *The Iliad*, Zeus approaches the Keres of Achilles and Hector who, as the scales begin to tip towards the end, reveals his inevitable death.

Harpies

The Harpies were well-coifed, winged monsters. They were predatory deities –in Greek *arpaktiko* is rapacious, the root of raptors– who snatched mortal souls for Hades. They personified gales.

The Harpies were the daughters of Thaumas, son of Pontus and Gaea, and the oceanid Electra. They were sisters of the gods' herald Iris. Other writers mention their father as being either Poseidon or Typhoeus.

Bronze head of a griffin (seventh century B.C., Delphi Museum). Imaginary, offensive animals, griffins were decorative elements during the archaic period and from the fifth century onwards they are found on helmets and breastplates.

Homer mentions one harpy: Podarge (Fleetfoot), who was the mother of Achilles's horses. Hesiod mentions two: Aello and Ocypetes or Ocythoe; other writers add a third, Celaeno.

The best-known myths surrounding the Harpies concern Phineus and the abduction of the daughters of Pandareus, who was from Miletus of Crete or Ionia.

According to Apollonius Rhodius, Phineus was the son or grandson of Agenor and king of Salmydessus in Thrace. Apollo had given him the gift of prophecy, but because he revealed the will of the gods, Zeus blinded him and condemned him to eternal hunger. In another version, he was punished for blinding the sons of his first wife Cleopatra, Oreithus, and Crambes. Phineus received an additional punishment: the Harpies would snatch away whatever food he was brought by people seeking a prophecy and would infect whatever they left with a terrible stench. Phineus patiently bore his punishment because he knew he would be kidnapped by the Argonauts. When they arrived, he asked the sons of Boreas, Zetes and Calais, to free him. The heroes chased the Harpies as far as the Floating Isles in the Ionian Sea and would have killed them had Iris not intervened. She promised that these monsters with the female head and bird body would not bother Phineus any more. Zetes and Calais left them on the islands and returned back; the isles, which are off the coast of Zakynthos island, were then renamed Strophades (from the Greek *strophe* or turn), and the Harpies fled to Crete.

Another widely-known myth about the Harpies is mentioned by Penelope in *The Odyssey*. Aedona, Cleothyra (or Clytie or Cameiro), and Merope were orphaned at an early age so they were raised by the goddesses Athena, Aphrodite, Artemis, and Hera. When they became old enough to marry, Aphrodite asked Zeus to find suitable husbands for their proteges, but the Harpies snatched them and gave them to the horrid Erinyes as handmaidens.

Erinyes (Furies)

The winged Erinyes were horrible, subterranean goddesses of destiny and

Bronze head of a griffin (Delphi Museum). This creature a lion's body, eagle's head and wings, and the tail of a snake or a scorpion. It was associated with Apollo and Dionysus as well as with mysteries originated from the East.

revenge. According to Hesiod, they were born from the drops of blood that fell to earth when Uranus was castrated by his son Cronus. Aeschylus presents them as daughters of Nyx (Night), while Sophocles presents them as daughters of Gaea and Erebus and later writers as the daughters of Hades and Persephone. Regardless, the Erinyes persecute all those who upset the natural order of things, for instance those like Orestes who commit matricide and those like Oedipus who commit patricide, and those who do not respect their parents.

The number of Erinyes has varied through the centuries. Euripides mentions three, who since Alexandrian times have been named Alecto (she who is not mollified), Tisiphone (the avenger of murders), and Megaera (the spirit of hatred).

Black and black-clad, they have a fierce look, foul-smelling, fiery breath, foam around their mouths, snakes in their hair and hands; they fly through the air chasing their victim. Neither gods nor mortals can escape their rage. These terrible goddesses pursue even Hades because he helped the Trojans against the will of his mother Hera.

On the other hand, the Erinyes protect beggars and strangers. Even though they spread disease and disaster in their wake, they can also change into benevolent goddesses, the Eumenides, who protect the earth from drought and ill winds, thus they are only a threat to the guilty.

The Eumenides were worshipped at Sicyon, Argos, and Megalopolis. Temples dedicated to the Eumenides existed in Athens, near the Acropolis, and at Colonus, where sacrifices to the goddesses were held at night, where they were offered libations from honey and milk or water and honey.

Charon

The son of Nyx (Night) and Erebus, the ferryman Charon would deliver the souls of the dead to Hades in return for a fee of one obol.

Over time, the ferryman who would transport the souls across the Acheron River became a personification of death and the underworld.

Hypnos (left) and Thanatos (right) remove the dead Sarpedon from the battlefield under the watchful eye of Hermes. Sons of Nyx, the brothers lived in Tartarus and are depicted as bearded youths carrying a swords. Thanatos is often confused with Hades and Charon, even by Hermes, and was hated by both gods and mortals.

GODS OF FIRE

Cabeiri

Most contemporary researchers believed that the name *Cabeiri* is derived from the Semitic *caber*, which is translated into Greek as *"great"*, the epithet of the Cabeiri, according to the ancient Greek writers. Commentators – whose information is confirmed by Strabo and Stisimbrotos – mention that their name is derived from Mount Cabeiros in Phrygia, from where their cult spread to Samothrace.

The number and origin of the Cabeiri is a subject of disagreement. Preserving the views of Acousilaos and Pherecydes, Strabo writes that Cadmus, the father of the Cabeiri, was the son of Cameiro and Hephaestus. The Cabeiri, in turn, fathered the Cabeirian nymphs. According to Pherecydes, the Cabeiri were born from the union of Hephaestus with Cabeiro, daughter of Proteus, granddaughter of Apollo and Rhyteia, who lived on Samothrace.

The cult of the Cabeiri has been associated with several gods, but especially with the cult of Hermes. The Cabeiri have also been linked to the cult of Artemis, as temples dedicated to the goddess at their worship sites. The Cabeiri have also been linked to Demeter and Kore – an association underscored by the ritual names of these deities. Other accounts attribute the establishment of the Cabeirian mysteries to Rhea, the great Phrygian goddess, or to Astarte-Aphrodite, which

Sanctuary of the Cabeiri on the island of Samothrace, the main cult center of the Great Gods, also known as the Samothrace gods or the Samothracians.

is also the mother of the Cabeiri in Phoenician mythology.

The association of the Cabeiri with the goddess of love –a link symbolized by the star of daybreak and evening– explains the particularly prevalent view that identifies the Cabeiri with the Dioscuri, the guiding stars and saviors of seamen.

Since information about the Cabeiri is confused, it is not easy to describe their exact nature. Many writers identify them with the heroes Dardanus and Iasion, sons of Zeus and Electra. Strabo, who lists them among the priests and healers of other gods, disputes their divine status.

As deities, the Cabeiri are benign; they are patrons of seamen, solvers of disasters, and avengers of those who slander the gods.

On Lemnos, the Cabeiri were honored as divine sons of Hephaestus and were depicted as boxers with protruding stomachs and crooked legs – hence their name as *Crabs*. Pausanias informs that the temple of the Cabeiri in Boeotia was near the woods of Cabeiraea Demeter and Kore. There was also a temple dedicated to the Cabeiri in the Boeotian city of Anthidona. This reinforces the view of Herodotus that the Greeks were taught the Cabeirian mysteries by the Pelasgians.

Archaeological excavations and Plutarch supply evidence that confirms that the cult of the Cabeiri in Macedonia. Plutarch mentions that Philip II met and fell in love with Myrtali-Olympiada, mother of Alexander the Great, at the Cabeirian mysteries on Samothrace.

During the Cabeirian mysteries held on Samothrace – or, the "secret drama" as it was described by Alexandros Klimis – priests known as *anaktotelestes* would re-enact the passions and murder of a Cabeiros (Hermes, Cadmelus, or Iasion) by one of his brothers, as well as his resurrection thus expressing the idea of rebirth through the passions of life and death. It is worth noting that part of the ritual involved prophecies.

The cult of the Cabeiri was also widespread in Asia, either because Asia was its birthplace or because Dardanus spread it there. The Phoenician historian Sanchoniathon writes in his *Theology* –which became known through Christian priests, specifically Eusebios– that the seven Cabeiri and Asclepius (who was

Cabeiros offers his beetle to Paidas, the youngest of the Cabeiri, who is drawing wine from a crater. To the left, are Cratea and Mitos and a child, Pratolos (fragments of black-figure pottery from the Cabeiri sanctuary at Thebes, fourth century B.C., National Archaeological Museum).

named *Esmonos* in Beirut) were sons of Sydyk (Hephaestus) and Astarte (Aphrodite). His belief is confirmed by Damaskios.

Telchines

The Telchines were evil demons, cunning, jealous, but also very clever; they had close-knit eyebrows, a trait that is popularly believed to be found in those with the ability to cast the evil eye. The Telchines were sons of Thalassa or Gaea and Pontus who, along with Oceanus's daughter Capheira raised Poseidon who had been entrusted to them by Rhea.

The sea-god married the Telchines' sister, Halia, with whom he had six sons and one daughter, Rhode.

According to some mythological accounts, the Telchines made the island Rhodes barren by wetting it with the waters of the river Styx. Other accounts mention that the telchine Lycus sought refuge in Lycia where he built the temple of *Apollo Lyceiou*. By some accounts, they were punished with death by Zeus because of their meanness or because their evil eye destroyed the crops.

The Telchines were said to have been the dogs of Actaeon who were changed into demons after devouring their master. By some accounts, they were said to be sons of Nemesis and Tartarus; while another account says that, like in the Erinyes, they were born from the blood that dripped to the ground when Cronus was castrated by his son.

Sorcerers and charmers, the Telchines made magic potions, and were able to make rain, snow, and hail. They also had the power to change into amphibian monsters, which is why they are depicted with amphibian characteristics.

Other writers mention that the Telchines were mortals, noted inventors and craftsmen who discovered gold, silver, bronze, iron, and other ores and invented several implements: the scythe with which Cronus castrated his father Uranus; Poseidon's trident; and, several sculpting tools that the ancients called *telchineia*.

Sanctuary of Cabeiri on the island of Samothrace. According to Herodotus, their cult spread from the islands to the Pelasgians.

THE LESSER GODS

GODS OF HEALING

Asclepius

Asclepius is one of the newer gods of the Greek pantheon. He is the function personification of the ideal doctor. In the prevalent version of the myth surrounding Asclepius, he is the son of Apollo and Coronis, daughter of King Phlegyas of Thessaly. In his third Pythioniko –which is dedicated to the Syracuse tyrant Hieronas– Pindar writes that the nymph lay with Ischys, son of Elatus, despite being pregnant by the god. Her infidelity outraged Apollo, who asked his sister Artemis to kill her. Many of Coronis's compatriots died with her in a terrible plague. But just as her body was to be laid on the funerary pyre, Apollo swooped down and removed his son from Coronis's body. He then turned the infant over to the centaur Cheiron to raise. Asclepius learned the art of healing from Cheiron and used it to save people. His skills were so great that he could even raise the dead, prompting the jealousy of the Olympian gods and the rage of Zeus, who struck him with a lightning bolt.

To link the myth of the birth of Asclepius with their city, the Epidaurians claim that Coronis happened to be in Epidaurus around the time she was due to give birth. She then abandoned the newborn Asclepius at Mount Myrtium, where he was guarded by a dog and breastfed by a goat.

Statue of Asclepius at the Asclepieion at Epidaurus (fourth century B.C., National Archaeological Museum).

A Messenian myth recorded by Pausanias and Pindar cites Arsinoe as the mother of Asclepius. The healing-god's inclusion in the Thessalian cycle includes his participation in the Argonauts' expedition and the hunt for the Caledonian boar; it thus clearly aims at establishing the liberation myth of the mortal-doctor.

Whether as a hero or as a god, Asclepius was worshipped throughout the Greek world and its colonies, especially in Classical and later periods. Homer only mentions him as the father of two heroes-doctors of Elis, Machaon and Podaleirius.

Despite evolving into a deity of Greek mythology, Asclepius never abandoned mortals. In Delphic theology, he replaced Apollo-healer in popular worship, as health is a personal, rather than social need of humans. Epidaurus was thus recognized as the metropolis of the cult of Asclepius.

The most famed Asclepieion was located at Epidaurus, where the god's cult was established around the *egatakimissi*, or patients' stay within the temple where the god appeared to them in their sleep, examined them, and recommended the appropriate cure.

Sanctuaries of Asclepius were also built at healthy environments – for instance in woods or near thermal spas. Baths, diet, and exercise were all part of the cure applied at the Asclepieion. There were also prominent sanctuaries in Athens where, an epigraph, states it was founded in 421 B.C.; there were also sanctuaries dedicated to the healing god in Piraeus (408 B.C.), on the island of Cos, and at Trikala.

The god's favorite plants were the cypress tree, the pine, and the olive tree. Animals dedicated to the god were the rooster, the goat, and the snake, which he is said to have bred himself at Pelion. Indeed, a snake wrapped around a staff was the primary symbol of Asclepius.

Hygeia (350-340 B.C., National Archaeological Museum). Hygeia is sometimes mentioned as the daughter (and, less frequently as the wife) of Asclepius. She personifies health, which originally did not have its own personification but was a trait embodied by other deities such as Athena.

The children of Asclepius

Machaon, the hero and doctor of Elis who cured Philoctetes (one of the Achaeans who hid inside the Trojan Horse), was considered a son of Asclepius. According to one myth, Eurypylus murdered Machaon and Nestor brought his bones to Greece.

Machaon had a brother, Podaleirius. One the return journey from Troy, he was shipwrecked on the coast of Caria and settled in the city of

THE LESSER GODS

Syrna. According to a different account, a shepherd named Bybassus rescued Podaleirius. Podaleirius cured the daughter of the Carian king, Damaethus, who had been injured in a fall; he then married the girl and received part of her father's kingdom as dowry. Podaleirius later founded the cities of Syrna and Bybassos, which he named after his rescuer.

On Cos, local mythology maintains that both sons of Asclepius settled on the island and became the eponyms of the *Asclepieiades*, doctors who formed a guild and passed along their knowledge to their descendants through secret rituals.

Hygieia is also mentioned as the daughter of Asclepius – or, less frequently, as his wife. Hygieia is the personification of good health, which was not originally a separate divine entity but was identified with other goddesses such as Athena. Other children of Asclepius encountered in Greek mythology include Panacea, Acesso, Alexinor, Aeetos, Ianiscus, and Telesphorus.

Votive relief dedicated by a patient to the healer Asclepius.

The Asclepieion of Cos (fourth century B.C.), which became a center for healing and developed a considerable tradition in medicine.

Heracles

HERACLES

Heracles was the greatest, most glorious, and best-loved of all the heroes of Greek mythology. Although his myths revolved around Thebes or Argos, the tales of his exploits were known throughout the Greek world.

A national hero of the Dorians, Heracles is a purely Greek hero who represents human power to tame nature – a power that is nonetheless combined with benevolence and justice, and is thus able to free humankind from its torments.

Heracles was the son of Zeus and Alcmene. After his death, he ascended to Mount Olympus and became a god. His cult was spread throughout the Greek world as the Dorians expanded their domain.

The birth and childhood of Heracles

Heracles was of Argive extraction, since his mother was Alcmene, daughter of the Mycenaean king Electryon (the son of Perseus and Andromeda). Alcmene was married to Amphitryon whose father Alcedes was also a son of Perseus and Andromeda. Heracles's mortal family had been forced to flee Argos because Amphitryon had killed his father-in-law.

The family thus settled in Thebes. There, Zeus came to earth and, disguised as gold snow, law with Alcmene, who became pregnant with Heracles. By a slightly different version, Zeus took the form of Amphitryon –who was away fighting the Taphians– and seduced Alcmene, whom he convinced he was truly her husband. Zeus is said to have stayed with Alcmene for three whole nights, which is why Heracles is sometimes called *triesperos* (from *tria*, or three, and *esperos*, or evenings).

The next day, when the real Amphitryon returned and learned what had transpired, he was mollified by the seer Teiresias, who told him that it was Zeus who had laid with Alcmene. Amphitryon and Alcmene also lay together on his return and from that union Alcmene bore Iphicles.

But Hera, who made a habit of harassing her husband's lovers, captured Heracles. According to a different version, Hera overheard Zeus bragging that the Perseid (descendant of Perseus) who would be born that day would rule all the Perseids (or all of Greece). Having received Zeus's assurance that this would be true, Hera then delayed Alcmene's labor and shortened by two months the pregnancy of the wife of Sthenelus, who was also a descendant of Perseus. Thus the prematurely-born Eurystheus was born before Heracles and became king of the Mycenaeans. He also played a pivotal role in the life of his cousin, Heracles.

One of the mythological accounts that mentions Alcmene's difficulties while in labor says Hera had sent the childbirth-goddess Eileithyia to sit cross-legged in Alcmene's room. The ancient Greeks believed sitting cross-legged prevented childbirth. Eileithyia stayed at Alcmene's side chanting magic words and had delayed Heracles's birth by nine days and nine nights. But then a childhood friend of Alcmene's, Galanthis, tricked Eileithyia by opening the door to the room and announcing that Alcmene had given birth to a son by the will of Zeus. Panic-stricken, Eileithyia rose from her position and the spell was broken. Alcmene then immediately went into labor and gave birth to Zeus's son, Heracles, and his twin brother by Amphitryon, Iphicles. Furious, Hera changed Galanthis into a cat. Hecate took pity on the woman and took her as an attendant. When Heracles reached adulthood, he dedicated a temple to her at Thebes, and Thebans offered sacrifices to her once a year.

Hera did not rest after Heracles's birth and relentlessly pursued the infant in an attempt to kill him. When Heracles was eight months old, she sent two enormous snakes to strangle him. As soon as Iphicles saw the snakes, he was terrified and began to wail. Heracles grabbed them by the neck and choked them.

According to a different myth, Hera breastfed the infant Heracles in her sleep without being aware of it. The drops of milk that spilled when he removed his mouth from her nipple were said to form the galaxy known as the *Milky Way*.

Heracles's childhood and adolescence

Amphitryon and Alcmene made various arrangements for the education of Heracles, whom they had initially named Alcaeus. Lycus, a son of Apollo, tutored him in music and taught him to read and write. Amphitryon taught Heracles how to drive a chariot. Autolycus, son of Hermes, taught him how to wrestle. Eurytus, king of

Heracles (detail from the metope of the Temple of Zeus at Olympia, 470-465 B.C., Olympia Museum).

Oechalia, taught him archery. Castor taught him how to use weapons. Rhadamanthys taught him to be virtuous and fair. But one day the young Heracles was angered when admonished by Lycus, so he threw an object at his tutor. Lycus was killed on the spot and Amphitryon, fearing a similar fate, sent Heracles off to Mount Cithaeron.

Heracles reached manhood on the mountain. He grew to four *pychis* (about twelve feet) tall and became very strong. Indeed, he even killed a lion that was decimating his father's herds as well as those of Thespius, king of Thespiae. As Prodicus, one of the *sophists* or traveling teachers that flourished in Athens in the fifth century B.C., writes, during this period Heracles chose the long and rough path of Virtue rather than the easy and hedonistic path of Evil.

When Heracles turned eighteen, he fathered his first child with one of Thespius's fifty daughters. The king of Thespiae extended his hospitality to Heracles for fifty nights, sending a different daughter to his bed each night even though Heracles thought he was sleeping with the same women. Thespius explained his actions by stating that he wanted all of his daughters to bear a child by the son of Zeus.

Heracles and Erginus

On his way back from Mount Cithaeron to Thebes, Heracles ran into the emissaries of Erginus, king of Orchomenus, who were on their way to Thebes to collect the annual tax of one hundred cattle imposed on the Thebans after their defeat by the Minyans of Orchomenus. Heracles cut off their noses and ears, tied their hands, and sent them back to Erginus with the message that this was the tax paid by the Thebans.

This insult triggered a war between Orchomenus and Thebes, during which both Erginus and Amphitryon were killed. Thanks to Heracles and the support of the goddess Athena, the Thebans won and were thus released from having to pay this hefty duty. In return for his assistance, Creon, the king of Thebes, gave Heracles the hand of his daughter Megara. The hero's brother Iphicles married Megara's sister and Alcmene married Rhadamanthys.

Raging Heracles

Heracles acquired many children from his marriage to Megara. But Hera, whose jealousy had not subsided, drove him insane so that in a crazed fit he threw all of his children and two of his brother's children into a fire. When he came to and realized what he had done, he left Thebes and went to Thespiae to be purified in Boeotia. He then went to the Oracle of Delphi to seek Apollo's advice on what he should do and where he should settle.

Pythia called him *Heracles* –the hero had been known as Alcaeus until then– and ordered him to go to Mycenae to serve Eurystheus for twelve years, executing whichever commands he was given. The oracle assured Heracles that after completing these tasks he would become immortal. Eurystheus, of course, was none other than the son of Sthenelus, whose birth Hera had expedited after making Zeus swear that he would rule all the peoples around him.

THE ESSENTIAL GREEK MYTHOLOGY

THE LABORS OF HERACLES

According to the ancient writing Apollodorus the Athenian, Heracles completed his twelve labors in eight years and one month.

The lion of Nemea

The first labor Eurystheus commanded Heracles to complete was to bring him the hide of the Nemean lion. The lion that had been terrorizing the valley of Nemea was one of the monstrous children of Echidna and either Orthus or Typhoeus, or had fallen to earth from Selene (Moon). At first, Heracles tried to shoot it with his arrows, but seeing that the lion's pelt could not be pierced, Heracles attacked it with his clubs. The lion ran away and hid in a cave with two entrances. Heracles blocked the one entrance, then wrestled with the lion and strangled it. He then skinned it and wrapped himself in its skin, after first offering a sacrifice to *Zeus the Savior*. He then returned to Mycenae with the lion thrown over his shoulder. Seeing Heracles dressed in the lion's pelt, Eurystheus was so frightened that he ordered him to remain outside the city's walls and display the trophy of his labors there.

Athena supporting Heracles and Gaea supporting Apollo in their dispute over the Delphi tripod (530-520 B.C., Berlin Museum).

The Lerna Hydra

Heracles's second task was to kill the Lerna Hydra, daughter of Typhoeus and Echidna, and sister of Orthus and Cerberus. The Hydra, who lived in the marshes of Lerna, devoured people and animals. She was a horrifying monster with nine heads, eight mortal and one immortal. She had foul, poisonous breath that killed anyone who inhaled it.

Heracles's aide on this labor was his nephew and charioteer Iolaus, the son of Iphicles and Automedusa. They arrived together at the Amymone spring, which was the monster's lair. Heracles forced out by shooting flaming arrows into the lair. Much to his surprise, Heracles saw that for every head he shot off, two more sprung in its place. A giant crab also helped the Hydra by biting Heracles's leg.

Heracles killed the crab. He then sought Iolaus's help, instructing his charioteer to use a brand to burn the root of each of the Hydra's heads that he cut off to thus prevent new ones from growing. After he killed the Hydra, Heracles dipped his arrows in its poisonous blood. He buried the monster's immortal head in the road between Lerna and Elaeus, then placed a rock over it.

Although Heracles completed this labor, Eurystheus refused to count it because he claimed that Heracles had received assistance in killing the Hydra.

The Cerynitian hind

Heracles's third assignment was to capture alive the Cerynitian hind, which the nymph Taygete had dedicated to the goddess Artemis and which lived in the Sanctuary of Artemis on Mount Cerynea. This gold-horned deer had bronze legs, and it took Heracles almost a year to catch.

Heracles managed to capture the animal on the banks of the river Ladon, after having chased it as far as the land of the Hyperboreans. He carried the deer on his shoulders and brought it back to Arcadia, where he was accosted by an angered Apollo and Artemis. But Heracles appeased them by laying the blame for his acts on Eurystheus.

Heracles captures the Cerynitian hind (490-485 B.C., Delphi Museum).

The Erymanthian boar

For his fourth labor, Heracles was ordered to catch the boar that lived on Mount Erymanthus and was ravaging the land of Psophis (near present-day Kalavryta). Heracles first chased the boar out of his hiding place in the forest, pushed it into a snow-covered ravine, and then captured it in a net.

On his way back to Eurystheus, Heracles clashed with the centaurs who attacked the hero by throwing rocks and tree trunks at him after going mad from the smell of the wine Heracles had been offered by the centaur Pholus. Heracles mortally wounded the centaur Cheiron. Although immortal, Cheiron saw that his wound could not be healed so he resigned his immortality in favor of Prometheus.

The Augeian stables

Eurystheus assigned Heracles to clean the stables of Augeias, king of Elis and a son of Helius or Poseidon or Hellenus or Phorbas.

Augeias, who had taken part in the expedition of the Argonauts, had countless herds. When Heracles asked for one-tenth of Augeias's animals as his fee for cleaning the stables, the king agreed because he believed the task was impossible. But Heracles tore down a wall and diverted the waters of the rivers Alpheius and Peneius into the corral. The stables were cleaned, but Augeias refused to keep his promise to Heracles. Eurystheus also refused to count this labor because he claimed the task was completed in return for a fee.

The Stymphalian birds

According to one account, the Stymphalian birds fed on human flesh and lived in a marsh near the Arcadian city of Stymphalia. After forcing them from their lair by shaking bronze rattles made by Hephaestus and given to Heracles by Athena, the hero shot them with his poison arrows.

In some accounts, the Stymphalides were not birds but daughters of Stymphalus and Ornitha who had refused Heracles's hospitality.

Athena supporting Heracles as he cleans the Augeian stables (metope, Temple of Zeus at Olympia, 470-460 B.C., Olympia Museum).

Heracles seizing the Cretan bull (metope, Temple of Zeus at Olympia, 470-460 B.C., Olympia Museum).

The Cretan bull

By one account, the Cretan bull was the beast that had carried Europa from Phoenicia to Crete for Zeus.

In other myths, the bull was sent by Poseidon to Minos to be sacrificed as the Cretan king had promised Poseidon he would sacrifice anything that rose from the sea. But Minos was taken by the animal's beauty and instead sacrificed another bull, thus provoking Poseidon's rage.

The sea-god then drove the animal wild, which ravaged Crete. Heracles managed to capture it and after showing the bull to Eurystheus, released it.

The bull roamed around Laconia and Arcadia, crossed the Corinth isthmus, and ended up in Marathon, which it ravaged.

The mares of Diomedes

Diomedes, king of the Bistones of Thrace, was the son of Ares and Cyrene. He had four superb mares –Podargos, Lamboon, Xanthus, and Demos– that were wild and fed on human flesh. The horses would devour all strangers who were shipwrecked on the Thracian coast.

Heracles managed to capture the wild mares. After killing Diomedes and defeated the Bistones, he took the horses to Eurystheus. While completing this labor, the hero founded the city of Abdera in honor of his beloved Abderus, son of Hermes, who had been devoured by the mares of Diomedes while guarding them for Heracles. Eurystheus released the horses into the wild, and they ascended Mount Olympus where they became the prey of the mountain's wild animals.

In one account, the "mares" were actually the extremely ugly daughters of the Thracian king who forced strangers to lay with them, then killed them.

The belt of Hippolyte

Admete, the daughter of Eurystheus, asked her father to have Heracles bring her the exquisite belt of Hippolyte, queen of the Amazons. The belt had been a gift from Ares.

The hero thus set off on a campaign against the Amazons, the famed tribe of female warriors who lived in Themiscyra (now Termeh), which emptied into the Black Sea, according to Aeschylus and Strabo. The Amazons were daughters of Ares and the Naiad Harmonia. They spent two months of the year with the Gargareis of Ida in order to perpetuate their tribe. The Amazons wore helmets, armor, and the short robes of warriors. Their left breast was either uncovered, or by some accounts cut off, so as not to obstruct their use of the bow. Male children born to Amazons were either killed or given to their fathers.

Heracles tames the Cerynitian hind (490-485 B.C., Delphi Museum).

Hippolyte –or Melanippe, according to some writers– agreed to give her belt to Heracles. But Hera, who continued to track the hero, changed into an Amazon and spread the rumor that strangers wanted to kidnap their queen. The Amazons thus rushed to attack the supposed enemy. In the ensuing clash, Heracles killed Hippolyte and took her belt, which he later gave to Omphale. The belt was subsequently inherited by the kings of Lydia and handed down from one to the other through Candalus, before passing into the possession of the Carians.

The cattle of Geryon

The giant Geryon (or Gyroneus) was the son of Chrysaor and the oceanid Callirrhoe. He had three bodies –or, according to Hesiod, three heads– and lived on the island of Erytheia (now Cadiz) at the mouth of the river Tartessus, near Gadeira, far beyond the Pillars of Heracles –the promontories Calpe (Gibraltar) and Abyla (Jebel Musa)– which the hero set up as a memento of his journey.

According to Apollodorus, Heracles arrived on Geryon's island in a large golden cup he had been given by Helius. After killing the herdsman Eurytion and his two-headed dog Orthus who guarded the giant's herds, Heracles stole Geryon's cattle.

Hearing of the theft from Ares's herdsman Menoetes, Geryon rushed to confront Heracles but was killed by the hero's arrows in the battle that ensued.

Heracles took Geryon's bones to Olympia and buried them there. According to one account, Geryon was buried in Gadeira, where two trees that dripped blood grew over his grave. Other writers place the myth of Geryon in northwestern Greece, in Ambracia or Apollonia.

On the journey back to Greece, Heracles founded the city of Alycia. He squared off against the people who lived along the banks of the river Rhodanus and lay with the daughter of a local king, thus becoming the father of Celtes (Celt) and Galates (Gaul), who gave their names to the region. He also killed Poseidon's sons Ialebion and Ercynus, who tried to steal Geryon's cattle from him. Heracles also wrestled with the giant Cacus near Rome and took part in the battle with the Giants near Kyme in Lower Italy.

After he had arrived at the straits of Messene, one of the cattle escaped from the herd and crossed the sea to Sicily. Heracles swam after it and landed on the island and the city of Erice, where he fought with Eryx, a son of Poseidon (or the Argonaut Butes) and Aphrodite. Heracles killed Eryx.

Eventually, the Greek hero landed at Ambracia where he gathered Geryon's cattle and herded it to the Hellespont. Arriving at Scythia, he was united with the monster Echidna, who bore him three sons: Agathyrsus, Gelonus, and Scythes, eponym of the Scythians.

From an entire herd of cattle, Heracles only managed to bring Eurystheus one ox, which the Mycenaean king sacrificed to Hera.

The apples of the Hesperides

Heracles's eleventh labor was also filled with adventure. The task assigned by Eurystheus was to find and bring back to Mycenae the golden apples of the Hesperides. According to Hesiod, the Hesperides were daughters of Nyx, although writers describe them as daughters of Phorcys and Ceto, Atlas and Hesperis, or Zeus and Themis. Apollodorus mentions four Hesperides: Aegle, Erychtheia, Hestia, and Arethusa. Apollonius mentions only three: Hespera, Erythida, and Aegle. Diodorus mentions seven, who lived in a garden in the land of the Hyperboreans or near Atlas, who held up the sky at the far western end of the earth.

The apples of the Hesperides were a wedding gift from Gaea to Hera when she married Zeus. They were guarded by Ladon, an immortal dragon with one hundred heads who was the son of Typhoeus and Echidna.

During the journey to the land of the Hesperides, Heracles killed Ares's son Cycnus and wounded his father who had rushed to avenge his son's death. When he arrived at the Eridanus River, the nymphs told Heracles that he could find out the way to the Hesperides from the old man of the sea, Nereus. Heracles found him, but was forced to tie him up to receive the information he wanted. He then reached the river Tigges, where he killed the giant Antaeus, a son of Poseidon and Gaea, who drew strength from his mother so that he could wrestle with and kill strangers.

Heracles then reached Egypt, where he killed another son of Poseidon, the inhospitable Busiris, who also sacrificed strangers. Heracles's wanderings also led him as far as Arabia, where he killed King Emathion, a son

The Titan Atlas bringing the apples of the Hesperides to Heracles, who is holding up the sky on his shoulders. Behind him is his supporter, Athena (metope, Temple of Zeus at Olympia, 470-460 B.C., Olympia Museum).

of Eos and Tithonus and gave the throne to his brother Memnon. After crossing the Libyan desert, he arrived at the Caucasus where he killed Zeus's eagle and the freed the Titan Prometheus. He and Prometheus arrived in the land of the Hesperides together where Heracles killed the dragon and took the apples. According to other accounts, he was given the apples by the Hesperides. In one account, Heracles begged Atlas to go get the apples for him. While he was away, the hero would take the Titan's place holding up the sky.

After completing his labor, Heracles returned to Mycenae with the apples. Eurystheus confirmed that he had completed the task and the apples, which were a wedding gift to Hera and Zeus, were turned over to Athena who returned them to the Hesperides.

Capturing Cerberus

The last labor Heracles needed to complete in order to purify himself after the murder of his children was to bring the three-headed guard dog Cerberus, son of Typhoeus and Echidna, up from the Underworld.

Before setting off to complete his task, the hero was initiated into the Eleusinian mysteries. Accompanied by Athena and Hermes, he descended into the dark kingdom of the souls through a crevice known as the Taenarum. After freeing Theseus and killing Hades's herdsman Menoetes in a wrestling match, Heracles appeared before the rule of the Underworld and explained his mission. Hades allowed Heracles to take Cerberus with him on condition that he would not use his weapons to capture the dog and that he would return him. Thus, the hero donned his lion pelt and attacked Cerberus. Although the fighting was fierce as the snake that formed the hound's tail get biting Heracles, the hero managed to capture Cerberus. Accompanied by Hermes, he ascended to earth from a gap near Troezen or Coroneia or Hermioni. True to his promise, he returned Cerberus to the world of darkness after presenting him to Eurystheus.

The final labor. Heracles presents the legenday three-headed dog of the underworld, Cerberus, to Eurystheus. Frightened, Eurystheus hides in a clay storage jar or pithos (hydria, 530-525 B.C., Louvre Museum).

HERACLES'S FEATS IN BATTLE

After completing his twelfth labor, Heracles was free. He returned to Thebes were he married off Iolaus to his wife Megara and left for Oechalia. There is some confusion about Oechalia's location as several Greek cities in Euboea, Thessaly, Messenia, and Aetolia had this name.

Eurytus, an accomplished archer, was king of Oechalia. He declared that he would give the hand of his beautiful blonde daughter Iole as a prize to anyone who would compete against him and defeat him in archery. Heracles defeated Eurytus, but the king refused to keep his promise and threw the hero out of his kingdom. Heracles thus sent off for Tiryns. There he met Eurytus's son, Iphitus. The king's son demanded that Heracles return Eurytus's cattle as the king was convinced that Heracles had stolen them. But Heracles was innocent; Autolycus had stolen the cattle. Angered, he threw Iphitus off the walls of Tiryns. According to a slightly different version, Heracles offered his hospitality to Iphitus but in a fit of rage killed him.

After this murder, Heracles went to Delphi to be purified, but Apollo condemned him to be sold as a slave. The price Heracles fetched would be given to Eurytus as compensation for his son's death. Heracles was sold by Hermes to the queen of the Lydians, Omphale, who was the widow of Timolus.

Heracles and Omphale

Heracles was Omphale's slave for three years. During this time he performed several feats.
- he captured midget-thieves Cercopes;
- he killed Syleus who forced strangers to work in his vineyards;
- he tossed the giant Lytiersus, son of Midas, into the river Maeander because the giant killed strangers after forcing them to plow his fields.

Omphale admired Heracles's daring and courage so she freed him earlier than the time they had agreed she would remain in her service. According to the Latin poets, Heracles became soft living with the Lydian queen and succumbed to various pleasures, such as wearing women's garments while Omphale wore his famed lion's pelt.

The Trojan campaign

Some writers claim Heracles set off for Troy after completing his ninth labor –retrieving Hippolyte's belt– while others claim he set off for Troy after being granted his freedom by Omphale. The cause of his war against Troy was the refusal of Kind Laomedon to compensate Apollo and Poseidon for the construction of the city's walls. The two gods were enraged and punished him: Apollo sent the plague and Poseidon sent a sea monster that devoured the citizens of Troy. Laomedon sought advice from oracles, which suggested that Laomedon sacrifice his daughter Hesione to Poseidon in order to appease the sea-god. Thus, the young woman was tied to a rock to await her end.

Heracles appeared at that very moment. He promised her father that he would kill the sea-monster and free Hesione, but requested in exchange that Laomedon give him the superb horses the king had received from Zeus as compensation for the abduction of Ganymede. Laomedon agreed, and the hero killed the monster and saved Hesione. But the king then reneged on his promise. Thus Heracles went to war against Troy, defeated the city, and gave Hesione as a trophy to Telamon, who had entered the city first. Telamon allowed the girl to choose one of her compatriots to take with her. Hesione chose her brother Podarces (Priam) and purchased his freedom with a golden veil. She then married Telamon and bore him a son, Teucer.

During Heracles's journey back to Greece, Hera whipped up the seas and the hero was stranded on the island of Cos. There, after clashing with the island's residents, the Meropes, he married Chalciope, daughter of King Eurytus whom he had killed in battle. She bore him a son, Thessalus.

The campaign against Elis and the Olympic Games

After the sacking of Troy, Heracles went to war against Elis and King Augeias seeking vengeance for the king's refusal to honor a promise to pay Heracles a fee for cleaning the stables.

Heracles killed the king and his sons. He then went to Olympia where he organized a foot race with a *kotinos*, or wreath of wild olive branches, as the prize. He thus founded the Olympic

The east pediment of the temple of Aphea: Heracles expedition against king Laomedon (Munich sculpture Gallery).

Games and raised temples dedicated to the twelve gods of Mount Olympus and the hero Pelops.

The campaign against Pylos

Heracles's campaign against Pylos was prompted by the refusal of King Neleus to cleanse him of the murder of Iphitus. Heracles's principal opponent in the battle –in which the gods also took sides– was Periclymenus, one of the king's twelve sons who had inherited from his godfather Poseidon the power to change into different forms. He changed himself into a lion, snake, and bee and fought with Heracles in each of these forms. But in the end he was killed by the hero, who had the support and help of the goddess Athena.

Neither Periclymenus's father nor his brothers escaped the rage of Heracles. Only Nestor, one of Neleus's sons, survived because he was not at Pylos was the battle took place.

The campaign against Sparta

Heracles also waged war against Sparta to avenge the death of Oenus who had been murdered by the sons of King Hippocoon for killing a dog in self-defense.

The hero's friend Cepheus and his sons were killed during the battle with Sparta. Heracles's brother Iphicles was also killed, although the hero won the war. Sparta was sacked, Heracles killed Hippocoon and his sons and returned the exiled and legal king, Tyndareus, to power.

During the campaign against Sparta, Heracles had passed through Tegea, where he raped Auge, a priestess of Athena. She bore him a son, Telephus. After Auge gave birth, she exposed the infant in the peribolos of the temple where she served as priestess. Her father Aleus found the infant and ordered that it be taken to Mount Parthenius and abandoned. But Telephus survived because he was found by a deer that fed it with her young. There are several versions of this story. According to the most

Bronze statue of a runner, fifth century B.C. (Archaeological Museum of Olympia).

widely-known, Auge was adopted by King Teuthras of Mysia. Her son, Telephus, had remained in Arcadia and when he grew up felt the need to seek his roots so he sought the help of the Delphi oracle. He thus found himself in Mysia, where he helped Teuthras at a difficult time when he was in danger of losing his throne. As a reward, the king gave Telephus his adopted daughter, Auge. But just as Telephus was about to commit incest, mother and son recognized each other and returned, happy, to their homeland.

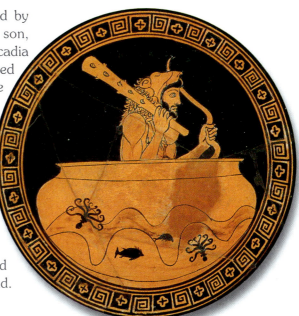

The death and apotheosis of Heracles

After taking part in so many wars and becoming involved in so many amorous adventures, Heracles went to Aetolia to seek the hand of Deianeira, daughter of King Oeneus of Calydon and sister of the dead Meleager.

After defeating the river-god Achelous who was his rival for Deianeira's hand, Heracles married his love. The couple lived for a while in Calydon, where they had their first child Hyllus. However, after Heracles's campaign against the Thesprotians and the accidental murder of Eunomus, a relative of his father-in-law, the family was forced to move to Trachis near King Ceyx, a close friend of Heracles and husband of Alcyone.

On the way to Trachis, they came to the river Evenus where the centaur Nessus would ferry travelers across for a fee. Heracles asked the centaur to take Deianeira across while he swam. But halfway across the river, the centaur tried to rape Deianeira. Heracles realized this and shot Nessus with an arrow, mortally wounding him. Before dying, Nessus told Deianeira to collect his sperm and blood and smear them on her husband's tunic to ensure his life-long fidelity and love. Naïve and in love, Deianeira believed him

Heracles kills the centaur Nessus (615 B.C., National Archaeological Museum).

THE ESSENTIAL GREEK MYTHOLOGY

Heracles uses his club to kill Cycnus, son of Ares. Athena (left) raises her aegis or shield as she charges with her spear, while Ares (right), raises his own against the hero (black-figure hydria, circa 510 B.C., Vatican Museum, Italy).

and created, as she would soon find out, a magic potion.

At Trachis, Heracles helped his friend Ceyx, the Malian king, in his fight against the Dryopes who had settled the slopes of Mount Oeta. He also helped the Dorian king, Aegimius, against the Lapiths and killed King Amyntor of Ormenium in a duel that place in Thessaly. He then raised an army and struck out against Eurytus, king of Oechalia, who many years earlier had reneged on his promise to give Heracles the hand of his daughter Iole. Naturally, this campaign was also successful. Heracles defeated Oechalia, killed Eurytus and his sons, and took the beautiful Iole as prisoner.

On the journey home, Heracles ran aground on Cape Cenaeum in northwestern Euboea, where he built an altar and decided to make a sacrifice to his father Zeus. For this purpose, he sent his herald Lichas to Trachis to bring him a white tunic. Learning that her husband had Iole with him, Deianeira became crazed with jealousy and decided to win back his love. Unaware of the consequence of her act, she used the potion she had made on the advice of the dying Nessus.

Heracles donned the garment and made the sacrifice. But as soon as the garment warmed to the touch of his skin, the centaur's poisonous blood entered the hero's body. Seared by pain, Heracles flung Lichas into the sea as he tried to tear the tunic off, but the venom had seeped into his skin and was burning through his skin like acid. In this pitiful state, the once powerful Heracles was taken back to Trachis. Seeing what she had done, Deianeira killed herself. Heracles ordered his son Hyllus to marry Iole, then climbed Mount Oeta where he collected timber for the funerary pyre. He asked those who had accompanied him to set light the fire and thus release him from his torment. No one dared. Finally, this terrible service was performed by a passerby named Poeas, who was the father of Philoctetes. But as the flames engulfed the hero, a cloud came down from the sky and the pyre was struck by a lightning bolt, which snatched Heracles. The hero was thus raised to Mount Olympus where he became immortal. There he was reconciled with Hera and married her daughter Hebe, with whom he had two sons: Alexiaris and Anicetus.

Myths about Athens

CECROPS

Cecrops was the founding father, king, and lawgiver of the world's first city, Athens, which was originally called Cecropia. Indigenous to the land, he was a son of Gaea and like all her children was half-human and half-snake. Various myths claim that Cecrops invented the founding of cities by organizing people who lived scattered about the land into settlements. Thus, in addition to Athens, he is said to have founded cities in Copais and Euboea.

Cecrops married Agraulus, daughter of King Actaeus of Attica. She bore him three daughters, Aglaurus, Herse, and Pandrosus. Erysichthon and Oreithyia were also children of Cecrops.

It was during the reign of Cecrops that Poseidon and Athena squabbled over who would become patron of Cecropia and give the city his or her name. Zeus asked Cecrops to mediate their quarrel and the gods gathered on the Acropolis where it was decided that whichever one gave the most valuable gift to the city would become its patron. Poseidon struck a rock with his trident and a saline spring appeared. Athena plunged her spear into the ground and an olive tree grew from the spot. The gods judged Athena to be the winner. She became the protectress of the city, which also took her name.

Cecrops built the first temple dedicated to the Athena in the city of Athens. His daughters became priestesses of the temple.

The Athenians worshipped Cecrops as a god. His priest was elected from the family of Amynandriads. A sanctuary dedicated to the city's founder as well as his grave were on the northwestern interior section of the Stoa of the Caryatids at the Erectheion, the most complex temple of the sacred Acropolis of Athens.

The Erectheion. Built between 420 and 407 B.C., it is an Ionian temple of unparalleled beauty and harmony that features six Caryatids as columns.
There was an underground sanctuary near the shrine of Zeus that was believed to be the grave of Cecrops

AGLAURUS

Aglaurus or Agraulus, as she is also sometimes called, was the daughter of Cecrops and Agraulus and sister of Herse, Pandrosus, and Erysichthon. According to Philochorus, the maiden was sacrificed for his homeland in keeping with a Delphic prophecy that suggested that Athens would be freed of its enemy if someone agreed to sacrifice himself for the city. The patriotic maiden thus voluntarily threw herself off the northern walls of the Acropolis. She was killed near a spring that provided water for the entire city, just above the temple of the Dioscuri. Athenians dedicated a shrine known as the Agrauleion inside a nearby cave.

A similarly brave act is attributed to the daughters of Erechtheus in the war between Athens and Eleusis and its ally Eumolpus. Cecrops's daughters are often confused with Erechtheus's daughters, to whom Athena entrusted the canister in with the infant Erichthonius. Aglaurus and Herse ignored Athena's order not to open the canister; seeing a snake –Erichthonius– inside they were scared out of their wits and jumped off the Acropolis.

According to another myth, Aglaurus became jealous of her sister Herse with whom Hermes fell in love. Ovid writes that she prevented the god from entering Herse's chamber and he punished her by turning her to stone. Pausanias claims that Aglaurus lay with Hermes and bore him Ceryx. Apollodorus writes that Aglaurus lay with Ares and gave birth to Alcippe.

The feasts of the *Plyntyreia* and the *Kallyntereia* were dedicated to Aglaurus because she was the first person to decorate statues.

On reaching maturity and arms-bearing age, Athenian youths, or *epheboi*, took the following oath to their homeland at the shrine of Aglaurus: *"I will not shame the sacred arms...let witnesses be the gods, Aglaurus, Enalios Ares, Zeus, Thallo, Auxo, Hegemone."*

In addition to Athens, there was also a shrine dedicated to Aglaurus at Salamis on Cyprus, where a human sacrifice was made each year. This horrible practice was banned by King Diphilus, who ordered it replaced with a sacrifice of cattle.

Sixth century B.C. Kore holding an apple, an offering to the goddess Athena (Acropolis Museum).

ERICHTHONIUS

The housebound snake in the Temple of Athena on the Acropolis is often identified with Erechtheus, who was a son of Hephaestus and Athena or –according to some Athenian myths– Hephaestus and Atthis, daughter of Cranaus since the Ionic version of this myth belied the virginity of their patroness. But the prevalent myth claims Erichthonius was the son of Hephaestus and Gaea, while Athena is said to have been charged with raising and protecting him by giving him two drops of the blood of the Gorgon –which in some cases caused death and in other gave life– and assigned two snakes to guard the infant.

The poet Callimachus mentions that the goddess of wisdom placed Erichthonius in a basket that she gave to the daughters of Cecrops –Aglaurus, Herse, and Pandrosus– to look after. Either Aglaurus or Herse ignored Athena's command not to open the basket and seeing a snake inside were scared out of their wits, and killed themselves by jumping off the Acropolis. The snake slithered off and took refuge on the Acropolis beneath the shield of Athena. This is why Erichthonius is often depicted as half-snake and half-human. Pandrosus, who obeyed Athena's orders, was rewarded with the unconditional love of the goddess.

Cecrops adopted Erichthonius, who succeeded him as the king of Attica. According to a different tradition, Erichthonius conquered Attica after deposing Amphictyon. Erichthonius wed the nymph Praxithea who bore Pandion, who became the fifth king of Athens.

The ancients attributed the invention of the four-horse chariot to Erichthonius as well as the habit of seating a warrior next to the charioteer. The Athenians also claimed Erichthonius invented coins or at least introduced currency into Attica, although this also attributed to Erechtheus, with whom Erichthonius was initially identified.

The goddess Athena with the newborn man-snake Erihthonius (440-430 B.C., British Museum).

ERECHTHEUS

As mentioned above, Erechtheus was initially identified with Erichthonius, although he was considered by some to be either a son or grandson of Pandion. Diodorus the Sicilian writes that Erechtheus came from Egypt and brought wheat to Athens, which was plagued by a famine. Grateful, the Athenians made him their king. Indeed, before his arrival, the city's inhabitants had been known as Cecropians but were renamed Athenians. Both the Panathenaic Festival and the Eleusinian Mysteries have been attributed to Erechtheus.

From Erechtheus union with Praxithea, Erechtheus had several children, among them Cecrops (the Second), Pandorus, Metion, Procris, Creusa, Chthonia, and Oreithyia.

During his rule, the Eleusinians –with the support of Eumolpus, son of Poseidon and Chione, who was made head of the Thracians– invaded Attica. After seeking the advice of the Delphi oracle, Erechtheus was forced to sacrifice his daughter Chthonia to save his land, while according to the same prophecy her sisters were forced to kill themselves. But according to a different version, Poseidon ordered that Chthonia be sacrificed because Erechtheus had killed his son and grandson in battle. Other writers mention that Erechtheus himself was killed in the battle and that the two sides were forced to declare peace.

The ancient myths differ on Chthonia's fate. According to one account, she married Butes, eponym of a tribe and first priest of Erechtheus.

As for Erechtheus's daughter Creusa, mythology and the tragedian Euripides mention her as the lover of Apollo and mother of Ion, founder of the Ionians.

The procession of the Panathinaia *as depicted on the Parthenon frieze by Pheidias and his students (430 B.C., Acropolis Museum). The* Small Panathinaia *were held every year, while the Great Panathinaia were held every four years during the month of Hecatombaionas (July) and lasted for twelve days.*

CEPHALUS AND PROCRIS

Apollodorus the Athenian narrates how Cephalus, the famed hunter son of Hermes and Herse (daughter of Cecrops) and husband of Procris, was kidnapped by Eos just after his marriage and held against his will for two months.

The Roman poet Ovid continues that Eos tired of hearing Cephalus speak of his love for his wife so she sent him away, but first made him doubt her fidelity. Thus Cephalus disguised himself as a stranger and wooed Procris with expensive gifts. When he thought that his marital honor might be in danger, she revealed himself to Procris and sent her away. Forlorn, the young woman roamed mountains and forests until Cephalus finally recognized his mistake and asked her forgiveness.

Another myth relates how Procris went to Crete where Minos gave her a dog and a spear that never missed her target – both presents from Artemis. She returned home, chopped off her hair and disguised herself as a boy, who became Cephalus's hunting companion. Seeing how effective the boy's dog and spear were, Cephalus asked for them as presents. The boy agreed, on condition that Cephalus would lay with him. When Cephalus accepted, Procris became livid with envy and revealed herself to her husband. Eventually, the two made up and Procris gave Cephalus the gifts he desired. But because she no longer trusted him, she spied on Cephalus from behind a bush. Mistaking her for prey, he shot her. When he realized his tragic mistake, he was inconsolable and threw himself off Leucas, a cape on the island of Lefkada.

He was sentenced to a life in exile by the Areopagus, or supreme court, for the accidental murder of Procris.

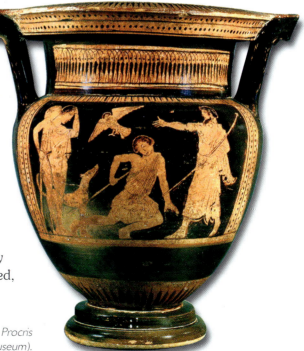

Cephalus and Procris (440-430 B.C., British Museum).

PROCNE AND PHILOMELA

According to Apollodorus the Athenian, the rule of King Pandion –son of Erichthonius and Praxithea– came between the rule of Erichthonius and the rule of Erechtheus. Pandion had two daughters with Zeuxippe: Procne and Philomela. Procne married Tereus, king of Thrace and son of Ares. She bore Tereus a son, Itys.

But Procne's husband fell in love with her sister, Philomela. Tereus deceived Philomela, telling her that Procne was dead. He then married her and cut out her tongue so she could not tell Procne that she had lain with her husband.

When Philomela realized that Tereus had lied to her about her sister's death, she wove a message to Procne into the fabric from which she made a dress. The two sisters then decided to take revenge on Tereus. Procne killed her son and served him to Tereus for dinner. The two sisters later left, but when Tereus realized what had happened he chased them, intended to kill them. Before he caught up to them, they had sent a prayer to the gods for help. The gods responded and changed them all into birds. Procne became a nightingale, Philomela became a swallow, and Tereus became an owl.

BOREAS AND OREITHYIA

The abduction of Oreithyia by Boreas (350 B.C., National Archaeological Museum).

Boreas, son of Eos and Astraeus was the king of the winds. He lived in Thrace and fell in love with Oreithyia, daughter of Erechtheus so he kidnapped her as she played with her girlfriends along the banks of the Ilissus River, according to Plato. Apollodorus Rhodius writes that she was either picking flowers along the Cephisus River or dancing with her companions. According to Acousilaos, Boreas snatched the young woman while she was walking up the Acropolis to make a sacrifice to Athena, while Aeschylus writes that Boreas abducted the girl after her father refused to give her hand to a Thracian. Boreas carried Oreithyia off to Sarpedon's Rock in Thrace or beyond the sea, where night is born at the edge of the world. She bore him two winged sons, Zetes and Calais, and two daughters, Cleopatra and Chione.

AEGEUS

A legendary king of Athens and father of Theseus, Aegeus was the son of the Erechtheid Pandion and Pylia, daughter of King Pylas of Megara. He succeeded Erechtheus's son Cecrops (the Second) on the throne of Athens. Apollodorus mentions that Aegeus was not the natural son of Pandion, a rumor subsequently taken advantage of by his nephews who sought to claim his throne.

After claiming the throne of Athens, which Metion's sons had usurped from his father, Aegeus married first Meta, then Chalciope, but did not have any children with them. Attributing his sterility on the goddess Ourania Aphrodite, he introduced her cult into Attica and sought help from the Delphi oracle. Pythia advised him not to lay with any woman before returning to Athens. Aegeus was puzzled by the odd prophecy. On the journey back, he stopped in Troezen, where he was

Procession of the Panathinaia *(section of the northern Parthenon frieze, 447-432 B.C., Acropolis Museum). Youths carry jugs of water for the celebration in honor of* Athena Polias.

welcomed by his old friend Pittheus in whom he confided what the oracle had said. The crafty Pittheus got Aegeus drunk and got him to lay with his daughter Aethra. But Poseidon also lay with Aethra that night, although Plutarch writes that this was just an invention by Pittheus since Poseidon was the patron of Troezen.

Before Aegeus set off the next morning, he made Aethra swear that if she had become pregnant and gave birth to a son she would not reveal the father's identity before the boy turned sixteen because Aegeus feared that if his fifty nephews –sons of his brother Pallas– learned he had a successor, they would kill the child. The King of Athens then hid his sword and sandals beneath a huge boulder.

Aethra gave birth to a son, Theseus, to whom she revealed the identity of his father when he turned sixteen.

When Aegeus returned to Athens, the city came under attack from King Minos of Crete who sought to avenge the death of his son Androgeus by a bull at Marathon. The Athenians were forced to surrender. A blood tax was levied against them by Minos, who demanded that every year seven youths and seven maidens be sent to Crete to be fed to the Minotaur.

Meantime, Aegeus was living with Medea who, after killing her children, had sought refuge in Athens. A son, Medus, was born of their union.

Theseus then arrived in Athens seeking to meet his father. Medea, a sorceress, realized that the youth was the son of her lover and fearing that her own son would be excluded from succeeding to the throne, convinced Aegeus –who did not know the true identity of Theseus– that the boy should be killed.

But Aegeus recognized his son during a symposium, when Theseus used the knife his father had hidden under the boulder before leaving Troezen. Theseus thus discarded the poison wine that he had been preparing to offer his guest. Realizing that he had been tricked by Medea, he banished both her and Medus from Athens. Theseus then undertook to free Athens from its blood tax and sailed with the other youths to Crete.

The ship that carried the Athenian youth to Crete had black sails. Aegeus, who was concerned about his son's fate and the outcome of the mission he had undertaken, asked for the ship's sails to be changed with white ones if Theseus was successful.

But on the way back, Theseus was drunk with the joy of success and forgot to instruct the sailors to change the sails. Aegeus, who had gone to the cape Sounion to look for the ship, saw it return with black sails. Overcome with despair, Aegeus threw himself off the cliff and drowned in the sea, which took his name – the Aegean.

Theseus

Theseus was the great hero of Athens and the second most important Greek hero after Heracles. He was also the last of the nine ancient kings of Athens.

The son of Aegeus and Aethra, Theseus was born at Genethleios, a city of the Argolid, near the temple of Ares and a spring dedicated to Poseidon. He was lovingly raised by his grandfather Pittheus and Connidus, who trained Theseus in wrestling.

According to one myth, Theseus was the only child who was not frightened by the sight of Heracles's lion pelt when the hero happened to pass through Troezen and was put up by Pittheus at the palace. On the contrary, the seven-year-old Theseus lunged out at the lion, which he thought was alive.

When Theseus reached adolescence, he went to Delphi, where he cut off his hair and dedicated it to Apollo. This ritual later became known as the *Theseia*.

When Theseus turned sixteen, his mother Aethra revealed the identity of his father to the youth. Theseus thus decided to go find his father in Athens. Despite the advice of his mother and his grandfather, he chose to go overland, ignoring the risks. On his journey to Athens, Theseus completed his first feats.

A sixteen-year-old Theseus bids his mother Aethra and grandfather Pittheus farewell under the watchful gaze of his true father Poseidon (right) and sets off for Athens (pottery illustration, 470-460 B.C., British Museum).

The feats of Theseus

Theseus encountered his first opponent near Epidaurus. This was the notorious Corynetes, a son of Hephaestus, who killed travelers with his club (*coryne*). Theseus killed him and took his club as a trophy.

A little further along the road, Theseus came across Sinis, who was also known as Pityocamptes (pine-bender). Sinis would bend back two pines, then capture travelers and tie each of their legs to one tree. He would then let the pines snap back into place, thus tearing the traveler apart. Theseus overcame Sinis and punished him with the same treatment he had reserved for strangers.

Theseus had his first erotic contact with Sinis's daughter, Perigune. When she saw her father dead, she ran to hide in the woods where she hid among the shrubs, where she vowed that if they protected her, then she would never harm them. Theseus called to Perigune, assuring her that he would not harm her. He finally persuaded her to come out of the shrubs. A son, Melanippus, was born from their union.

Near Corinth, by the Kakia Skala, Theseus encountered Sceiron, also a son of Poseidon, who would force travelers to wash his feet. As they bent over to comply, he would toss them off the rocks into the sea, where they were devoured by a huge sea turtle.

Outside Eleusis, the hero fought with and killed another son of Poseidon, Cercyon, who forced travelers to fight with him to the death. At Eleusis, Theseus overpowered Damastes, a son of Poseidon known by the nickname Procrustes because he would tie his victims to a bed, then either lop off their limbs if they were too long or stretch their bodies to fit the bed if they were too short.

At Megarida, Theseus killed Phaea, the Crommyonian sow – a monstrous offspring of Echidna and Typhoeus that ravaged the town of Crommyon. Plutarch writes that Phaea was a prostitute who lived off robberies and that her nickname –sow– reflected her lifestyle.

The labors of Theseus (interior of a red-figure kylix, 440-430 B.C., British Museum).
In the center, the hero is depicted slaying the Minotaur. Along the top from the right, Theseus wrestles with Cercyon; he brandishes an axe to strike Procrustes, who is begging the hero to spare him; threatens Sceiron as the sea turtle below awaits its prey; captures the Marathon bull; bends a pine to which Sinis is tied; and attacks the sow Phaea (440-430 B.C., British Museum).

Theseus in Athens

When Theseus reached the outskirts of Athens, he offered a sacrifice to *Zeus Meilichius* and was purified of the killings he had committed on the way by the Phytalides on the banks of the Cephisus River.

Tales of his feats had already reached the palace of Aegeus, who at the time was living with Medea. She talked the king into poisoning the young stranger in an attempt to prevent Aegeus from recognizing his son so that her own son, Medus, would be assured of the throne.

Aegeus thus invited the youth to a symposium. During the meal, Theseus pulled out a knife to cut his meat. Aegeus recognized the blade as being the same one he had buried under a boulder before leaving Troezen. He realized that the stranger was his son, and poured out the poisoned wine. He then officially recognized Theseus in front of the people of Athens and banished Medea and her son.

After being declared the heir to the Athenian throne, Theseus faced and defeated his cousins, the sons of Pallas (Aegeus's brother), who had decided to kill Theseus as his sudden appearance on the scene spoiled their plans to succeed Aegeus on the Athenian throne.

Theseus then captured the Marathon bull that had killed Minos's son Androgeus. He brought the beast to Athens and sacrificed him to Apollo Delphinius. A little earlier, he had established the *Hecaleia* in memory of Hecale, an old woman who had vowed to make a sacrifice to Zeus if the youth succeeded in his mission.

Theseus is also credited with establishing the *Isthmian Games* at Corinth in honor of the sea-god Poseidon.

Theseus in Crete

Relations between Athens and the Minoans had been severely disrupted by the death of Androgeus. The death had been attributed alternately to the Marathon bull and travelers on the road to Thebes, while by some accounts Androgeus had been killed by Aegeus who had become increasingly wary of the close relations between the Minoans and the sons of Pallas. In any case, as a result of Andreogeus's death, a tribute was imposed on Athens, which for nine years was obliged to send seven youths and seven maidens every year to feed the Minotaur – a horrible monster who lived in a labyrinth built by Daedalus.

Theseus volunteered to take part in one such group of young Athenians, who were chosen by lot. The young hero said he would either defeat the beast or die with the other youths.

According to another myth, the young Athenians were not chosen by lot but were handpicked by Minos, who chose the successor to the Athenian throne. In this version, Minos fell in love with an Athenian maiden, Eriboea, whose honor Theseus decided to defend. To explain his bravery, Theseus declared that he was a son of Poseidon. Minos demanded proof of the claim, and challenged Theseus to retrieve from the seabed a ring he had just tossed into the water. Theseus dove into the sea and with the help of either dolphins or Triton went to the palace of Poseidon and Amphitrite, where he was greeted with honors. He was given a seal and a wreath, while the nereids also gave him the Cretan king's ring. Thus Minos no longer doubted the Athenian hero's divine roots.

When the boat carrying the Athenian youths arrived on Crete, Minos's daughter Ariadne saw Theseus and fell in love with him. By one account, she met him at an athletic competition, then helped him defeat the Minotaur by giving him a ball of thread that would help him find his way back out of the labyrinth.

Theseus killed the Minotaur and set sail for Athens with Ariadne and the other youths. They stopped at Delos, where they made a sacrifice to Apollo and danced a circular dance around his altar.

There are several myths about Ariadne:
- Theseus abandoned her on the island of Naxos, where she married Dionysus.
- Dionysus demanded that Theseus let Ariadne go ashore.
- Ariadne killed herself or was killed by Artemis.
- Ariadne died while giving birth to Ammathounda (Ammochostos) on Cyprus, where Theseus's ship was wrecked during a storm. She was buried in a woods consecrated to Aphrodite Ariadne.

Theseus returned to Athens, but forgot to change the ship's sails from black to white, as had been agreed with his father in case of victory. The mistake led Aegeus to take his own life from grief.

Theseus and the Amazons

Many ancient writers relate the tale of how Theseus set out with Heracles to battle the Amazons when Heracles went to get the belt of the Amazon queen Hippolyte as one of his labors. Theseus then abducted Ares's daughter Antiope.

According to Plutarch, Antiope's abduction was perpetrated by a fraud. The Amazons greeted Theseus with gifts and he invited Antiope, who was carrying these presents, aboard his ship, then raised anchor and set sail. Antiope bore Theseus a son, Hippolytus. But he became smitten with Phaedra, Ariadne's sister, which enraged the Amazons who launched a campaign against Athens. The Amazons were defeated after a tough battle near the Areopagus in which their queen was killed.

Theseus and Phaedra

Phaedra bore Theseus two sons, Acamas and Demophon. But Phaedra, a victim of the goddess Aphrodite, fell in love with her stepson Hippolytus, who she met at the palace of Pittheus in Troezen. But the youth was devoted to

Theseus abducts Antiope (metope from the Athenian treasury at Delphi, 490-485 B.C., Delphi Museum).

Artemis and did not respond to Phaedra's advances. Despondent, she killed herself, but left a letter for Theseus, who was away on a trip, in which she claimed that Hippolytus had insulted her honor. Despite Hippolytus's denials and because of his vow not to reveal what had really transpired, Theseus became so enraged that he used one of three wishes he had been granted by Poseidon to ask for his son to be destroyed. Theseus then banished Hippolytus from Troezen. The sea-god then sent an enormous monster –or a bull– that startled the horses of Hippolytus's chariot. He was thrown from his seat, became entangled in the reins, and was dragged to his death.

In Troezen, Hippolytus was honored as a god. Girls would dedicate a lock of their hair to Hippolytus before their wedding as a symbol of their purity.

The abduction of the Amazon Antiope by Theseus (segment of bronze plate, 570 B.C., Olympia Museum).

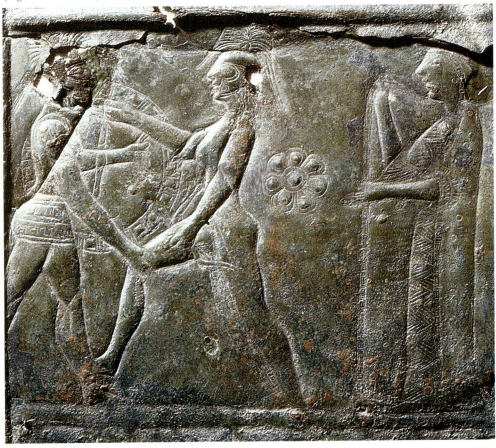

Theseus and Peirithous

Peirithous was a king of the Lapiths. On hearing of Theseus's feats, he decided to measure his strength against the hero, so he went to Marathon and stole a herd of cattle that belonged to the king of Athens. Theseus rushed to find the thief and punish him, but instead of becoming adversaries, the two men ended up becoming close friends. Theseus proved his devotion to Peirithous at his wedding to Hippodameia or Deidameia, when he helped Peirithous bring the inebriated centaurs, guests at the wedding, back under control.

Together, Theseus and Peirithous kidnapped Helen, the beautiful daughter of Zeus and Leda when the girl was just seven or eight years old, although her abductors were in their fifties. Other myths claim that her true kidnappers were Idas and Lygeus, who entrusted her to Theseus to guard and that he, in turn, refused to give the girl to the brothers Castor and Polydeuces. Another account relates how the girl's mortal father Tyndareus handed her over to Theseus to protect her from Hippocoon who wanted to kidnap her.

Pausanias relates how Theseus hid Helen at Aphidnae so the Dioscuri could not find her, but that they discovered her hiding place, besieged Aphidnae, and destroyed Athens.

While Castor and Polydeuces freed Helen –who according to one myth bore Theseus a daughter, Iphigeneia, who she entrusted to her sister Clytemnestra to raise– the two friends descended to the Underworld to kidnap Persephone. But the moment they were seated on the throne proffered by the king of the underworld, they realized that they were stuck to their seats, while snakes wrapped themselves around their bodies. In a slightly different version, Theseus and Peirithous were captured after a fight. When Heracles descended to the underworld to steal Cerberus he freed Theseus, but the gods did not allow him to save Peirithous too.

In his biography of Theseus, Plutarch claims that he and Peirithous did not descend into Hades but instead raised an army and set off on a campaign against the king of Epirus, Aidoneus, to kidnap his daughter –who was named Persephone. They were captured by the king of the Molossians, who held Theseus hostage until he was finally freed by Heracles. Aidoneus, however, fed Peirithous to his dog, which he called Cerberus.

The unworthy death of Theseus

When Theseus returned to Athens, he was captured by insurgents led by Menestheus, a descendant of Erechtheus. He was expelled to the island of Scyrus by his unruly and ungrateful subjects. He hoped to find welcome on the island by Lycomedes, king of the Dolopes, but he pushed Theseus off a cliff and into the sea. The hero's bones were taken to Athens by Cimon after the Persian Wars and placed in the city center at the Theseion, which became a refuge for the weak, for slaves, and all those oppressed by the powerful.

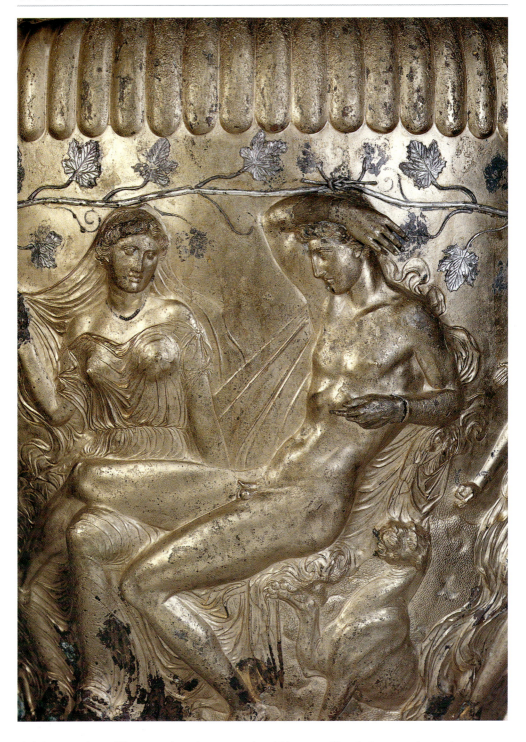

Ariadne seated near Dionysus, whose leg rests on her thigh – a position that represents marriage. The sacred panther, Dionysus's favorite animal, lays at the couple's feet (detail from bronze, gold-leaf Derveni crater, 330-320 B.C., Thessaloniki Archaeological Museum).

Gods of Thessaly

PELEUS

Peleus was the son of Aeacus, the first and last king of Aegina, and Endeis, daughter of the wise centaur Cheiron. Peleus was forced to abandon his homeland after the murder of his half-brother Phocus and seek refuge in the Thessalian city of Phthia.

In Phthia, Peleus was received by King Eurytion, who purified Peleus of the murder and gave him the hand of his daughter Antigone along with one-third of his kingdom as dowry. But Peleus accidentally killed his father-in-law during the hunt for the Caledonian boar, and was forced to flee to Iolcus, where he received by King Acastus, son of Pelias, who purified him of the killing.

But Acastus's wife Astydameia fell in love with Peleus, who rejected her advances. To avenge the insult, she told Peleus's wife Antigone that her husband was getting ready to marry. Astydameia also denounced Peleus to Acastus, claiming that Peleus had tried to take her as a lover. Antigone killed herself and Acastus, who could not kill a man he had purified, sent Peleus to Mount Pelion to be devoured by wild animals.

Peleus survived thanks to a wonderful knife that had been a present from Hephaestus. He returned to Iolcus and killed Astydameia, who had slandered him. Some accounts claim he also killed Acastus.

Thetis struggles to escape the embrace of Peleus by changing forms, symbolized by the dolphin on her right and the snake biting the hero (interior of red-figure kylix, 460 B.C., National Archaeological Museum).

Peleus and Thetis

The gods decided that Peleus should marry an immortal. They settled on the sea-god Nereus's beautiful daughter Thetis, with whom both Zeus and Poseidon had fallen in love. Neither had consummated his love for her because of Prometheus's prophecy that a child born to Thetis would become more powerful than its father. There is also a version of the myth in which Thetis rejected Zeus's advances out of respect for Hera who had raised her; this angered Zeus, who decided to marry her to a mortal. Yet Thetis helped Zeus when Hera, Poseidon, and Hades tried to overthrow him, just as she helped other gods. One of them was Hephaestus, whose pieces she collected after Zeus tossed him off Mount Olympus. Another was Dionysus, after he jumped into the sea to evade the king of Thrace, Lycurgus.

In spite of her initial negative reaction to the marriage that was imposed upon her by the gods, Thetis acquiesced and her wedding to Peleus took place on Mount Pelion in great splendor. Peleus and Thetis had only one child: a son, Achilles, who grew up and became the great hero of the Trojan War.

The death of Peleus

Peleus distinguished himself at the games organized by king Pelias of Iolcus. He also took part in the Argonauts' expedition, as well as in Heracles's campaigns against Laomedon in Troy and the Amazons. He died at an old age, after the death of his son.

According to other myths, Peleus was persecuted by the sons of Acastus from Iolcus and took refuge on the island of Cos, where he met his grandson Neoptolemus and left for the Elysian Fields. According to Euripides, however, Peleus continued to live with Thetis in Nereus's palace in the sea.

The marriage of Peleus and Thetis.

JASON AND PELIAS

Jason was the son Aeson and Polymede, and grandson of Tereus, king of the Thessalian city of Iolcus. According to the prevalent account Aeson's half-brother, Pelias (son of Poseidon and Tyro), usurped the throne of Iolcus. Concerned about the fate of his son Jason, Aeson entrusted his upbringing to the wise centaur Cheiron. When Jason turned twenty, he went to Iolcus on the occasion of a sacrifice Pelias was making to Poseidon. Along the way, he lost one of his sandals as he crossed a river while carrying Hera, disguised as an old woman, on his shoulders. He thus appeared before his uncle with a single sandal. Pelias, who had been told by the Delphi oracle that his throne would be threatened by "a stranger but also a citizen who will arrive in Iolcus wearing one sandal," was disturbed by the sight of Jason and asked him what he would do if he were in Pelias's position. Jason naively answered that he would send the stranger to Colchis to bring him back the golden fleece. Pelias took advantage of this response and assigned precisely that mission to Jason. thus Pelias lead the largest naval expedition of antiquity. But who was Phrixus and what was the origin of the golden fleece that played such an important role in the tale of the Argonauts?

Phrixus and Helle

Phrixus and Helle were the children of Athamas and Nephele. Their stepmother, Ino, tried to kill them by persuading all the women of Thebes to bake the seeds that were to be used for sowing, thus creating a famine. The emissaries told him the oracle had said the famine would only end if he sacrificed his son Phrixus at the shrine of Zeus. But just as the sacrifice was about to take place, Nephele sent a golden-fleeced ram –which had been born from the union of Poseidon and the mortal Theophano and given to Nephele by her brother Hermes– to carry her children away. During their journey across the sky, Helle fell into the sea and drowned in a strait that became known as the Sea of Helle or Hellespont. Phrixus continued the journey to Aea, the capital of Colchis, a land of Helius near Oceanus, the cyclical river that wrapped itself around the earth. In this barbarian land, Phrixus was received by King Aeetes and married the king's daughter Chalciope. Phrixus sacrificed the ram to Zeus Phrixus and gave its fleece as a present to his father-in-law. Aeetes hung the fleece on an oak in a woods consecrated to Ares and placed a sleepless dragon by the fleece to guard it.

Helle on the golden ram flying over the sea that was named after her.

The Expedition of the Argonauts

The Argonauts' expedition has provided quite a bit of background mythology for the epic poetry of the ancient Greeks, including large segments of Homer's *Odyssey*, as witnessed by the rhapsodies and narration of the sorceress Circe.

The legend of the seafaring Argonauts also inspired the lyric poets such as Pindar, who relates the tale in his *Pythian IV*, as well as the tragic Attic poets such as Euripides (*Medea*). Herodorus from Pontoheracleia, whose works have been dated to the late fifth century B.C., also wrote about the expedition in his *Argonautica*. Writing in the fourth century B.C., the poet Antimachus the Colophonius includes in his first book a lengthy poem entitled *Lyde*, while the Alexandrian poet Philitas was also likely referring to the Argonauts' expedition in his lost poem *Telephus*.

Yet most of our information about the Argonauts' adventure comes from Apollonius Rhodius's wonderful Hellenistic epic *Argonautica*.

The building of the Argo (first century clay relief, British Museum). On the left, Argus works on the boat;s bow while Athena helps Tiphis raise the sail on the mast.

The building of the Argo

With Hera's support and inspiration, Jason agreed to raise a mission to bring the golden fleece to Pelias. Athena and Aphrodite also rushed to Jason's support. Athena even helped with the building of the five-masted ship, the *Argo*, in the Thessalian harbor of Pagasae.

The ship was built by Jason and Argus, the son of Phrixus and Chalciope. The boat is believed to be named after him, although in some accounts it is named after the Argive hero Argus, son of Zeus and Niobe. By some accounts, the *Argo* was built at Thespiae, in Corinth, or in Argos. It was made of pine timber from Mount Pelion, and Athena fixed to a piece of sacred oak from Dodona to its bow to warn sailors of dangers that lay ahead.

The *Argo*'s name means fast and bright, and it was the fastest and steadiest of all boats ever built, as well as the lightest so the Argonauts could carry it on their shoulders when they were on land. After the expedition's return from Colchis, the *Argo* was dedicated at the Corinth isthmus to the Temple of Poseidon.

The Argonauts

The heroes who joined the *Argo*'s crew became known as Argonauts and were the first sailors in the world. The crew members' names are drawn from various mythological cycles and their number varies from ten, according to Pindar, to sixty, according to Apollodorus.

There are, however, 28 names of Argonauts that appear consistently throughout all the ancient texts:
- the sons of Zeus, the Dioscuri Castor and Polydeuces, and Heracles;
- the sons of Hermes, Echion, Eurytus, and Aethalides;
- the sons of Ares, Ascalephus and Ialmenus;
- the son of Apollo, Orpheus;
- the sons of Dionysus, Phlias and Eumedon;
- the winged sons of Boreas, Zetes and Calais.

Also mentioned as members of the *Argo*'s crew are the mortal seers Amphiaraus and Mopsus, Meleager, Periclymenus, Telamon, Peleus, Idmon, Tiphys, and Pelias's son Acastus.

Apollodorus the Athenian writes that Atalante also took part in the expedition, but Apollonius Rhodius refutes this and claims that she was forbidden from coming aboard by Jason, who feared the effect of a lone woman among so many men. Jason was elected to lead the expedition, and the oars were assigned by lots although the middle bench was unanimously given to Heracles and Augeias.

After making a sacrifice to the god Apollo, the *Argo* set off on its journey to the seas of the east.

The Argonauts on Lemnos and Samothrace

The first stop on their journey was Lemnos, an island without men because Aphrodite had punished its women for not worshipping her by making them smell bad. Thus their men could not get near their women, so they imported women from Thrace. This angered the Lemnos women, who killed their men. But seeking to please Hephaestus, who hoped to see his favorite island populated again, Aphrodite made the Argonauts extend their stay on the island to enjoy the charms of the Lemnos women. Jason became the lover of the island's queen, Hypsipyle, and had a son, Euneus by her. But because the men kept delaying

Amphora with maritime scenes (1700 B.C., Aegina Archaeological Museum).

THE EXPEDITION OF THE ARGONAUTS

their departure, Heracles was forced to pull the crew to order so they could continue on their quest.

The Argonauts and Cyzicus

Some writers mention that the Argonauts' next stop was Troy, where Heracles freed Hesione whose father, Laomedon had offered her as prey to a sea monster to rid his land of a plague. All accounts, however, agree that the *Argo* next dropped anchor in the land of the Thracian tribe known as Doliones, where they were warmly welcomed by King Cyzicus.

During a visit to Mount Dindymus, which was sacred to the great goddess Cybele, to enjoy the panoramic view, bad giants blocked the harbor with boulders in an attempt to steal the *Argo*. Heracles, who had stayed behind, valiantly fought them off and, with the aid of his fellow Argonauts, was able to defeat them.

After sailing from the land of king Cyzicus, a storm once again brought the Argonauts' ship to the coast of the Doliones. Not recognizing the *Argo*, the Doliones feared they were under attack and launched a counter-attack. Cyzicus was killed in the battle.

In the morning, the two sides were grief-stricken to realize the results of their confusion and held a grand burial for the king, whose wife Cleite killed herself out of grief.

Gales forced the Argonauts to stay with the Doliones for twelve days. The storm subsided after Jason, on the advice of the seer Mopsus, offered a sacrifice to Hera.

The Argonauts and the Bebryces

The Argonauts' next stop was

Pentikontoros; an ancient Athenian battleship.

Mysia, where the nymphs kidnapped the handsome Hylas, son of the Mysian king Theiodamas. Inconsolable, Heracles stayed behind in Mysia to look for his friend, but the Argonauts sailed on after a prophecy by Zetes and Calais, sons of Boreas, that Heracles was destined for other feats. (In some accounts, the prophecy was made by the sea-god Glaucus).

Continuing on their journey, the Argonauts reached the land of the Bebryces on the coast of Lampsacus on the Hellespont. Amycus, a son of Poseidon and king of the Bebryces, would challenge strangers to a wrestling match, then kill them. Polydeuces accepted the king's challenge and defeated him. In some myths, Polydeuces fought Amycus to the death, while in others the Argonaut spared the king's life after making him swear that he would become hospitable in the future.

The Argonauts in Bithynia

Arriving in Salmydessus at Bithynia, the Argonauts encountered the aging Thracian king, Phineas, who had been blinded by Zeus for revealing the will of the gods to mortals. Condemned to a life of hunger because the Harpies snatched away his food, Phineas was freed of his torment with the help of two Argonauts, Zetes and Calais, who chased away the winged demons. To reciprocate their help, Phineas advised the Argonauts on the best way to sail through the Clashing Rocks, or *Sympligades* – two tall rocks that the winds would push together, then part, making it impossible for any vessel to sail into the Black Sea.

On Phineas's advice, the Argonauts released a dove outside the Clashing Rocks and observed it as it flew through them. The dove cleared the rocks, and only its tail was caught in them. The Argonauts followed the dove's example and, with Hera's help, sailed quickly through the rocks. The tip of the *Argo*'s stern was crushed by the rocks, causing only light damage. The *Clashing Rocks* then became rooted in their place as it had been decreed by the gods that they would stop clashing if a vessel managed to sail through them.

The Argonauts in Colchis

The Argonauts finally reached their destination in Colchis: Aea. Jason and the sons of Phrixus, Telamon and Augeias, presented themselves before King Aeetes, who promised to give them the golden fleece if they completed a labor he would assign them in a single day. The labor was to yoke two bulls with bronze legs and bronze, fire-breathing mouths. The bulls had been a present from Hephaestus to the son of Helius. As part of the labor, Jason had to sow the teeth of a monstrous giant – a gift from Athena – from which would spring giants that Jason would then have to slay.

Jason agreed, and managed to complete the labors thanks to help he received from the sorceress Medea, daughter of Aeetes who fell in love with the handsome Greek. Thus Jason used a magic potion that made him invincible and managed to yoke both fire-breathing bulls and slay the giants.

But Aeetes had no intention of keeping his promise to give Jason the golden fleece. He decided to kill Jason during the night, but his plan was foiled by Aphrodite who filled the king with a sudden desire for his wife. That very night Jason sneaked off to the tree where the golden fleece hung. Using magic chants and herbs, Medea lulled the dragon that was guarding the fleece to sleep and Jason stole the precious prize, the golden fleece.

The Journey home

After stealing the golden fleece, the Argonauts immediate boarded the *Argo* and set sail. They took Medea with them because her love for Jason had caused her to betray her father's house and her brother Absyrtus. But Aeetes chased after the Argonauts. Medea did not hesitate to kill her brother, chop his body into pieces, and toss it into the sea, forcing her grief-stricken father to stop his pursuit of the Argonauts in order to pick up the pieces of his son's body.

The Argonauts' journey home followed different routes in the texts of various writers, depending on their knowledge of geography at the time they were writing.

In Apollonius's account, the Colchians led by Absyrtus chased the Argonauts down the rivers Ister (Danube), Eridanus, and Rhodanus to the Tyrrhenian Sea and the island of

Jason retrieves the golden fleece with Medea's help. The dragon mesmerized by the Colchian sorceress is shown wrapped around the tree, while the Dioscuri observe the scene (Classical-era red-figure amphora, National Museum of Naples).

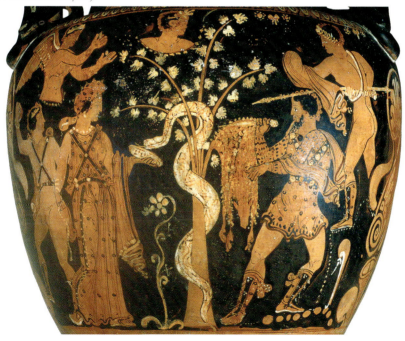

Circe, who purified Medea and Jason. Learning that Medea is her niece and the events that brought the Argonauts to her island, Circe sent them away. The *Argo* then sails by the islands of the Sirens, or Seirenes, who fail to lure the Argonauts with their song as Orpheus manages to drown out their voices with his music. Only Butes, son of Aenetus, dove into the sea and swam to their island. But Aphrodite saved him from the Sirens and led him to Sicily, where she had a son with him who became the Sicilian hero Eryx, later king of the Elymians.

Thetis and the nereids helped the Argonauts pass through the rocks of Scylla and Charybdis. After sailing past Thrinacie (Sicily), they arrived on Corcyra, land of the Phaeacians. But although they could see the coast of the Peloponnese from here, a storm washed their boat all the way over to Libya, where they were forced to put the *Argo* in dry dock for twelve days for repairs. The chances of ever reaching home seemed even more remote than ever, when Triton –or, by other accounts, Poseidon's son Eurypylus– appeared and gave the Boeotian Argonaut Euphemus a clump of soil. Euphemus tossed the clump into the sea, and the island of Thera (Santorini) appeared.

Setting sail from Libya, the Argonauts arrived on Crete, where Medea killed the bronze giant Talus by removing the nail that kept his only vein closed. Other writers, like Apollodorus, claim that Talus was killed by the Argonaut Poeas, who shot him in the ankle with an arrow.

The *Argo* remained on the island of Aegina for quite some time, then eventually returned to Pagasae from where it had set sail.

Jason and Medea in Iolcus

During Jason's four-month absence, Pelias had decided to kill Jason's family. His aging father Aeson asked Pelias to be allowed to end his one life himself, and committed suicide by drinking the blood of a bull. Jason's mother came to a tragic end as she was hung, while Jason's brother Promachus was also killed.

Jason gave Pelias the golden fleece and left for Corinth, where he dedicated the *Argo* to Poseidon. Medea, however, found a way to avenge the death of her father-in-law. She convinced Pelias's daughters that their father would become immortal is they threw him in a vat of boiling water in which she would have placed the pieces of a ram that would come alive in the water. So Pelias's daughters killed their father and threw him a vat of boiling water, but the miracle of immortality did not occur.

The residents of Iolcus buried Pelias, then persecuted Jason and Medea who sought refuge in Corinth.

Medea's infanticide

Medea has been etched in Western culture as the best-known and most heinous murderess. But her infanticide was no more than a deep and determined intervention of the tragic poet Euripides in the ancient myth, according to which Medea accidentally killed her children while trying to use her sorcery to make them immortal. Inspired by the narration of the myth of Procne, Euripides transformed the Colchian sorceress into the impassioned heroine of his tragic play, *Medeia*, in which she avenges her husband's infidelity in the most horrendous way.

Jason and Medea spent ten quiet years in Corinth, until one day king Creon offered the hand of his daughter Creusa to Jason. Jason accepted and Medea was sent into exile. She found refuge in Athens, where king Aegeus took her in. Seeking revenge on Jason and Creon, she sent the bride-to-be a robe and a tunic her two children Mermerus and Pheres. As soon as Creusa donned the robe, it burst into flames and the girl died writing in pain, along with her father who had tried to help her.

Realizing that her children's fate had been sealed, Medea fought the feelings of jealousy, rage, reason, maternal love, pain, and guilt that had consumed her being to complete her vengeance against the treacherous Jason by killing their children. She then rode off on the magic chariot of her grandfather Helius, after establishing the worship of her murdered children in Corinth.

According to a different myth, Medea's children were murdered by the Corinthians inside the temple of Hera where Medea had sought to hide and protect them. The Corinthians were punished for their sacrilege by an illness, which was lifted after the Delphi

Jason and Medea present the golden fleece to Peleus. The hero is crowned by Nike for his victory, while Hermes (top right), patron of travelers, observes (crater, 350-340 B.C, Louvre Museum).

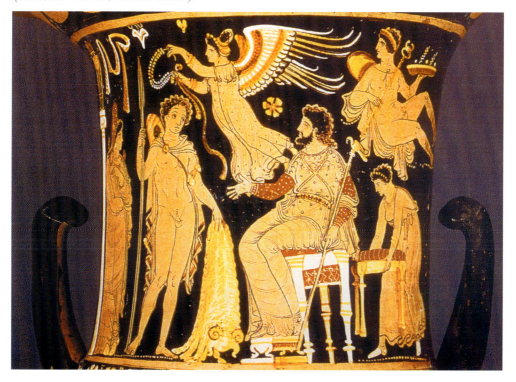

Oracle instructed them to establish a cult to Medea's children in order to purify themselves of the murder and placate Hera.

Medea in Athens

Medea sought refuge in Athens, which was then ruled by the aging Aegeus. He fell in love with Medea and she bore him a son, Medus. But the arrival of Theseus upset Medea's dreams that Medus would succeed Aegeus. She thus persuaded Aegeus to poison the stranger. At the crucial moment, father and son recognized one another, so the murder was averted. Aegeus then banished Medea and Medus, who returned to Colchis and helped Aeetes reclaim his throne, which had been taken by his brother Perses.

Jason's death

The ancient writers disagree on how Jason died. One writes that he followed Medea's advice to rest on the *Argo*'s bow, where he was hit on the head by a mast. Another writes that he killed himself out of despair, while by another account he was rejuvenated by one of Medea's potions and returned to Colchis with her. There, he helped Aeetes reclaim his throne and later succeeded him as king of Colchis.

Myths about Aegina

AEGINA AND ZEUS

Zeus, the father of gods and mortals, fell in love with Aegina, the most beautiful of the river-god Asopus's twenty daughters. Zeus changed into an eagle, grabbed Aegina from Phlius (east of Arcadia), and took her to an uninhabited island known as Oenone in the middle of the Saronic Gulf. Aegina bore Zeus a son, Aeacus. He became the first and last king of the island that later took his mother's name, Aegina.

Hellanius or Panhellenius Zeus, father of the eponym and settler of Aegina, was worshipped on Mount Hellanion, the highest point on the island and the area of the Saronic Gulf.
The oldest shrine in Europe is located atop this mountain and is dedicated to the rainmaker Zeus.

AEACUS AND HIS DESCENDANTS

Aeacus was the first mythical settler of the island of Aegina. He enjoyed great paternal benevolence and became the protector of both his island and all Greece as the eponym of the famed tribe of the Aecians.

But Zeus's legal wife Hera became quite jealous of Aegina, so she sent poisonous snakes to the island, where they released their venom into the water, thus killing all of the island's inhabitants. Aeacus prayed to his father Zeus for companions, so Zeus transformed the ants of a sacred oak into people, who became known as the *Myrmidons* (from the Greek *myrmingi*, or ant). The Myrmidons later settled Phthia and led by Aeacus's descendant

Kolonna, the sole ruins of the late sixth-century B.C. Temple of Apollo on Aegina.

Achilles launched a campaign against Troy in Asia Minor.

According to Plutarch, Aeacus was the most respected and fair of all mortals. Thus, when the gods decided to punish the Greeks with drought and famine for the murder of King Stymphalus by Pelops or Androgeus, the oracles said that the only hope to appease the gods was for Aeacus to pray to *Hellanius* or *Panhellenius Zeus*. Aeacus responded to the Greeks' pleas and prayed to his father, who sent rain. To commemorate Aeacus's assistance, the Greeks held the Aeaceia, festivals in which athletes from throughout Greece participated.

Pindar mentions a myth in which the Trojans called on Aeacus to cooperate with Apollo and Poseidon in building the walls of the city of Troy. After the walls were completed, three snakes attacked the fortifications. Two of the snakes fell dead, but the third slipped into the city through the section built by the king of Aegina. Apollo interpreted this as a sign that the city would be conquered by the first and fourth descendant of Aeacus, who would invade from precisely that point.

According to a tradition mentioned by Pliny, Aeacus was the first to discover silver. He has thus been associated with the early coins minted on Aegina. Serbius relates how Aeacus built the first temple dedicated to Zeus in Arcadia, while Stephanos Byzantios writes that Aeacus founded the cult of Thessalian Zeus and became king of Thessaly.

With Endeis, daughter of the sage centaur Cheiron –or, according to some, daughter of Scyrius, son of the king of Megara Pylas– Aeacus had two sons, Peleus (father of Achilles) and Telamon (father of Ajax). Aeacus also lay with the nereid Psamathe –who changed into a seal to avoid his

Marble base of a statue with bas-relief representations. In the center, a representation of a couple wrestling (late sixth century B.C., National Archaeological Museum).

advances– who bore him a third son, Phocus, whose half-brothers claimed to have accidentally killed during a discus competition. To avoid their father's rage, Peleus moved to Phthia and Telamon moved to Salamis. Telamon was racked by remorse over the death of Phocus, so they sneaked back to Aegina and built him a grave. He then sought his father's forgiveness. Aeacus would not allow Telamon to land on the island, so he built a barrier outside the port from where he offered his apology. But Aeacus was not convinced of Telamon's sincerity, so he refused his forgiveness.

After Aeacus died, his sense of fairness –which could not even be swayed by blood ties– was rewarded as he was made the gatekeeper of Hades and judge of the Europeans, in contrast to Rhadamanthys who became the judge of the Asians, while Minos only intervened in controversial cases.

The Temple of Aphaia on Aegina, one of the best examples of Archaic architecture (500 B.C.). Built in the Doric style, the peripteral structure has six columns on its narrow ends and twelve columns along its length. The temple was dedicated to a local deity, Aphaia, whom the Cretans worshipped as Dictynna, a daughter of Zeus and Carme who jumped into the sea to avoid the advances of king Minos.

Myths about Crete

MINOS

Three generations before the Trojan War, around 1300 B.C., Crete was ruled by king Minos, son of Zeus and Europa and brother of Rhadamanthys. According to other accounts, Minos was the son of the Crete's King Asterius. Minos vied against his brother Sarpedon for the Cretan throne. He prayed to Poseidon for a sign of the gods' will and promised, in return, to sacrifice to the sea-god anything that emerged from the sea. Minos's prayer was answered and Poseidon sent him a beautiful bull. Sarpedon was thus convinced that he was not favored by the gods; defeated, he left for Lycia. Minos thus became king of Crete. But charmed by the bull's beauty, he regretted his vow to sacrifice it, so he tried to deceive Poseidon by sacrificing a different beast. This enraged the god, who took revenge by instilling in Minos's wife Pasiphae, daughter of Helius and Perseis, a gnawing lust for the bull. To sate her passion, Pasiphae asked the craftsman Daedalus for help. He built the queen a replica of a cow and concealed Pasiphae inside. She thus united with the bull and later bore the Minotaur (Bull of Minos), a beast that was half-man and half-bull.

Minos had several children with Pasiphae: Catreus, Deucalion, Glaucus, Androgeus, Acacallis, Ariadne, Xenodice, and Phaedra. He also had several more children with other women. After the Athenians killed his son Androgeus, Minos imposed a tribute under which the Athenians were obligated to send

Prince with lilies (wall painting, Palace of Knossos, 1500 B.C., Archaeological Museum of Iraklio, Crete).

every year (or, in other accounts, every three or nine years) seven youths and seven maidens to feed the Minotaur. Theseus ended the tribute.

In some accounts, Minos fell in love with Theseus so he made a compromise with the Athenians and also gave Theseus the hand of his daughter Phaedra.

Other myths mention the Cretan king's love for Miletus, who chose instead to follow Sarpedon. Minos was also said to have fallen in love with Britomartis, daughter of Zeus and Carme, and favorite of the goddess Artemis. To escape Minos's advances, Britomartis fell into the sea and became tangled in fishermen's nets. She was rescued by Artemis, who made her a goddess whom the Cretans worshipped as *Dictynna* (from the Greek *dicty*, or net). Britomartis was also worshipped on Aegina, where local myths claim she rose from the sea near their island and became invisible, or *aphaia*. In a slight variation on the Cretan version, Britomartis was rescued from the sea by fishermen who took her to Greece. During the voyage, they made advances, so in order to avoid them she jumped into the sea near Aegina, swam ashore, climbed a hillock, and disappeared into the pine woods.

Minos's infidelities prompted Pasiphae to resort to sorcery to transmit a mysterious illness that would cause the death of any woman who lay with him other than herself. Minos was able to lift the spell with help from Procris.

Minos was the first Greek ruler to

King Minos's throne in the throne room and the mural of the griffins (mid-16th century B.C., Palace of Knossos, Crete).

expand his empire across the sea. After conquering nearby islands, especially the Cyclades who were named Minoides and the sea was named Minoan, he founded many cities and colonies, forcing the Carians and the Lelegians into submission. He even used the Lelegians to counter piracy. Minos also lay siege on Athens, which he conquered while the city was suffering from a famine brought upon as punishment for the murder of his son Androgeus. He also conquered Megara, which fell after fierce fighting after being betrayed by Scylla, daughter of King Nisus, who fell in love with Minos.

According to ancient sources, Minos ruled Crete fairly. He divided the island into three regions, with Cnossus as the capital. He built his palace at Cnossus. Minos also divided his subjects into classes: warriors, farmers, and so on.

Minos was also honored as a lawgiver, and it is said that the laws, traditions, and rites he introduced were handed down to the Cretan king by Zeus. Every nine years, Minos would summon Zeus to a sacred cave on Mount Ida and seek the god's advice on laws or other matters. The sobriety and fairness with which Minos ruled earned him the right to hold a golden scepter and be seated on the bench of Dikaiosyne (Justice) in Hades, where he presided upon the judgement of people with Rhadamanthys and Aeacus.

THE MINOTAUR

After Pasiphae united with the bull sent to Minos by the sea-god Poseidon, she gave birth to a man-eating beast with a human body and a bull's head. The beast became known as the Minotaur.

Minos ordered Daedalus to build an underground residence known as the Labyrinth in which the beast was kept. The Minotaur was fed with seven youths and seven maidens sent as a blood tribute by Athens as compensation for the murder of Minos's son Androgeus.

Theseus voluntarily participated in either the second or third mission. He managed to slay the Minotaur and with help from Ariadne, Minos's daughter, find his way out of the Labyrinth, thus ridding his city of this heavy tax.

The Minotaur, born of Pasiphae's lust for the Knossos bull (National Archaeological Museum).

DAEDALUS AND ICARUS

According to ancient Greek tradition, the greatest painter, architect, and first sculptor was an Athenian known as Daedalus, a descendant of Erechtheus and relative of Theseus. Before Daedalus, statues were no more than amorphous wood or clay idols. Daedalus gave statues shape and made them so beautiful that simple citizens would avoid them because they thought they were real, so they bound them with chains so they would not flee. It is even said that on seeing a statue of himself at Pisa, Heracles thought it was real and pelted it with rocks.

The entire world admired Daedalus's art and inventions. But he was envious of his sister's son Perdix, a student of Calus or Talus, for inventing the saw, timber mill, and pottery wheel first. Daedalus thus killed his nephew and buried his body on the southern slope of the Acropolis. But the murder was discovered and the Areopagus, or supreme court, sentenced Daedalus to death. The inventor fled to a *demos*, or administrative district, of Athens that had adopted his name –Daedalidae– and from there to Crete, whose powerful king Minos became his protector. On Crete, Daedalus built many wonderful projects, from *xoana* (wooden idols) of gods to Pasiphae's wooden cow and the *Labyrinth*, an enormous underground palace with such a complex arrangement of corridors that it was impossible for anyone to find their way out. For the palace of Cnossus, Daedalus built a *choros*, a palatial suite where performances were staged. Crete was thus identified with the inventions of this great artisan, who in later texts is considered a native of the island. But Minos was angered by Daedalus, either for giving Ariadne the ball of thread that she then gave to Theseus so he could find his way out of the Labyrinth or for building the wooden cow that Pasiphae hid inside in order to mate with Poseidon's bull. He jailed Daedalus with his son Icarus, whom he had fathered with the Cretan slave Naucrate. But the ingenious inventor and artisan would not rest until he found a way out for him and his son. Using feathers, flax, and wax, he built two pairs of wings. He put on one pair and instructed his son to put on the other; the two then flew out of jail and off the island like birds in the sky.

Daedalus instructed his son to fly beside him and not to float too close to the sea or soar too close to the sun to avoid getting the feathers wet and melting the wax. But Icarus ignored his father. Drunk on the sheer pleasure of freedom, he soared too close to the sun. The wax melted and his wings fell apart; the boy then plunged into the sea, which was named in his honor. Quite some time later, his body washed up on the shores of an island, where it was found by Heracles who named the island Icaria, after Daedalus's son.

Daedalus continued on to Italy. He landed at Cyme, where he built a temple to Apollo to whom he dedicated his wings. Later, he arrived in the Sicilian city of Camicus, which was ruled by king Cocalus. Daedalus created magnificent works in Camicus that drew the admiration of the king's daughters.

Minos raised an army for a campaign against Camicus, demanding that Daedalus be surrendered to him. Cocalus's daughters advised the king against rejecting Minos's demand and told him to extend his hospitality to the Cretan ruler. Minos came to the palace, but while he was bathing, Cocalus's daughters doused him with a cauldron of boiling water. The powerful Cretan king died, writhing in pain.

The fall of Icarus (wall-painting, 10 B.C., National Museum of Naples).

RHADAMANTHYS AND SARPEDON

Rhadamanthys was the brother of Minos and a son of Zeus and Europa. He was the personification of even-handedness and justice. The ancient Greeks credited Rhadamanthys with the formation of the code of penal justice, and considered him as the one who introduced the concept of *"equal punishment"* which became known as the *Rhadamantheian law* according to which *"it was considered just to impose on the perpetrator the same treatment he had imposed on his victims"*. Heracles used this principle to justify his murder of Linus, as it was widely accepted that *"the law forgives the person who kills because he is forced to use violence against violence"*.

Plato only acknowledges a limited role for Rhadamanthys, claiming merely that he was a virtuous man who became an excellent judge because he was a student of Minos. By contrast, Diodorus Siculus relates how Minos envied his brother's reputation, which is why Rhadamanthys was forced to flee to remote islands and from there to Boeotia, where he married Heracles's mother Alcmene, widow of Amphitryon.

According to a different myth of Theban origin, Alcmene died in Thebes and Hermes, on orders from the gods, carried her to the Elysian Fields where she married Rhadamanthys, who in the afterlife had become a judge alongside Minos and Aeacus.

Minos and Rhadamanthys had another brother, Sarpedon. He, too, was forced to leave Crete because Miletus chose him over Minos. But Herodotus writes that after Minos became the ruler of Crete, Sarpedon was expelled from the island and go to the land of the Mylians, Lycia, in Asia Minor where he became king. The Lycians had taken their name from their first king, Lycus, whose brother Aegeus had banished from Athens, so he returned to the Lycia and joined the court of Sarpedon.

Apollodorus the Athenian writes that Zeus extended Sarpedon's life to three times the average mortal life span, which is why he is often confused with the son of Zeus and Laodameia, daughter of Bellerophon, who took part in the Trojan War.

TALUS

According to Plato, Minos assigned Rhadamanthys the task of monitoring the implementation of the law in Cnossus, while the giant Talus was responsible for seeing that the laws were followed on the rest of the island. Thus, Talus would pass through all Cretan city-states three times a year to see whether the laws were being implemented. Indeed, because he traveled with bronze tablets on which the laws had been inscribed, he became known as the bronze man.

Apollodorus the Athenian writes that Talus was a living bronze giant made by Hephaestus, who presented him to Minos as a gift to guard Crete. This enormous robot had just a single vein that ran down his body and which was kept shut by a bronze nail that did not let the blood spill. Talus covered the length of the island three times a day, and never allowed a stranger to land. Those who dared were met with a horrible death in his fiery embrace or from his fiery breath.

But the Argonauts' arrival on Crete brought about the death of Talus. The giant saw their ship, the *Argo*, approach and threw rocks at it to force it to change course. The sorceress Medea, who was sailing back with Jason, killed the giant by giving him a poisonous herb or, according to others, by removing the nail that kept his vein closed.

Supported by the Dioscuri Castor and Polydeuces, the bronze giant Talus –a sun-god who was demoted to a hero– slowly dies (detail from red-figure crater, 400-390 B.C., Museo Jatta).

The Theban Cycle

CADMUS

Cadmus was the son of the king Agenor of Sidon. He was the brother of Europa, Cylix, and Phoenix. When Zeus abducted his precious daughter, Agenor sent his three sons to find them and told them not to dare return without her. While searching for Europa, Phoenix founded Phoenicia, Cylix founded Cilicia, and Cadmus landed in Greece, where he settled in Thrace with his mother.

After his mother's death, Cadmus went to Delphi to seek the oracle's advice and was told to follow a cow

Cadmus threatens the dragon dedicated to Ares. In front of him stands Athena, his patroness, and behind him Harmonia and Ares (450 B.C., Metropolitan Museum of New York).

THE THEBAN CYCLE

that would cross his path and found a city where the cow fell. He followed the divine prophecy and tracked a cow to Thebes, where the animal fell down exhausted. Just as Cadmus was preparing to sacrifice it, a giant dragon dedicated to Ares attacked him. Cadmus and the dragon, which was guarding a spring, fought fiercely, but Cadmus managed to overpower the beast. With his dying breath, the dragon told Cadmus that he would be changed into a dragon one day.

The goddess Athena advised Cadmus to sow the dragon's teeth in the ground. Fully-armed warriors sprung from the ground where he planted the teeth. The warriors immediately engaged each other in battle and all were killed except five: Udaeus, Chthonius, Pelorus, Hyperenor, and Echion. Cadmus formed a lifelong friendship with these warriors who helped him build *Cadmeia*, the acropolis of the seven-gated city of Thebes, home of the *Sparti*, or Sown-Men, who formed the city's noble line.

Cadmus's punishment for killing the dragon was to serve Ares for eight years. With Athena's help, he later became king of Thebes and Zeus gave him Harmonia, daughter of Ares and Aphrodite, as his wife. The wedding was quite grand, as it was attended by the Olympian gods who offered the bride brilliant gifts while the Muses chanted songs.

Cadmus became one of the richest and most powerful kings of Greece. With Harmonia, he fathered five children: Polydorus, Ino, Semele, Agave, and Autonoe. But the gods also had much sorrow in store for the king, who lost his daughters Semele and Ino and watched his grandson Actaeon, infant son of Autonoe, fall victims to the rage of Artemis.

When Cadmus grew old, he was totally grief-stricken; he left Thebes with his wife Harmonia and roamed the world. He often thought of the dragon's prophecy and wished for it come true. The gods heard his pleas and changed him into an enormous snake that wrapped itself around Harmonia's body. The gods also changed her into a dragon. She and Cadmus then became the guardians of the seven-gated city (Thebes).

According to Herodotus, Cadmus introduced Greek writing into Thebes along with Phoenician writing. The city was named *Cadmeia* in his honor.

Several Greek traditions link Cadmus with Illyria, while others link him to Samothrace and the battle against the Titans – especially the fight against Typhon. Later myths deny that Cadmus was the one who introduced the Greek alphabet. They also claim he was from the Boeotian city of Cadmeia, from which he took his name. These myths interpret the name Cadmus as stemming from the word *quadmon*, which means oriental.

DESCENDANTS OF CADMUS

Ino and Athamas

Cadmus's daughter Ino married Athamas, the son of Aeolus and Enaraete or Minyas and Phanosoura. He was the king of Boeotia or Orchomenus and, according to a different myth, had two children –Phrixus and Helle– from a previous marriage to Nephele.

Ino bore Athamas two son, Learchus and Melicertes. Wishing to destroy her stepchildren, she persuaded the women of Thebes to bake the wheat seeds used for sowing. As a result, the crops did not grow and there was a famine. Athamas went to the Oracle of Delphi to seek advice on how to end the famine. Ino intercepted his messengers and plotted with them to tell Athamas that the land would only become fertile again if he sacrificed Phrixus. Athamas led Phrixus and Helle to the shrine of Laphystian Zeus and prepared to sacrifice the boy. Just then, Nephele snatched her children and placed them on a golden-fleeced ram she had been given by Hermes. Phrixus and Helle rode the ram into the sky and over the sea, away from Thebes.

Tragedy struck the family again after Ino agreed to raise Dionysus, the son of her dead sister Semele and Zeus. Furious, Hera drove Athamas mad; he killed his son Learchus. Hera also drove Ino to madness; she threw Melicertes into a boiling cauldron, then clutching her dead child plunged into the sea.

Athamas was expelled from Boeotia. The Delphi Oracle advised him to settle in the land where he would be welcomed by wild animals. He settled in Athamania (Copais or Phthia), where he married Themisto. She bore him four sons: Leucon, Erythrius, Schoeneus, and Ptous. According to Strabo, Athamas also founded the Thessalian city of Aloe.

Herodotus mentions a tale in which the Achaeans decided to sacrifice Athamas to purify the city, but that Athamas was saved by his grandson Cytissorus, son of Phrixus, who had arrived from Colchis. Athamas's descendants were subsequently forbidden from entering the prytaneio.

The myth of Ino and Athamas inspired the great tragic poets Aeschylus and Sophocles to write the plays *Athamas* and Euripides to write the tragedy *Ino and Phrixus*, none of which have survived.

Semele

Semele, daughter of Cadmus and Harmonia, lay with Zeus and bore one of the most important gods worshipped in ancient Greece: Dionysus. But Hera, who was consumed with jealousy over her husband's latest infidelity, disguised herself as Semele's nurse and persuaded the young women to ask Zeus to prove his love by appearing before her in the godly form he appeared before his wife Hera. Zeus tried to dissuade her, but she was insistent. Zeus appeared in his godly form, and everything around them caught fire when he fell upon her enveloped in lightning and thunder. Semele was consumed by the lightning, but Zeus managed to save their unborn child by removing it from her womb and sewing it into his thigh until it reached term.

Agave

Daughter of Cadmus and Harmonia, Agave married Echion and bore him Pentheus, who became king of Thebes. After the death of her sister Semele, Agave told everyone that she had been struck by Zeus's thunderbolt because she had tried to conceal the identity of her mortal lover by falsely claiming that Zeus was the father of her unborn child. Her son Pentheus supported his mother's opinion, and refused to allow the introduction of the Dionysian cult in his kingdom.

Nonetheless, Dionysus decided to prove his divine lineage and punish the hubris and slander of his relatives. So, he drove the Theban women crazy, including his aunt Agave, who took to the mountains with her sisters Autonoe and Ino. There, they joined in the orgiastic rituals of the Dionysian cult. Pentheus climbed Mount Cithaeron to spy on the maenads, as the female votaries of Dionysus were called, but was torn apart and devoured by his mother in her frenzy. Agave then went around holding up the head of her dead son, believing it was the head of a lion.

After her son's murder, Agave fled to Illyria, where she married king Lycotherses. Later, she killed him so she could hand over his kingdom to her father, Cadmus.

Actaeon

Grandson of Cadmus and son of Autonoe and Aristaus, Actaeon was raised by the centaur Cheiron and become one of the most skilled hunters in Greece.

Once, exhausted from hunting, he descended to the sacred valley of Artemis, Gargaphia, and fell asleep. When he awoke, he saw Artemis bathing in a spring with the nymphs. Outraged that a mortal had seen her naked, the goddess doused him with water and changed him into a deer. She then made his dogs rabid, and they chased after the deer, which they tore apart quite ignorant of the fact that the deer had been their master. Afterwards, they raced through the woods barking and looking for him. Cheiron took pity on the dogs and made them an idol of Actaeon to calm them.

According to different versions of the myth, Actaeon's violent death was precipitated by his desire to lay with Artemis –or Semele– thus provoking the wrath of Zeus.

A tradition of Boeotian Orchomenus held that after Actaeon's death, a criminal ghost appeared that ravaged the land. After consulting the Oracle of Delphi, Orchomenus's citizens built a copper statue of Actaeon and tied it to a rock, where it was seen by the traveler Pausanias. In addition to describing the statue, he wrote that Actaeon's father,

Aristaeus, abandoned Boeotia after his son's death and settled in Sardoe (Sardinia). Autonoe, Actaeon's mother, went to the village of Ereneia near Megara, where she lived until her death.

THE ROYAL HOUSE OF THEBES

Labdacus

Polydorus, son of Cadmus and king of Thebes, had a son with Nycteis. The son's name was Labdacus and he became the eponym of the Labdacids, whose line was plagued by an unknown curse.

Laius and Oedipus

Laius was a son of Labdacus, who died when the boy was barely a year old. He succeeded his father on the Theban throne, with Lycus as regent – a post he had also held under Labdacus. But after Lycus and his wife Dirce were punished by Zethus and Amphion, Laius was expelled and sought refuge from King Pelops at Elis.

But Laius took advantage of the king's hospitality: he kidnapped the king's son Chrysippus and took him back to Thebes. Filled with pain and rage, Pelops cursed the kidnapper to die childless or to be killed by his own son – a curse that Hera supported.

Apollo advised Laius not to have children, but the advice was ignored. Laius married Jocasta, daughter of Menoeceus, and had a son with her. Frightened of the curse, he made holes in the soles of the infant's feet and left it in the woods of Mount Cithaeron to be eaten by wild beasts. The infant was

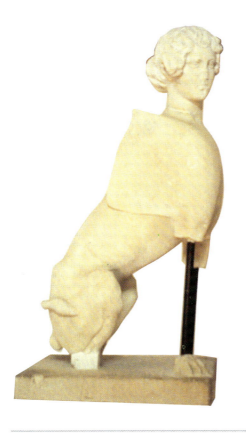

Marble sphinx by the Boeotian sculptor Calamis. Tousled hair add a demonic element to the sculpture and suggest some type of mythical monster (460 B.C., Aegina Archaeological Museum).

found by a goatherd from Corinth, who took the infant to his childless master, King Polybus of Corinth, and his wife Merope. The couple decided to name the child Oedipus, from the holes on the soles of his feet. They raised the boy as their own child.

Fearing that he may be overthrown by his father-in-law Menoeceus, Laius went to Delphi to seek the oracle's advice. Oedipus had, in the meantime, reached manhood. Having learned at a feast that he was not the natural-born son of Polybus and Merope, he went to the Temple of Apollo to seek the identity of his real parents and was told by the oracle that he would kill his father and marry his mother.

Frightened that the prophecy might come true, Oedipus decided not to return to Corinth. As he roamed about Phocis, he killed Laius in a chance fight, without realizing Laius's true identity. Destiny then led Oedipus to Thebes, which he rid of the monstrous Sphinx that had settled on Mount Phicium and devoured all passing Thebans who were unable to solve the riddle it posed.

King Oedipus

After solving the riddle of the Sphinx, Oedipus was made king of Thebes. He married the widow Jocasta, not knowing that she was his mother. Jocasta bore him two daughters and two sons: Antigone, Ismene, Eteocles, and Polyneices.

But destiny had great tragedy in store for Oedipus and his family. Plagued by a terrible disease, the city of Thebes became a huge cemetery. Seeking to ease the suffering of his subjects, Oedipus dispatched his wife's brother Creon to Delphi to ask the oracle for a prophecy that will rid the city of the disease. The oracle says that the killer of Laius must be driven from Thebes because it is his sick deeds that have plunged the city into misery.

The blind seer Teiresias revealed the guilty party, His testimony was confirmed by the slave who had handed over the infant Oedipus to the Corinthian herdsman. Oedipus is horrified when he realizes that he is the killer of his father, husband of his

Oedipus wearing a heat sits and listens to the riddle of the sphinx (red-figure kylix, fifth century B.C., British Museum).

mother, as well as father and brother of his children. Jocasta hangs herself. Seeing his mother hanging, Oedipus takes one of his gold brooches and puts out his eyes so he will not be able to see.

Oedipus at Colonus

Blind, disabled, and suffering the tragedies with which the gods have afflicted him, Oedipus is sent into exile by his subjects and children – who meantime have their eye on his throne. Led by his daughter Antigone, he follows the commands of the Delphi oracles and arrives in Athens and takes refuge in the sacred woods of the Eumenides at Colonus. Soon after, his daughter Ismene arrives to inform him that his sons have been fighting over the succession to the throne. She also tells Oedipus that Creon is on his way to bring him back to Thebes as the oracle had predicted that the throne would be won by the person who is on the side of Oedipus.

Theseus offers his hospitality to Oedipus, and Creon returns to Thebes alone. Oedipus, who had been condemned to such tragedy by the gods, now becomes their chosen one. His decline is slowly reversed and by the end of his tortuous wanderings he has become a hero. As he lies dying, he offers Theseus the prediction that Athens will remain impenetrable and will defeat the Thebans since the city will be protected by his spirit from his grave at Colonus.

The Naxos sphinx (Naxian votive offering, 2.50 meters tall, 570 B.C., Delphi Museum).

The riddle of the Sphinx
– What animal walks on four legs in the morning, on two legs at noon, and on three legs at night?
– Man. When he is young, at the dawn of his life, he crawls on all fours. At noon, in other words when he is grown, he walks on two legs, while at night, when he has aged and needs a walking stick for support, he walks on three legs.

The Seven Against Thebes

After Oedipus was exiled, his sons Eteocles and Polyneices agreed to take turns ruling, rotating the throne every year. As part of their agreement, when one brother ruled, the other would leave Thebes.

Being the eldest, Eteocles assumed the throne first. But when his year was up, he refused to step down and turn power over to his brother. He also banned his brother from returning to Thebes and ordered all the city's gates to be closed. Polyneices went to Argos, where he married king Adrastus's daughter Deipyle. He decided to return to Thebes to claim the city's throne with the help of his father-in-law and five friends: Tydeus, son of the King Oeneus of Calydon and brother-in-law of Adrastus; the Argive seer Amphiaraus; Capaneus, king of Mycenae; Hippomedon of Tiryns; and, Parthenopaeus of Arcadia.

By the time the army they had raised arrived at Nemea, the soldiers were thirsty. But water was nowhere to be found because Zeus, who opposed the campaign, had ordered all the nereids to shut all the springs. As the soldiers fanned out to look for water, they came upon Hypsipyle, the former queen of Lemnos whose subjects had sold her to King Lycurgus of Nemea to punish her for saving her father, king Thoas, from being killed with the other men on the island. Hypsipyle was now a slave who had been charged with raising Lycurgus's son Opheltes. Hypsipyle left the child and led the soldiers through the woods to a secret spring. While she was gone, a snake slithered out from under the bushes and strangled the infant. Lycurgus lunged at Hypsipyle, who was defended by Tydeus. The heroes buried the infant Opheltes and organized games in his honor. This athletic competition later evolved into the *Nemean Games*. The seer Amphiaraus interpreted the infant's death as a bad omen for the campaign. He named *Opheltes Archemorus*, which means *"he who brings death"* and tried, in vain, to dissuade the others from continuing their campaign.

The seven leaders finally arrived near Thebes and sent Tydeus ahead to negotiate with the city's rulers. They challenged him, so Tydeus wrestled with them and won, with the help of Athena. They became enraged, so they sent fifty warriors to ambush Tydeus, who not only escaped unscathed by also killed all except one, whom he let return to Thebes to relate Tydeus's feat. The Thebans vowed to fight the seven leaders. After making a sacrifice to the war-god Ares, they vowed they would either see the city's walls unbreached or see the Theban land soaked with their blood.

The Argive army split and took positions outside each of the city's seven gates. On the opposite side of the wall from Polyneices was his brother, Eteocles. The battle was fierce, and the gods were on the side of the Thebans. The Argive warriors were forced to retreat, while the two brothers –Polyneices and Eteocles– fought to the death, as they each fell upon the other's corpse.

The only Argive leader to survive the carnage was Adrasteus. The Thebans buried their dead with honors, but left their invaders unburied and refused to return the bodies of the Argive dead to their wives and mothers. They asked Theseus for help, who raised an army to march on Thebes, where he forced the Thebans to turn over the bodies of the Argive dead to their families. The Argive warriors were cremated with honors at Eleutherae, and their leaders were cremated at Eleusis. Theseus then presented their ashes to the Argive women. Only the ashes of Capaneus, who was killed by one of Zeus's lightning bolts, remained in Eleusis because his wife Euadne, who could not bear to live without him, had thrown herself on the funerary pyre.

Antigone

After Polyneices and Eteocles killed each other, Creon assumed the throne of Thebes. He ordered that Eteocles be buried with full honors, but that Polyneices's body be left exposed to the hounds and vultures. No citizen dared disobey the king's law. Unable to flout a higher, moral law concerning the burial of the dead, Creon's niece Antigone decided to bury her brother by herself after her sister Ismene refused to help. Antigone appealed to the gods, placing their laws above those of the mortals and acting out of sisterly love. Her action was uncovered and Creon ruled that Antigone be punished by being buried alive in the grave of the Labdaciéds.

Haemon –Antigone's cousin, fianc, and son of Creon and Eurydice– rushed to meet his beloved when he learned of her fate. But he was too late. He found Antigone hanging. Unable to bear the pain of separation, he killed himself in front of his father by plunging his sword into his heart.

Eurydice was informed of her son's tragic death by a herald. Silent, she also took her own life. Arriving at the palace with his dead son in his arms, Creon learned of his wife's death. His arrogance, thirst for power, and insult of the gods of the Underworld had created this destruction. Despondent, he called to death to come take him and put an end to his torment, his pain, his guilt, and his loneliness.

The Sons of the Seven Champions

Ten years after the campaign of the seven Argive leaders against Thebes, their children decided to avenge the deaths of their fathers. This time the gods were on their side and the Delphi Oracle predicted that they would be victorious if Alcmaeon, son of the seer Amphiaraus, took part in their campaign.

Thersander, who was charged with the task of persuading Alcmaeon, bribed his mother Eriphyle with one of Harmonia's dresses that had been woven by the goddess Athena.

The sons raised an army and the oracle near Potniae also predicted that they would be victorious. In the battle that ensued, only Aegialeus –son of Adrastus, sole survivor of the earlier campaign against Thebes– was killed.

The sons of the seven champions defeated the Thebans, who followed the advice of the seer Teiresias –who died near the spring of the nymph Telphusa– and abandoned their city. They fled to Hestiaea in Thessaly. The sons dedicated Teiresias's daughter Manto and lavish gifts to the Oracle at Delphi. They then returned home, while Thersander, the son of Polyneices, rebuilt Thebes and became its king.

A relief dedication to Argive, 375 B.C., at Amphiaraus Oropos (National Archaeological Museum).

THE ESSENTIAL GREEK MYTHOLOGY

Boetian Tradition

ALCMAEON

After the victorious campaign of the sons of the seven champions against Thebes, Alcmaeon, son of the seer Amphiaraus, returned to Argos to fulfill his father's dying wish and kill his mother Eriphyle, who had sent her husband to war. With her dying breath, Eriphyle cursed her son that no land would ever welcome him. Thus the matricidal Alcmaeon was forced to wander around Greece, persecuted by the Erinyes, until he reached Phocis in Arcadia. There, he was purified by king Phegeus and married the king's daughter Arsinoe.

But his mother's curse continued to follow him. Famine and disease descended on Phocis. The Delphi Oracle advised Alcmaeon to cleanse himself in the Achelous River. The river-god purified Alcmaeon of the sin of murder and Alcmaeon wed Achelous' daughter Callirrhoe. Alcmaeon then settled on a sandy islet near the river's mouth – a land that did not exist when Eriphyle had cursed him.

But Alcmaeon was still plagued by bad luck. When Callirrhoe learned of Harmonia's dress that Polyneices and Thersander had given Alcmaeon's mother, she demanded that her husband bring it to her. Alcmaeon when to Phegeus and asked him for the dress, saying that he wished to dedicate it to the Oracle of Delphi. Phegeus believed Alcmaeon and gave him the dress. Later, when he heard from a slave that Alcmaeon intended to give the dress to Callirrhoe, Phegeus asked his sons Pronous and Agenor to cleanse the family of this insult. Pronous and Agenor killed Alcmaeon, but their sister Arsinoe –who still loved her husband– cursed them. They, in turn, handed Arsinoe over to King Agapenor of Arcadia; they accused her of killing her husband, and she was executed.

When Callirrhoe learned of Alcmaeon's murder, she decided to take revenge against Phegeus and his sons. But her children –Acarnan and Amphoterus– were still infants, so she prayed to Zeus for help.

Zeus heard her wish and overnight Acarnan and Amphoterus grew up and avenged their fathers' death by killing Phegeus and his sons. With their mother's permission, they dedicated their grandmother's cursed relics to Apollo at Delphi. They then settled a new land, which was named Acarnania after Acarnas, and created a new kingdom there.

ZETHUS AND AMPHION

Antiope, daughter of the river-god Asopus and sister of Aegina, lived in Thebes. Zeus fell in love with her and she bore him two sons: Zethus and Amphion. Because Antiope was frightened that her father might find out about her amorous adventure, she abandoned the infants in the forest. They were found by a herdsman who, unaware of their identity, raised them. Zethus became a brave warrior and fearless hunter, while Amphion became an accomplished musician who played a lyre given to him by the god Apollo.

Meantime, their mother was the prisoner of king Lycus of Thebes and his wife Dirce, and was chained in their palace. With help from Zeus, she made a miraculous escape and sought refuge in the hut of the herdsman who had raised her children. But Dirce, who had been roaming the mountains with the other women of Thebes engaged in a Dionysian ritual, saw Antiope. She persuaded Zethus and Amphion to tie her to the horns of a wild bull so she

A river god (Cladeos or Alfeos, from the east pediment of the temple of Zeus at Olympia, 460 B.C.., Museum of Olympia).

would be killed. Fortunately for Antiope, the herdsman arrived in time and told Zethus and Amphion that Antiope was their mother. The youths punished Dirce in the same way that she had sought to punish Antiope. They then killed Lycus and became kings of Thebes, whose walls they built in their own way. The muscular Zethus carried the enormous stones and placed them one atop of the other. Amphion charmed the stones with his music, and they stacked themselves into a large, strong fortification.

The brothers' fame spread throughout the world. Zethus married Aidona, daughter of king Pandareus of Ephesus, and Amphion married Tantalus's daughter Niobe. Both women brought great misfortune to the sons of Antiope and their families.

NIOBE

Niobe, wife of the Theban king Amphion, was the daughter of Tantalus and Dione, a sister of Pleiades. Contented, she was very proud of her six handsome sons and six beautiful daughters. But she made the mistake of boasting that she was better than Leto, who had only given birth to two children, Apollo and Artemis. Niobe's hubris prompted her punishment. Apollo and Artemis shot and killed all Niobe's children with their arrows. The children were not buried for none days because Zeus would turn to stone anyone who approached the bodies to bury them. On the tenth day, the twelve children were buried by the gods themselves. Their father Amphion could not bear the pain and killed himself. Niobe was so stunned by their deaths that she remained still and silent. Eventually, her pain turned her into stone. She was carried away by a storm and set down in Lycia on Mount Sipylus, where she has stood for centuries, weeping.

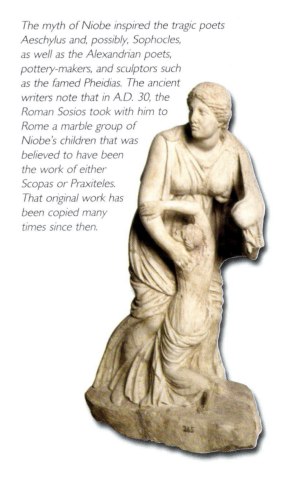

The myth of Niobe inspired the tragic poets Aeschylus and, possibly, Sophocles, as well as the Alexandrian poets, pottery-makers, and sculptors such as the famed Pheidias. The ancient writers note that in A.D. 30, the Roman Sosios took with him to Rome a marble group of Niobe's children that was believed to have been the work of either Scopas or Praxiteles. That original work has been copied many times since then.

The Arcadian Cycle

ATALANTE

The Atalante featured in the Arcadian myths also plays an important role in Boeotian tradition, according to which Hesiod tells us she was the daughter of Schoeneus and Clymene. From a very young age, she was very fast, had a passion for hunting, and wanted to remain a virgin. When a man wooed her, she would make him agree to race against her; she would then beat and kill her prospective fiancés. Atalante was finally defeated by Hippomenes, who distracted her during the foot race by tossing three golden apples he had been given by Aphrodite by her feet. The pair finally united at the shrine of *Zeus Callinicos*, but was punished for their sacrilege by being changed into lions.

According to Arcadian tradition, Atalante was the daughter of Schoeneus or Iasus and Clemene or some attendant of Artemis. She lived on Mount Maenalus in Lycia or Tegea. Her father had wanted a son, so when she was born he left her on the mountain where she was raised by a bear. She later married Melanion and bore him a son, Parthenopaeus.

Atalante took part in the hunt for the Caledonian boar, which she killed. She then took the boar's hide and head back to Arcadia, where she beat Peleus at wrestling, according to Apollodorus. She also wanted to join the Argonauts' expedition, but in the end was not allowed aboard by Jason who feared the effect of a woman in the midst of so many men, writes Diodorus.

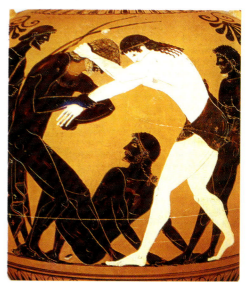

Atalante, or the "untamed" in Greek, is an Arcadian version of the myth of Artemis. Here she is shown beating Peleus at wrestling (sixth century B.C., Munich Archaeological Collection).

Myths about the Peloponnese

CORINTHIAN HEROES

Sisyphus

Sisyphus was notorious for his slyness. The son of Aeolus and Enarete, Sisyphus was married to Atlas's daughter Merope. He founded the city of Ephyra, which was later known as Corinth. Some ancient writers, however, note that he only built the Corinth acropolis, Acrocorinth, and fortified the isthmus, thus forcing travelers to pay tolls.

Sisyphus was condemned by Zeus to an eternity of pushing a boulder to the top of a mountain, only to have the boulder roll back down. Zeus chose to punish Sisyphus this way because Sisyphus told the river-god Asopus that Zeus had abducted Asopus's daughter Aegina. Zeus was infuriated and ordered Thanatos (Death) to take Sisyphus away, but the wily hero managed to overpower Thanatos and tie him up. Thus, no one on earth died. Hades freed Thanatos, who took Sisyphus with him to the Underworld. But the crafty Sisyphus managed to escape, as he had had the foresight to instruct his wife Merope not to conduct any funerary rites. Arriving in Hades, he convinced Pluto to allow him to return to earth for a short while to punish his wife for failing to honor him. But once he returned to the earth, he went back on his promise and lived to a ripe old age. When he returned to Hades, he was condemned to rolling a boulder that would prevent his return to life.

Sisyphus's slyness is illustrated by his encounter with Autolycus, son of Apollo and notorious thief who dyed the hides of the animals he stole. When king Laertes of Ithaca fell victim to Autolycus, he asked Sisyphus for help. Sisyphus made marks on the animals' hooves, then later used these marks to prove that the animals had been stolen by Autolycus. It is said that Laertes's wife Anticleia was the lover of Sisyphus and that he was the real father of Odysseus. Sisyphus is credited with founding the *Isthmian Games*.

Glaucus

Glaucus, the son of Sisyphus, was passionate about his horses, which he fed human flesh because he believed this would make them stronger. After his defeat in a chariot race at Olympia, he fell off the chariot's seat and was devoured by his own mares that were gripped by a frenzy, either because they had drunk water from a sacred well or because they had eaten a magic herb. In other accounts, his mares were made mad from hunger or by Aphrodite to punish Glaucus for not allowing them to mate with stallions. Glaucus is often confused with a sea deity of the same name. His tragic death is believed to have been the subject of a drama by Thespes.

Bellerophon

Bellerophon, or Bellerophontes, was the son of Glaucus and grandson of Sisyphus. He has also been identified as the son of Poseidon. He was initially named Hipponous, but became known by the epithet *Bellerophontes*, or killer of Bellerus, after he murdered his brother Bellerus.

The Corinthian hero sought refuge in Tiryns where he was purified by king Proetus. But there he fell prey to the slander of Proetus's wife Anteia, or by other writers Stheneboea, after rejecting her advances. Furious, Proetus sent Bellerophon to Lycia to deliver a sealed letter to his father-in-law king Iobates, or Amphianactas, which instructed the king to kill the bearer of the message. Iobates received Bellerophon with great honors and extended the palace's hospitality for nine days. On the tenth day, Bellerophon presented the letter to Iobates. But the king was unable to kill anyone to whom he had extended hospitality, so the task of killing Bellerophon was given to Chimaera.

Chimaera, daughter of Typhoeus and Echidna, was a monstrous, fire-breathing creature with a goat's waist, a lion's body from the waist up, and a dragon's body from the waist down. Bellerophon managed to defeat this horrible creature by riding Pegasus, a horse he had tamed near the Corinthian spring Peirene with a golden bridle sent by the goddess Athena.

After this success, Iobates sent Bellerophon to fight the Solymi, which he defeated. He also defeated the Amazons and destroyed all the soldiers that the Lycian king had sent to ambush him. Iobates then accepted Bellerophon's victory as the will of the gods and showed him the letter from Proetus. Iobates gave Bellerophon the hand of his daughter Philonoe (or Cassandra, or Anticleia, or Alcmene) and part of his kingdom. Bellerophon returned to Corinth and punished Stheneboea by throwing her off Pegasus. By other accounts, Stheneboea took her own life when she learned of Bellerophon's successes.

But towards the end of his life the hero provoked the rage of the gods because he became too proud of his feats and wanted to ascend to Mount Olympus. To punish him for his arrogance, the gods made Pegasus buck as he was carrying Bellerophon towards Olympus. The hero plunged to the ground. Paralyzed –or, by some accounts, blinded– he lived out the rest of his life in squalor. His children – Isander, Hippolochus, and Laodameia – all died before him.

Bellerophon was worshipped in Corinth and in Lycia as a god, and was depicted on local coins. In Corinth, there was a cypress woods in which there was a statue of the hero with Pegasus. A fountain spouted from one of the horse's hooves. Many dramatic poets drew inspiration from the myth of Bellerophon, including Socrates (*Iobates*), Euripides (*Bellerophontes* and *Stheneboea*), Astydamas, Theodectes (*Bellerophontes*), and Eubolus.

THE ARGOS CYCLE

Inachus – Phoroneus – Io

Inachus was the son of Oceanus and Tethys. He united with the nymph Melia, with whom he had many children, including Phoroneus and Io.

Phoroneus is believed to have fathered the line of the Pelasgians. He was the first man to gather the inhabitants of the Peloponnese and teach them how to use fire, both to honor the gods with sacrifices and to improve their lives.

Io fell prey to Hera's rage and jealousy when Zeus fell in love with her and lay with her in the marshes of Lerna. The young woman told her father what had happened, and he was forced to banish her so as not to avoid being struck by lightning in accordance with prophecies by the oracles of Delphi and Dodona.

To protect his lover, Zeus changed her into a cow, although he subsequently turned her over to Hera. She, in turn, assigned the task of guarding Io to the many-eyed monster Argus, who was killed by Hermes. Hera then turned Argus into a peacock and decorated the bird's tail with his eyes.

After being freed from Argus's watch, Io crossed the sea, which was named Ionian in her honor. She also crossed the Bosphorus, which took its name from the Greek for "bovine" (*boos*) and "crossing" (*perasma*), to reach the Caucasus where the Titan Prometheus was chained. He predicted that she would continue her wanderings, but also her final destination.

Io finally reached Egypt, where she was changed back into human form by Zeus when he touched her on the forehead. From this contact, Io gave birth to Epaphus, who was abducted by the Curetes on Hera's orders. Zeus, however, destroyed them in retaliation.

Epaphus returned to Egypt, where he married Memphis, daughter of the river Nile. He also founded the city of Memphis. His mother Io married king Telegonus of Egypt.

Danaus

Danaus was the hero and eponym of the Danaoi, as the Argives were called (and as Homer called all Greeks). He was the grandson of Epaphus and son of Belus. His mother was Anchinoe or Anchirrhoe, daughter of the god Nile. Danaus received part of Libya as dowry and founded the famed oracle of Ammon in the Egyptian desert. He married Elephantida, Aethiopida, Memphida, Piereia, Herse, Crino, Melia, the hamadryads Atalanteia and Phoebe, and the naiad Polyxo, with whom he fathered fifty daughters. According to a different account, Europa was the mother of all the Danaidae.

Either because of an oracle's prophecy or because of his fear of the sons of his brother Aegyptus, Danaus decided to leave his homeland and go to Greece. With help from the goddess Athena, he built the first five-masted ship, which was named *Danais* and is believed to be older than the *Argo*. Danaus and his fifty daughters then set sail for Rhodes, where he dedicated a statue to *Athena Lindia*, and from there continued on to Argos. King Gelanor of Argos extended his hospitality to the new arrivals and took them under his protection.

According to another myth mentioned by Pausanias, Danaus became king of Argos after an omen from Apollo: Danaus and Gelanor fought over power and the god sent a wolf to ravage Gelanor's herds outside the city. The Argives interpreted this as a sign that Apollo was on the side of Danaus and chose him as their king.

Danaus is credited with many important inventions and advancements such as the introduction of the alphabet into Greece (before Cadmus), the irrigation of fields, the collection of water in reservoirs, and the construction of springs – from where the myth of the Danaidae stems.

According to a different version, Danaus was a Greek, the son of the Argive Eos and brother of Aegyptus, whom he expelled from Argos because out of jealousy because his brother had fifty sons while he had fifty daughters. Aegyptus sought refuge in the land that later took his name (Egypt), and his sons persecuted Danaus and married his daughters, only to be killed by their wives on their wedding night.

Danaidae

Persecuted by Aegyptus's fifty sons, Danaus's fifty daughters followed their father to Rhodes. Three of them remained on the island, while the rest continued on to Argos. When Danaus became the city's king, his nephews –and persecutors– went to him and said they wanted to make peace. As a gesture, they each asked to marry one of the Danaidae. Danaus accepted, but on their wedding night, he advised the

Danaidae to kill their new husbands. Only the eldest, Hypermnestra, did not kill her husband Lynceus and was imprisoned by her father for a year.

Hypermnestra's sisters later married the Argives who had won some local competition. They gave birth to the line of Danaoi. Amymone also bore Poseidon –who had made the Lerna spring bubble– a son named Nauplius. In a different version, Lynceus killed Danaus to avenge the death of his brothers.

According to a later tradition, the Danaidae were punished in Hades by being forced to fill a jar that had a hole in it –hence the Greek saying "*Danaidaeon jar*", which means that the effort being made is futile.

The myth of the Danaidae is obviously rooted in the Greeks' belief that the dead continued their earthly activities in the Underworld. The Danaidae may have also symbolized the nymphs of the Lerna springs that bubbled over the dried Argive land.

The Danaidae initiated the Argives into the mysteries of Demeter, and their myth inspired Aeschylus to write *The Suppliants*. They also inspired two other works by the tragedian, *Danaidae* and *Amymone*, neither of which has survived.

Proetus and the Proetidae

Proetus was one of the twin sons of Abas (son of Hypermnestra and Lynceus) and Aglaea. The brothers were separated by a deep-rooted hatred that caused them to clash over the right inherit their father's throne.

The contest between them was tied, so Acrisius was given the throne of Argos and Proetus was given the throne of Tiryns, although Apollodorus the Athenian writes that the competition was won by Acrisius, who banished his brother from Argos. According to this version, Proetus sought refuge in Lycia, where he married Anteia or Stheneboea, then seeking to assume his father's throne returned to Greece and forced Acrisius to share his kingdom.

When Proetus's daughters Lycippe, Iphianassa, and Iphinoe reached adolescence, they took ill and began to roam about the Peloponnese. Their illness –perhaps, epilepsy– was attributed to Hera because they had claimed that they were more beautiful than the goddess or, by other accounts, because they had belittled Hera's temple as being poorer than their palace or for stealing the statue of the goddess. Their disease has also been attributed to Aphrodite because the girls ignored men or to Dionysus because they resisted joining in the bacchants' cult.

The seer Melampus was summoned to cure the girls. He initially asked Proetus to give him one-third of his kingdom, then asked for another third to be given to his brother Bias as other Argive women had been afflicted with the same disease. Proetus was forced to acquiesce to Melampus's demands. The seer then located Proetus's daughters near Sicyon. The oldest, Iphinoe, died but the other two were cured with a bath in the river Anigrus, whose waters then became quite smelly.

The girls married Melampus and Bias.

Acrisius and Danae

Proetus's twin brother Acrisius had a daughter by Eurydice or Aganippe. The daughter's name was Danae, and Acrisius imprisoned her and her nurse in a bronze-fitted underground chamber because the Delphi oracle had told him that the child he fathered would kill him.

Zeus fell in love with the beautiful Danae, changed into a shower of gold, and lay with her. Danae bore Zeus a son, Perseus. Acrisius did not believe Danae's claims about her son's father, locked his daughter and her baby in a chest, and tossed it into the sea.

The currents carried the chest to the island of Seriphus, where it was found by a fisherman named Dictys, brother of King Polydectes. Dictys took in Danae and her child, but Polydectes, who had fallen in love with the beautiful maiden, sought a way to get rid of Perseus. He thus told the boy to bring him the head of Gorgon or Medusa. When Perseus returned, he found out that his mother and Dictys had taken refuge at the altars of the gods to escape Polydectes. Perseus used the Medusa's head to turn the king into stone, handed over the rule of Seriphus to Dictys, and returned to Argos with his mother.

The mortal Gorgon Medusa (late Hellenistic floor mosaic from Kos, Rhodes Archaeological Museum).

Gorgo or Gorgon, a winged monster with a horse's body, could turn humans to stone with a single look (detail from the Nessus amphora, 620 B.C., National Archaeological Museum).

Perseus

Danae's son Perseus agreed to bring Polydectes the head of the hideous Gorgon Medusa. Hermes and Athens helped him complete this feat.

Medusa, one of the monstrous creatures of Greek mythology, was the mortal daughter of Phorcys and Ceto. With her two immortal sisters, Stheno and Euryale, Medusa lived beyond Oceanus at the furthest point of the west. Like the other Gorgons, she had snakes instead of locks of hair. Medusa also had enormous teeth, bronze hands, and gold wings; anyone who looked at the Medusa would turn to stone.

Perseus followed Hermes's advice and met first with the Graeae, who were also daughters of Phorcys and Ceto. These two old hags shared an eye and a tooth, which Perseus stole, then forced them to show him the way to the nymphs, who had the necessary magic items that he needed to defeat the Medusa: Hades's helmet that made the wearer invisible; a pair of winged sandals; a sword with a blade of steel; and a sack.

After obtaining these items, he arrived in the land where the Gorgons lived and killed Medusa while she slept. To avoid being turned to stone, he did not gaze directly at the Medusa but looked instead at her reflection on Athena's bronze shield. Perseus used the magic sword to behead the monster, put it in the sack, then donned Hades's helmet, and fled on the winged sandals so that Medusa's sisters were unable to chase him.

The divine horses Chrysaor and Pegasus spring from the Medusa's headless body; they were born from Medusa's union with Poseidon. Athens collected the Medusa's blood, which had the ability to take or destroy lives; according to Euripides, the goddess gave it to Erichthonius, while according to Apollodorus, she gave it to Asclepius.

Returning to Greece, Perseus passed through Ethiopia, where he freed Andromeda whose father king Cepheus had tied her to a rock in accordance with the advice of the Oracle of Zeus Ammon. Andromeda was meant as prey for a hideous monster sent to Ethiopia by Poseidon after Cepheus's wife Cassiopeia had bragged that she was more beautiful than the nereids. Perseus married Andromeda and took her with him to Greece, where they had seven children.

Arriving back on Seriphus, Perseus found his mother Danae and her rescuer Dictys had become suppliants at the temple of Zeus in order to escape from Polydectes. Perseus used the Medusa's head to petrify their persecutor, then named Dictys king, and took Danae with him to Argos. Acrisius had deserted the land and had settled in Thessalian Larissa. Perseus met his grandfather, reconciled with him, and persuaded him to return to Argos.

Meantime, funerary games had been declared in honor of the father of the king of Larissa. Perseus took part, but in the discus competition, his throw went astray and killed Acrisius. The oracle's prophecy was thus fulfilled.

Grief-stricken over his grandfather's accidental death, Perseus made an agreement with Proetus's son Megapenthes to exchange the kingdom of Argos with the kingdoms of Tiryns and Mycenae.

Tantalus

Tantalus was the son of Zeus or Timolus (Sipylus), the mountain of Phrygea which he ruled. Very wealthy and quite happy, he enjoyed the benevolence of the gods often joined them at symposia. But his extreme happiness caused him to become arrogant: he told the gods' secrets, stole their nectar and ambrosia, and tried to become their equal so he rejected Helius's cover, kidnapped Ganymede, then killed Pelops's son and invited the gods to dine on his flesh. The gods realized the heinous crime Tantalus had committed and did not touch the meal, except for Demeter who absent-mindedly ate a piece of Pelops's shoulder. The gods struck Tantalus with lightning and thunder, then brought Pelops back to life, replacing the missing piece of his shoulder with ivory.

Tantalus was punished in the Underworld by being condemned to eternal hunger and thirst. Every time he reached over to pick up food or water, the food and drink would move away; when he walked past trees laden with fruit, the branches would suddenly be out of reach. Additionally, everywhere he went, a boulder hovered over his head.

Pelops

The Peloponnese owes its name to Pelops, the son of Tantalus who fled from Lycia to Greece to avoid being persecuted for his crimes. According to Homer, Pelops was the son of Hermes. The ancient texts mention Clytie, Euryanassa, or Dione as his mother, while a local myth from Elis claims that Pelops was the son of Hermes and Calyce, daughter of the god of winds Aeolus and wife of the mortal Aethlio who was king of Elis.

Thus Pelops's descent from Tantalus, whose origin was from Asia Minor, contradicts local traditions according to which Pelops was an Achaean from Olenus or Elis rather than from Lydia-Phrygia-Paphlagonia. The myth of Pelops being killed and dismembered by Tantalus also originated in Asia Minor.

According to this last myth, after Pelops was revived and put back together by the gods, he married the beautiful Hippodameia after using a ruse to defeat her father Oenomaus, a son of Ares, in a chariot race. Oenomaus was the king of Pisa in Elis. Pelops promised the king's charioteer Myrtilus, a son of Hermes, that he would let him lay with Hippodameia for a night if he helped him beat Oenomaus. The charioteer removed a linchpin from one of the royal chariot's wheels so that the chariot would veer off course. It did; Oenomaus fell off the seat, became entangled in the reins, and was dragged to his death. As he lay dying, he cursed his charioteer to die at the hands of the race's victor. Oenomaus's curse was fulfilled as Pelops killed the charioteer immediately after the race. According to other accounts, Pelops spared Myrtilus's life at the behest of Hippodameia, but killed the charioteer later by throwing him over a cliff. By some accounts, Pelops killed Myrtilus because he tried to kiss Hippodameia. In another version, Hippodameia was in love with Myrtilus, but when he rejected her advances, she told Pelops that the charioteer had tried to seduce her. Regardless, the murder of Myrtilus was the cause of the tragedies that befell the descendants of Pelops.

Pelops is credited with dedicated the

The myth of Pelops as depicted on the eastern pediment of the Temple of Zeus at Olympia. Pictured from the right are Hippodameia, Oenomaus, Zeus, Pelops, and Stereope (fifth century B.C., Olympia Museum).

Olympic Games to Zeus. Heracles, who was a fourth generation descendant of Pelops, established the hero's cult at Olympia where the Pelopeion with his grave was located. The traveler Pausanias claims that Pelops's bones were kept in a bronze chest in a structure next to the Temple of Artemis Kordakas and were taken from there to Troy in accordance with a prophecy about the city's sacking. Pausanias writes that only Pelops's shoulder was taken to Troy, and was lost in a storm during the Achaeans' journey back to Greece. Many years later, it was found by the fisherman Damarmenus, who on the counsel of the Delphi Oracle returned it to Elis that was suffering from a plague. After the sacred relic's return, the disease disappeared and Damarmenus and his descendants were charged with the task of guarding them.

The chariot race between Pelops and Oenomaus was a source of inspiration for several ancient works of literature and art. The myth was depicted on the eastern pediment of the Temple of Zeus at Olympia, which is now on display at the Archaeological Museum of Ancient Olympia.

Atreus – Thyestes

Atreus and Thyestes were sons of Pelops and Hippodameia. Their families was burdened by a curse placed either by Hermes to avenge the murder of his son Myrtilus by Pelops or as a result of their murder of their half-brother Chrysippus at the behest of their mother Hippodameia. According to the later version, after Chrysippus's death, the two brothers were forced into self-exile from Pisa and took refuge at either Mycenae or Macesto in Triphylia, where Atreus married Cleolla who had two sons –Agamemnon and Menelaus– from her previous marriage to Pleisthenes.

At Mycenae, Atreus and Thyestes were received by King Eurystheus or Sthenelus. After his death, they shared the throne and ruled Mycenae alternately. But Atreus acquired greater power as a result of a gold-fleeced lamb he was given by Hermes as a symbol of royal power. Thyestes then plotted with his lover Aerope –wife of Atreus and grand-daughter of Minos– to steal the lamb and take the throne. Zeus then reversed the course of Helius and the Pleiades across the sky, thus signaling his favor towards Atreus. Thyestes was then forced to leave Mycenae.

When Atreus discovered Aerope's infidelity and his brother's plot, he invited Thyestes to dinner, where he served Thyestes the flesh of his children Tantalus and Pleisthenes. The crime was so heinous, that even the sun hid; Thyestes was killed or banished, while the adulterous Aerope killed herself by jumping into the sea.

According to this version, the exiled Thyestes raped his daughter Pelopia, who was a priestess of Athena. From this act of incest was born Aegisthus, who was adopted by Atreus (who in the meantime had married Pelopia). Atreus sent Aegisthus to kill Thyestes, without telling Aegisthus that Thyestes was his real father. But father and son recognized each other; Aegisthus then murdered Atreus and turned the throne over to Thyestes.

The myths of this tragic family are related in Sophocles's lost tragedies *Atreids, the Mycenaeans, Thyestes Sicyonian,* and *Thyestes Defteros (2nd).*

Tyndareus and Leda

Tyndareus was the first-born son of Oebalus, king of Sparta, and Bateia. He was deposed by his brother Hippocoon and forced to seek refuge in Aetolia, where he married the beautiful Leda, daughter of King Thestius. Tyndareus had several children with Leda: Castor, Clytemnestra, Philonoe, Timandra, Helen, and Polydeuces. The last two are often considered children of Zeus who was known as Zeus Tyndareu in Laconia. This gave rise to the myth of Leda and the swan, a form which Zeus had taken to unite with her. From their union was born an egg with Helen and Polydeuces or two eggs, one with Helen and the other with Castor and Polydeuces. In a slightly different account, Helen and Clytemnestra were born from the same egg.

Heracles restored Tyndareus to his throne. After the apotheosis of the Dioscuri, Menelaus became king of Sparta.

Leda and the swan, a subject that has inspired countless artists through the centuries.

Dioscuri

Castor and Polydeuces (or Pollux) were known as the Dioscuri and, according to the prevalent myth were the twin sons of Zeus and Leda, who were born from a single egg. The ancient Greeks worshipped the Dioscuri as gods of light or as heroes. They were often called *Tyndarides* (in line with the myth that they were sons of Tyndareus). The ancients' wish to interpret the phenomenon of natural light that rises and sets was represented by the dual nature of the Dioscuri: they were simultaneously immortal and mortal, corrupt and incorruptible, while Castor was said to be the son of Leda's mortal husband and Polydeuces was said to be the son of Zeus.

The Dioscuri were skilled horsemen, charioteers, and athletes – Castor in races and Polydeuces in boxing. For this reason, they were honored as gods of sport in Sparta. The Dioscuri were credited with inventing the *pyrrichios*, a dance performed with full armor.

Patrons of warriors, the Dioscuri would rush on horseback into battle to save fighters. They were also considered the saviors of seamen and said to hang from the masts of ships to guide them through night and storms.

The Dioscuri were also identified with the Cabeiri in the Samothrace mysteries, while the Athenians called them *Anaces*.

The Dioscuri appear in several myths, such as the hunt for the Caledonian boar, the expedition of the Argonauts, the campaign against Athens mounted after Theseus kidnapped Helen, the battle against the sons of Aphareus –Idas, and Lynceus– in which Castor was killed and Polydeuces shared his immortality with him.

The mighty sons of Aphareus, brother of Tyndareus, and Arene hated their cousins, the Dioscuri. According to Apollodorus the Athenian, their suspicion over some battle spoils they had acquired together led Idas to kill Castor and Polydeuces to kill Lynceus to avenge the death of his beloved brother. Polydeuces then went after Idas, who threw a stone at Polydeuces and knocked him out. Zeus struck Idas with a bolt of lightning and took Polydeuces to heaven.

Pindar tells a slightly different version of the myth. He attributes the cause of the disagreement to the theft of Idas's cattle by Castor. A different version claims that the dispute was caused when the Dioscuri kidnapped Phoebe and Helaeira (personifications of bright and pure light), the daughters of Leucippus who were betrothed to their cousins.

In areas where the Dioscuri were worshipped as heroes, it was claimed that after their deaths, Zeus transformed them into the constellation known as Gemini. The symbol of the Dioscuri was a *dokano*, two parallel sticks that the Spartans carried with them on their campaigns. Other symbols were their hats in the shape of half an eggshell (symbolizing the egg from which they were born), two amphorae with snakes wrapped around them, two stars (symbolizing the Dioscuri as saviors of seafarers), and the branch of a palm tree (a symbol of victory in races).

Helen

Helen, the most beautiful woman in the world, was the cause of the Trojan War; even her name, which stems from the root *elo* or conquer, signaled disaster and destruction. Helen was the daughter of Leda and Zeus or, according to the Cycleian epics, was the daughter of Zeus and Nemesis who changed into a goose as part of futile attempt to escape the god's advances. Zeus then changed into a swan that was supposedly being chased by Aphrodite, who had changed into an eagle. In the form of a swan, Zeus found refuge in the arms of Nemesis and from their union was born an egg, which Helen was born. The egg was found by a herdsman who took it to King Tyndareus, who gave it to Leda. In slightly different versions, the egg fell from the sky into Leda's arms or was given to her by Hermes. In one account, Helen was the daughter of Oceanus and Tithys.

Homer does not offer any physical description of Helen, perhaps because the world's greatest poet sought to allow his readers to shape the most beautiful woman according to their own imaginations. Helen's beauty had been renown since her childhood. According to Plutarch's *Life of Theseus*, her beauty prompted Theseus to kidnap her when he was fifty years old and he happened to see the seven-year-old Helen (in other accounts, she was eleven) dancing at the Temple of Artemis Orthyia at Sparta. Her brothers, the Dioscuri, then seized Aphidnae in Attica, then lay siege to Athens to rescue Helen. She then returned to Argos, where she gave birth to a daughter, Iphigeneia, whom she gave to her sister Clytemnestra to raise.

When Helen reached marrying age, 29 suitors vied for her hand, among them Odysseus, Philoctetes, Ajax, Patroclus, Asclepius's sons Podaleirius and Machaon, and Ares's sons Ascalaphus and Ialmenus. Tyndareus was in a difficult position because he feared that no matter whom he chose as Helen's husband, the others would turn against him. Odysseus provided a way out of the dilemma when he suggested that Tyndareus ask all the suitors take an oath that no matter whom the king chose for his daughter's husband, that the rest would defend the groom and whoever insulted his marriage. Tyndareus then chose Menelaus as Helen's husband.

The couple lived quite happily together and had a daughter,

A clay head of Athena (490 B.C., Museum of Olympia).

Hermione, while some writers also mention a son, Nicostratus. Their marital bliss lasted until the day when Paris arrived in Lacedaemon. Aphrodite had promised Paris that Helen would become his if he chose her as the most beautiful in a contest against Athena and Hera.

Menelaus extended his hospitality to Paris, and left for Crete. During Menelaus's absence, Paris kidnapped Helen, who did not resist; she left with him, taking several of Menelaus's treasures with her. The two lovers made a stop on the islet of Cranae, in the Laconian Gulf, then set sail for Troy, although winds forced them to land in either Sidon or Egypt.

Herodotus mentions a myth in which Helen did not follow Paris to Troy, but stayed behind in Egypt, where she was reunited with Menelaus after the Trojan War and the returned with her husband to Greece.

But in the most widespread version of this myth, Helen went to Troy with Paris. The Achaean kings, true to their oath to Tyndareus, raised an army against Troy. The Trojan campaign thus took place, which ended in the sacking of Troy. Afterwards, Helen, who after Paris was killed had married his brother Deiphobus, then followed her first husband back to Sparta, where the couple lived out the rest of their lives.

There are many accounts of how Helen died. One tradition holds that after the death of Menelaus, their sons Nicostratus and Megapenthes expelled Helen from Sparta. She sought refuge on the island of Rhodes where her friend Polyxo lived. To avenge the death of her husband Tlepolemus, Polyxo forced Helen to hang herself. The Rhodians purified themselves of Helen's death by building a temple in honor of Helen Dendritida, or Helen of the Tree.

Another tradition held that after her death, Helen lived with Achilles on the islet of Leuce at the mouth of the river Danube. The winged Euphorionos was born from their union. Zeus later fell in love with the Euphorionos, but struck him down with lightning on the island of Melos after the youth rejected the god's advances.

Helen likely personified the

Cretan-Mycenaean moon deity. Her cult was widespread throughout Greece, but was especially strong in Sparta where she was worshipped at shrines in Platanista and Therapne.

Clytemnestra

Clytemnestra was the daughter of Tyndareus and Leda, and sister of Helen and Timandra. All three sisters were adulterous because their father Tyndareus did not offer a sacrifice to Aphrodite.

Euripides mentions Tantalus as Clytemnestra's first husband, but in both *The Iliad* and *The Odyssey* she is the unfaithful wife of Agamemnon; Clytemnestra and her lover Aegisthus then kill Agamemnon when he returns from Troy with Cassandra. In some versions, Aegisthus murders Agamemnon alone, while in Aeschylus's *Oresteia* Clytemnestra murders Agamemnon. In his play *Electra*, Sophocles excuses Clytemnestra's murder of Agamemnon as revenge for the murder of Iphigeneia.

Eight years after Agamemnon's murder, Clytemnestra's son Orestes avenges his father's death; at the urging of Apollo, he kills his mother and her lover Aegisthus. He is then persecuted for matricide by the Erinyes and seeks refuge in Athens, where he is cleared by the Areopagus (supreme court) with the support of Athena.

Orestes knifes his mother Clytemnestra, while her lover Aegisthus becomes a suppliant at the altar (section of bronze plate, 570 B.C., Olympia Museum).

The Trojan War

MYTH AND HISTORY

The Trojan War provided considerable material for poets and recorders of myths. It was immortalized by Homer in *The Iliad*. Historical and archaeological evidence suggests the Trojan War took place in the early twelfth century B.C., and is depicted and described by the campaign of the Greek tribes beyond the borders of the Greek world that had been established in the tenth century B.C. –in other words, after the end of the Mycenaean era (1600-1100 B.C.), which followed the Bronze Age and the dominance of the Achaeans in the Greek world.

The campaign is attributed in poetry by Paris's abduction of Helen, which prompted the Greeks to restore the honor of the cuckolded Menelaus. But this tale is nothing by the beautified narration of the colonization of the eastern Mediterranean basin, which was prompted by the constrained Greek space and the clashes within the Greek mainland, especially after the arrival of the Dorians (circa 1100 B.C.), who forced the Achaeans to seek new lands along the western coast of Asia Minor.

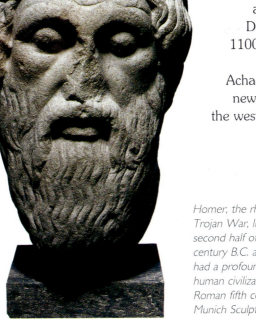

Homer, the rhapsodist of the Trojan War, lived during the second half of the eighth century B.C. and his work had a profound effect on human civilization. (Bust, Roman fifth century copy, Munich Sculpture Gallery.)

As far as mythology is concerned, the seeds for the Trojan War were sown at the wedding of Peleus and Thetis. Angered that she had not been invited, Eris, the goddess of discord, tossed a golden apple into the party. The apple was inscribed with the words *"For the most beautiful"*. The goddesses Hera, Athena, and Aphrodite began to argue over the apple and decided to settle the issue in a beauty contest to be decided by Alexander-Paris, son of the king of Troy. As is the case with many beauty pageants, each contestant tried to sway the judge with various bribes. In this case, Hera offered Paris power, Athena offered him wisdom, and Aphrodite offered him the most beautiful mortal, Helen.

Young and carefree, Paris was most impressed by the offer of Helen. His choice proved fatal for himself and his country. With help from Aphrodite, he set off for Sparta, where Helen –who happened to be married– lived.

Paris enjoyed the lavish hospitality extended by Helen's husband Menelaus. But as soon as Menelaus left on business, Paris snatched Helen –in some accounts, he kidnapped her against her will, while in other versions Helen willingly went with him– and ran away. He also took many of the Spartan king's treasures. Returning home, Menelaus could not bear the stigma of the cuckold. H recalled the vow that all Helen's suitors when seeking her hand from King Tyndareus to help whoever became her husband should the marriage ever be breached.

Of course, no one was in a rush to go after the unfaithful Helen. Many years had passed since they had taken the oath and many of her former suitors had since married and started families. Menelaus, they said, should have been more careful about taking strangers into his home. However, the young barbarian had also insulted Zeus Xenios and they had taken a sacred vow. Thus, what was a purely family affair of the Atreidae because the cause of all the Greeks, who decided to take decisive action against this Asian insult. These arguments swayed even those who had been the most reluctant to

help Menelaus, and the Trojan campaign was decided. Menelaus's brother, King Agamemnon of Mycenae, was placed in charge of the army and the Achaeans fleet.

But the gods did not seem to favor the campaign. The fleet and army had been immobilized for months at Aulis by a mysterious lack of winds.

The seer Calchas was forced to divulge the reason and the solution. Long ago, the commander-in-chief had shot Athena's favorite deer and had promised to purify himself of the crime by sacrificing his most precious acquisition that year. The goddess was now demanding that he live up to his vow: his most precious acquisition had been his daughter, Iphigeneia, who was now twelve years old.

Distraught, Agamemnon dared not make such a sacrifice. His heart could not bear the thought of sacrificing an innocent girl for the sake of an unfaithful woman. So, while he had initially summoned his wife and daughter to Aulis, with the pretext of seeking to marry Iphigeneia to Achilles, Agamemnon had second thoughts. He sent them a message to return to Mycenae. But the army revolted as the reputation of Greece was at stake: if they did not undertake the campaign against Troy, the Asians would then feel that they could come and snatch their wives and daughters.

Agamemnon continued to have qualms. The ever-resourceful Odysseus intervened. He caught up with the herald and switched the message. Clytemnestra and Iphigeneia arrived at

Bent over a table where he has placed an animal's innards, the seer Calchas examines its liver. (Etruscan mirror, fourth century B.C., Vatican Museum, Italy).

Aulis filled with joy at the prospective wedding.

There were several tense confrontations between Clytemnestra and Agamemnon. But Iphigeneia decided to sacrifice herself for the sake of Greece. Just as the knife was raised over the young girl, the goddess Athena enveloped the shrine in a cloud and carried Iphigeneia away. When the cloud lifted, a deer was in her place. The winds billowed the ships' sails so that the Greek army could finally set sail for Troy.

The Achaeans fought for ten whole years to conquer the city of Priam. The gods had been split into two camps, each one supporting a different side in the war. The Greeks fought for their honor, while the Trojans fought to defend their city. Helen, whom the Trojans had come to hate, enjoyed the destruction being created in her name.

Casualties were high on both sides. Hector and Achilles, both true leaders, lay dead, yet the citadel of Troy still stood.

But wit finally accomplished what weapons could not achieve. Odysseus devised the plan to build a wooden horse, which became known as the Trojan Horse. Warriors were hidden inside the large, hollow belly of the monumental statue. The plan was for the Achaeans to pretend to set sail for Greece, while leaving behind the wooden monument as an offering to the goddess Athena. The Trojans would then wheel the horse into the city at night; as they celebrated their victory, the warriors would climb out of the horse's belly and open the city's gates so the Achaeans could sneak in and sack Troy.

Everything went according to Odysseus's plan. Troy was razed, the Trojans massacred, and their women taken as slaves back to Greece where they became domestics and concubines in wealthy homes.

Three thousand years, Heinrich Schleimann, a former general store employee and son of a German priest with a deep love for Homer, decided to study archaeology. With the help of his Greek wife, Sophia Castriotou, he set off on a quest to find Troy. On August 1, 1890, he excavated Troy and proved that *The Iliad* was not just a rhapsody, but a true story. The feats of the heroes who had been ground to dust had been brought to life among the ruins of the city of Priam.

The Trojan Horse depicted on a clay amphora (650 B.C., Myconos Archaeological Museum). The wooden horse made by the Greeks according to the instructions of either Athena or Odysseus allowed them to penetrate Troy. Epeios is mentioned as the builder of the horse in which Greek warriors who opened the city's gates hid.

THE HEROES OF THE TROJAN WAR

The Greeks

Agamemnon

Commander-in-chief of the Achaean forces, Agamemnon was the son of Atreus and Aerope and brother of Menelaus. He became king of Mycenae, which developed into a powerful city under his rule. An indication of the city's strength was its fleet, which contributed sixty ships to the Trojan campaign.

Agamemnon had married Helen's sister, Tyndareus's daughter Clytemnestra. They had three daughters –Chrysothemis, Laodice, and Iphianassa– and one son, Orestes. Accounts written after Homer mention Electra and Iphigeneia as his daughters, but they are generally identified as Laodice and Iphianassa, respectively.

Agamemnon was placed at the head of the army raised by the Achaeans for the campaign against Troy. He offered 100 ships to the campaign, and offered another sixty on behalf of the Arcadians. He was also forced to offer his daughter Iphigeneia as a sacrifice in order to change the winds so the fleet could set sail.

In *The Iliad*, Agamemnon's autocratic behavior and his refusal to return Chryseis –whom he had taken as a spoil of war– to her priest father, provoked the rage of Apollo, who used his arrows to spread seakness among the Greek camp. Agamemnon's subsequent abduction of Briseis, a concubine who had been given to Achilles as a

Gold funerary mask from Grave Circle B at Mycenae (Grave V), which Heinrich Schleimann believed belonged to Agamemnon even though the artifact has been dated to 1600 B.C., thus precluded it belonged to the Achaian king who lived 400 years later
(National Archaeological Museum).

present, also provoked Achilles's anger as well as his decision to withdraw from the war with the Myrmidons. His hubris aside, Achilles fought valiantly and his bravery is praised in *The Iliad*'s rhapsodies.

After the sacking of Ilium, as the Phrygian city of Troy was also called, Agamemnon returned to Mycenae with Cassandra, Priam's daughter, as a slave. Clytemnestra and her lover Aegisthus murdered both.

Agamemnon was worshipped as a god in many parts of Greece. In Sparta, he was known as *Zeus Agamemnon*.

He was also worshipped in Chaironeia, where his scepter was kept, and elsewhere.

Menelaus

Menelaus was the son of Atreus, brother of Agamemnon, grandson of Pelops, and cuckolded husband of Helen. He had inherited the throne of Sparta from his father-in-law, Tyndareus. The most celebrated army in ancient Greek history was raised to uphold his honor.

Menelaus contributed sixty ships to the fleet, and was commanded the armies from Phari, Sparta, Mesi, Bryseies, Augeies, Mycles, Elos, La, and Oetilos. During the fighting at Troy, he dueled against his rival Paris, was wounded by Pandarus, and retrieved the body of Patroclus –an event to which one of the most eloquent rhapsodies of *The Iliad* is dedicated.

Menelaus was one of the warriors who hid inside the Trojan Horse. Inside the city, he killed Deiphobus, whom Helen had wed after Paris died.

Helen used her charm to dissuade Menelaus from killing her too. Instead, he took his wife back home with him. Their return journey lasted for eight years during which time they landed on Cyprus, Phoenicia, Ethiopia, Libya, and Egypt. They finally arrived at Sparta in time for the wedding of their daughter Hermione. There, they encountered Telemachus, who sought news of his father Odysseus.

According to mythology, Menelaus did not die but descended to the Elysian Fields alive. The traveler Pausanias mentions the existence of a mound dedicated to Menelaus and Helen at Therapne, near Sparta.

Achilles

Son of Peleus and Thetis, Achilles was the personification of valor and the heroic ideal. He was born in the Thessalian city of Phthia, of which his father was king. Seeking to make her son immortal, Thetis secretly dipped the infant in the waters of the river Styx –or, according to a slightly different account, in a cauldron of boiling water or into flames. But Peleus saw Thetis perform this ritual and cried out in fright. Achilles's immortality was never completed, and the hero was vulnerable at the ankle by which his mother had held him over the river (or fire). According to mythology, he was struck at this exact spot by Achilles's arrow. Achilles was also said to have been raised by the centaur Cheiron.

Hesiod, Apollonius Rhodius, Apollodorus, and Pindar give some of the background about Achilles. In *The Iliad*, Homer mentions that Achilles was raised in Phthia near his mother.

According to *The Iliad*, Achilles was dispatched to Troy by his father Peleus – who had been one of Helen's suitors. He was accompanied by his tutor Phoenix and Patroclus. According to slightly different accounts offered by Apollodorus and Ovid, Thetis had hidden Achilles on the island of Scyrus among the daughters of king Lycomedes. Achilles father a son, Neoptolemus, with Deidameia, before Achaeans heralds located him using a ruse devised by Odysseus.

In the *Cypriot Epics*, the Greeks'

first campaign against Troy failed as the Greek fleet landed at Teuthrania instead of at Troy. Here, Achilles wounded king Telephus, but because he helped heal him Telephus became the Greeks' guide in their second campaign that took place eight years later.

The second campaign against Troy was grounded by a lack of winds at Aulis. The winds blew after the sacrifice of Iphigeneia, whom Achilles had defended. Arriving at Tenedos, the Achaeans looted the island and Achilles killed Apollo's son Tenes for defending the honor of his sister Hemithea whom Achilles had desired. Achilles then killed Cycnus, son of either Poseidon or Ares.

Various feats performed by Achilles also took place during this period. He stole the herds of Aeneas, murdered Priam's son Mestor, and captured Mestor's brothers Isus and Antiphon. Achilles also sacked several cities, among them Peidasus, Hypoplacian Thebes, Tenos, Adramytius, Lyrnessus, and Lesbos.

A central force in Homer's epic is Achilles's deep-rooted rage against Agamemnon for seizing Briseis (after Chryseis was returned to her father). Reacting to arrogant and autarchic behavior of the Greeks' commander-in-chief, Achilles decided to withdraw his Myrmidon forces from the war and stubbornly remained ensconced in his tent, unmoved by the various applications of Achaean emissaries pleading with him to return to the battlefield.

Achilles's withdrawal had disastrous results for the Greeks, who were defeated despite of the valor of Ajax and Diomedes. The Trojans thus penetrated the Greek camp and torched one of their ships. At this crucial moment in the battle, Patroclus donned Achilles's armor and joined the fray. The Trojans thought that the hero had returned to the battlefield and fled, although not before Hector, with Apollo's help, killed Achilles beloved Patroclus.

Pain and a desire for revenge brought Achilles back to the battlefront, with new armor and weapons made for him by Hephaestus. He went on a rampage, filling the river Skamandros with dead bodies. He appeared unstoppable, and his rage only subsided

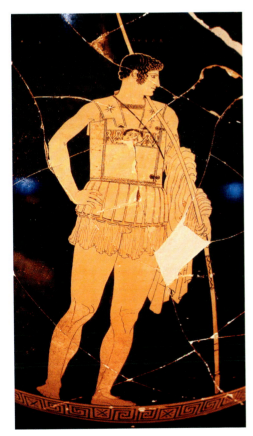

Achilles, the greatest hero of the Trojan War (red-figure amphora, circa 450 B.C., Vatican Museum, Italy).

after he killed Hector and dragged his body around for twelve days before heeding Zeus's orders to turn it over to the Trojans for burial.

Arctinus narrates the events that followed Hector's burial. Achilles killed the Amazon queen Penthesileia and Thersites, who mocked Achilles over his lament for the Amazon's lost beauty. He then went to Lesbos, where he made a sacrifice to Apollo and Leto, and was subsequently purified of these murders by Odysseus. Achilles then returned to Troy, where he killed Memnon, an Ethiopian king who was the son of Eos. Achilles was killed by one of Paris's arrows.

The circumstances surrounded the death of Achilles vary. According to one myth, Paris shot him while going to meet Priam's daughter Polyxena with whom he had fallen in love. Other accounts claim Achilles was ambushed on his way to negotiate a truce with Priam.

The Achaeans buried Achilles with great honors. The dead hero's soul went to the Underworld, where he was later encountered by Odysseus during his descent into the kingdom of the dead –or on the island of Leuce, where he lived with either Helen or Medea. Achilles was worshipped in Epirus and Thessaly, from where his cult spread to the Black Sea, Lower Italy, Asia Minor, and especially Troy. After his death, the Thessalians would send a ship to Troy every year, where rituals and games in Achilles's honor were held over his tomb.

Temples dedicated to Achilles existed in Tanagra, Brasiae, Elis, and along the Sparta-Arcadia road. From Miletus, his cult also spread to colonies in the Euxenus (Black Sea), Thrace, and the island of Leuce at the mouth of the river Istrus (Danube).

Achilles tending to his wounded friend Patroclus (interior of red-figure kylix, circa 500 B.C., Schloss Charlottenburg-Staatliche Museen, Berlin).

Ajax of Telamon

The son of Telamon and king of Salamis, Ajax was the second most celebrated hero of *The Iliad* after Achilles. Ajax was Achilles's first cousin since their parents were brothers and offspring of Aeacus, who were expelled by their father after killing their stepbrother Phocus. Peleus then settled in Phthia, while Telamon settled on Salamis.

Ajax's mother was Eeriboea, who took part in the mission of Athenian youths to the Minotaur. She had married Theseus, which is why Attic tradition traces the tribe's lineage to Athena, who had a place of honor in the public life of Salamis.

Ajax joined the Trojan campaign with twelve ships, according to *The Iliad*. During the voyage, he formed the far-left flank of the fleet. His strength, bravery, and valor matched his great height, while his pride and honesty made him stand out among the other Greek fighters. After Achilles's death, he became the bulwark of the Greek forces. Ajax performed brilliantly in the fighting around the dead body of Patroclus, defended his half-brother Teucer, and dueled with Hector. Despite Ajax's clear superiority, the two were forced to abandon their duel at nightfall, offering each other spoils of equal value: Hector gave Ajax his sword, while Ajax gave Hector his belt.

The story of Ajax's death is told by Homer in *The Odyssey*. Ajax had contested the right to be awarded Achilles's arms, but the Achaeans gave them to Odysseus. Despondent, Ajax was overcome by grief and in his frenzy attacked his fellow-warriors. Athena turned his sword against the camp's animals, but when Ajax recovered his senses he was so overcome by shame that he fell on his sword and killed himself.

Achilles playing with Ajax (black-figure amphora, 530 B.C., Vatican Museum).

Ajax was worshipped as a god. He was buried at Troy's cape and a shrine, the *Aianteion*, erected over it. His cult was also widespread in Attica and Megara, while there were many shrines and busts of the hero on Salamis. Games known as the *Aianteia* were also held on the island in his honor. A bust of Ajax was placed in Athens outside the Boulefterion.

Ajax of Locris

The second Ajax mentioned in *The Iliad* was the Locrian king and son of Oileus. Ajax of Locris participated in the Trojan campaign with forty ships. Although Homer refers to him as *"small"* or short to distinguish him from the son of Telamon, Ajax of Locris was a brave fighter. He was the best spear-thrower of the Greek army and fleeter than Achilles despite being beat by Odysseus in a footrace. But Homer describes his character as coarse and violent, which explains Athena's hostile stance towards him. According to a later tradition, Athena was enraged at him because he dishonored her in her temple with Cassandra, who had become a suppliant with the young Palladius in her arms.

On his return to Greece after the sacking of Troy, Ajax of Locris lost all his ships, although he survived thanks to the intervention of Poseidon. His arrogance led to hubris, and he bragged that he had escaped in defiance of the gods' will. The god's response was to punish him: as Ajax rested on a rock, Poseidon struck it with his trident and Ajax was drowned.

The Locrians and the Epizephyrian Locrians of Sicily worshipped Ajax, son of Oileus, by keeping his place for him at the head of troops as they headed into battle.

Diomedes

Diomedes was also one of the greatest heroes of the Trojan War. The son of the Aetolian king Tydeus and Deipyle, daughter of Adrastus, Diomedes was raised in Argos whose rule his father had also assumed after the death of Adrastus.

Diomedes had taken part in the campaign against Thebes mounted by the sons of the seven champions (Epigoni). His bravery had contributed to the capture of Thebes. He also took part in the Caledonian campaign and punished the sons of Agrius who had expelled his grandfather Oeneus from power. Diomedes brought Oeneus back to Argos with him. He cared for his grandfather until the old man's death; he buried Oeneus at the site known as Oenoe.

Diomedes took part in the Trojan campaign with eighty ships and his friend Sthenelus, son of Capaneus. He was head of the armies raised by Argos, Tiryns, Hermioni, Asine, Troezen, Epidaurus, and Masitas. He was a favorite of the goddess Athena. He survived the battle over the body of the Trojan warrior Pheleus, whom he had killed, although he was wounded in the shoulder by an arrow shot by Pandarus, son of Lycaon.

Diomedes's heroism and feats are sung in *The Iliad*'s rhapsody known as the *Diomedous aristeia* as well as other verses of the epic poem. He dueled with Aeneas, wounded Aphrodite and Ares, and worked closely with Odysseus in many missions, including the search for Achilles on Scyrus. He also cooperated with Odysseus in the arranging the sacrifice of Iphigeneia, the murder of the Trojan spy Dolon, the attack on the Thracian camp where he killed Rhesus and stole his horses, on Lemnos and the transfer of Philoctetes's body to Troy. He also helped build the Trojan Horse, steal the Palladium from Troy, and was one of the nine heroes who accepted Hector's challenge to a duel.

After the sacking of Troy, he returned to Argos in just four days but found that his wife Aegialeia or Aegiale had been overcome by a sexual mania. He thus took off with his companions for Libya, then set sail for Apulia in Italy.

Arriving, he offered his assistance to king Daunus against the Messapians. He later married the king's daughter Euippe and received as dowry a section of the kingdom which became known as the *Diomedian Fields*. The hero founded his own kingdom, known as Argyripa.

There are various myths about Diomedes's death. According to some, he became immortal and married Hermione. In other accounts, he disappeared on an island that became known as Diomedeia, while in some accounts he was killed by Danaus. Grief-stricken by his death, his friends turned into birds, usually described as swans or herons.

Odysseus

Odysseus, king of Ithaca, is often referred to in Greek as *polymichanos* in recognition of his resourcefulness. He is immortalized in Homer's epics, according to which he was one of the greatest heroes of the Trojan War as the Greeks sacked the city thanks to his inventive ruse with the Trojan Horse.

Odysseus was the son of Laertes and Anticleia. While visiting his grandfather Autolycus, he was wounded in a boar hunt. But the scar later helped his nurse Eurycleia recognize him. Later, he was dispatched by Laertes to Messene to arrange for compensation for herds stolen from the king's subjects. On this

The west pediment of the temple of Aphaia: The Trojan expedition. In the center is goddess Athena and on the right Aias, the grandson of Aiakos (sixth century B.C., Munich Sculpture Gallery).

A brass helmet of the fifth century B.C.

trip, he met Iphitus, who gave him the famous bow that he used on his return from Troy to kill Penelope's suitors.

Odysseus was one of the suitors who sought Helen's hand from her father Tyndareus. Like the other suitors, he had taken an oath to defend her marriage and this led to his participation in the Trojan campaign. He took part with twelve ships as the head of the Cephallonian army that was raised from the islands of Ithaca, Neritus, Zakynthos, and Sami. He proved to be a formidable fighter and tracker in most battles, as well as a valued emissary and advisor. After Achilles's death, Odysseus won his arms, precipitating a rift with Ajax, who went mad and killed himself.

Nestor

Nestor, the wise and responsible king of Pylos, was the son of Neleus and Chloris. He was raised in Gerenia in Elis and is thus sometimes called Gerenios. He was spared by Heracles, when the hero killed Nestor's father and brothers.

As a youth, Nestor took part in the war of the Lapiths against the centaurs, as well as in the Caledonian boar hunt and the Argonauts' expedition. He joined the Trojan campaign with ninety ships as head of the armies raised by Pylos and its neighbors. Despite his advanced age, he proved quite formidable in battle.

In *The Iliad*, Nestor stands out for his eloquence, humility, and conciliatory and his counsel was heeded with great respect. After the war, he returned home to live out the rest of his life in happiness.

Bronze statue of Promachos Athena, protectress of the Greeks in the Trojan War (470 B.C., National Archaeological Museum).

Idomeneus

A king of Crete and grandson of Minos, Idomeneus took part in the Trojan campaign with his nephew Meronius, the son of his half-brother Molus, with eighty ships under his command.

Idomeneus distinguished himself in battle for his valor and skillful use of the spear, while his bravery is also praised in *The Iliad*.

After the sacking of Troy, he returned home. According to later myths, he did face treacherous seas on his journey back, but prayed to Poseidon for salvation, promising to sacrifice the first thing he saw when reaching shore. True to his vow, Idomeneus was forced to sacrifice his son. The human sacrifice brought great famine to his land, so the Cretans expelled him. Idomeneus then went to Calauria, then settled in Colophon where he died.

Philoctetes

Philoctetes was the son of Poeas who lit the funerary pyre of Heracles. In return, he received the hero's bow and arrow. Philoctetes ruled the cities of Methone, Thaumacia, Meliboea, and Olezon.

A skilled archer, he took place in the Trojan campaign as the commander of seven ships and 350 archers. The Achaeans left him on the sacred island of Lemnos as a festering wound caused by a snakebite emitted an unbearable stench.

Philoctetes was transported to Troy near the end of the war after the Trojan seer Helenus predicted that the city would only fall if the battle was joined by the hero who had the bow of Heracles. Philoctetes was healed by Machaon, killed Paris, and after the sacking of Ilium sailed to Italy, where he founded many cities.

Nike by Paionios (420 B.C., Olympia Museum).

THE TROJANS

Alexandros-Paris

Paris, who provided the cause for the Trojan War, is often referred to by the name Alexandros or Alexander by Homer. He was the son of Priam and Hecuba. His decision in favor of Aphrodite at a beauty contest between the goddesses, his abuse of Menelaus's hospitality, and his abduction of Helen brought disaster to his land.

Although Paris was frequently admonished by his brother Hector for his detached stance on the war, he took part in many battles and distinguished himself as an archer. He was defeated by Menelaus in a duel, but saved at the last minute by Aphrodite. He later wounded Diomedes, Machaon, Eurypylus and others, while according to the *Cypria* he also killed Achilles, just as his brother Hector had predicted.

Hector

The bravest of the Trojan warriors, Hector led the Trojan forces into the war. He was the son of Priam and Hecuba, and married Andromache, daughter of Eetion, king of the city of Thebes on Mount Placus. Andromache bore Hector a son, Scamandrius.

To recognize his valor, the Trojans called him Astyanax (king of the city). The title suggests someone who saves and preserves and encompasses his virtue. Indeed, Hector is presented by

Hector, Andromache, Paris, and Helen (540 B.C., Wurzburg Museum, Germany).

Homer as the ideal hero. He is a great warrior, a considerate son, a respectful and dedicated husband, and good father – traits that are clearly highlighted in a rhapsody dedicated to Hector as well as the well-known scene where Hector and his family are parted.

Hector was a responsible politician and patriot who realized that the Trojans would lose the war but yet considered it his duty to defend his land to the last drop of blood. It is Hector whom Homer has deliver the famous words: *"A man fighting for his country is the best, the only omen."* Indeed, the Achaeans are cowed by the mere sight of Hector, who feared dishonor more than he feared death. He thus controls his slothful and indolent brother Paris, whom he manages to goad into battle.

Apollo and Ares protected Hector on the battlefield. He duels with Ajax, injures Teucer, breaks up the Achaeans, torches Protesilaus's ship despite its brave defense by Ajax. However, he is repelled by Patroclus

THE TROJAN WAR

Hector preparing for battle. Hector adjusts his armor plate while his mother, Hecuba, holds his spear and helmet. His father, Priamus, leans on a stick and delivers his final instructions, punctuating these by gesturing with his right hand. (red-figure amphora, 510-500 B.C., Staatliche Antiken-Sammlungen, Munich).

who is dressed in Achilles's armor. Hector retreats, then charges forward again, and engages Patroclus in a duel during which the Greek is killed. Hector died in a duel with Achilles, who returned to the battle to avenge the death of his dear friend Patroclus. Hector's body is desecrated by Achilles who, swept up in the triumph of the moment, strips Hector's body, ties it to the back of his chariot, and drags it around the walls of Troy. Achilles dragged Hector's body around Troy's walls for twelve days. But his protector, the goddess Aphrodite protected the corpse by embalming it with ambrosia, while Apollo also covered it with a golden *aegis*, or shield.

On Zeus's command, Achilles finally surrenders Hector's body to Priam for a ransom. The Trojan hero was then buried with great honors, accompanied by moving laments during a ten-day truce agreed by Achilles.

"The triumph of Achilles", *a painting by the Austrian artists Franz Matz from the Achilleion on Corfu. The painting depicts Achilles dragging the dead Hector behind his chariot around the walls of Troy.*

Aeneas

One of *The Iliad*'s greatest Trojan heroes was Aeneas, son of Aphrodite and the handsome Trojan shepherd Anchises with whom the goddess of beauty had fallen in love. Aeneas was raised by the nymphs of Mount Ida until the age of five, when his father turned the boy over to Alcathous. (Alcathous, who was killed during the Trojan War by Idomeneus, was the husband of Aeneas's oldest daughter Hippodameia).

Aeneas tended herds on the Trojan mountain, but during the war was persecuted by Achilles and took part in the fighting.

He was wounded while engaged in combat with the Greek hero Diomedes. Aeneas's mother, Aphrodite, rushed to his aid and covered him with her bright veil and removed him from the battlefield. She was wounded shortly afterwards. His uncle Apollo also intervened on his behalf, covering him with a cloud.

Aeneas later returned to battle and killed several Greeks. He also took part in the attack on the Achaeans camp, engaged Idomeneus in combat, and fought at Hector's side around dead Patroclus's body, causing a significant number of Greek casualties.

At Apollo's behest, Aeneas fought Achilles when he returned to battle. But Aeneas was almost killed in the clash. He was saved by the intervention of Poseidon who predicted a grand future for his descendants. The sea-god advised Aeneas not to risk fighting against Achilles and not to return to battle until after Achilles's death since Achilles was the only Greek who could kill him.

Later poets describe Aeneas as the leader of the Trojans after Hector's death. One version contained in Stesichorus's lost epic *Iliou Persis* (The Sack of Ilium), claims that after the fall of Troy, Aeneas left the burning city, carrying his aged father on his shoulders as well as his son Ascanius, the household gods, and the Palladium. He sought refuge at Ida, from where he left for Italy where he founded Rome.

Glaucus

There are three mythological heroes with the name Glaucus.

- Glaucus was the son of Hippolochus and grandson of Bellerophon. In *The Iliad* he appears alongside Sarpedon as the leader of the Lycians, allies of the Trojans. While dueling with Diomedes, the two fighters realize that their grandfathers were friends and had exchanged hospitality presents. The two immediately stopped fighting and exchanged armor.

In other rhapsodies, Glaucus killed the Achaeans Iphinoos and Bathycles, urged Hector to join the battle, was wounded by Diomedes, and healed by Apollo. Ajax finally killed him during a battle over the body of Achilles, according to Apollodorus. Apollo seized Glaucus's body from the funerary pyre;

THE TROJAN WAR

the body was carried on the winds to Lycia, where Apollo buried it next to the river of the same name.

- Glaucus was also the name of a Trojan hero and son of Antinoroos. He was expelled by his father for accompanying Paris to Sparta and helping him kidnap Helen. Agamemnon killed Glaucus, although according to one account Menelaus and Odysseus, who were old friends of his father's, saved him. In this version, Glaucus left Troy with Menelaus and was shipwrecked on Crete, where he founded the city of Aptera.

- A third hero with the name Glaucus is mentioned by Apollodorus. He was one of Priam's sons and was killed in battle by Diomedes.

Sarpedon

Sarpedon was the son of Zeus and Laodameia, and grandson of Bellerophon. He was the second leader of the Lycians and an ally of Troy. At the height of battle, with the Achaeans forced to retreat behind a protective moat and wall guarding their ships, Sarpedon persuaded his fellow king Glaucus to join him in assaulting the walls.

Patroclus killed Sarpedon. Dying, he asked his companion Glaucus not to allow his body to be desecrated by the Achaeans. A terrible battle, with many casualties, was thus mounted around Sarpedon's body. Commanded by Zeus, Apollo embalmed Sarpedon's body with Ambrosia and

Meeting of the gods about the Trojan War. Ares, Aphrodite, Artemis, and Apollo were on the side of the Trojans (525 B.C., Delphi Museum).

Helenus

Helenus, one of the bravest Trojan warriors and famous seer, was the son of Priam and Hecuba. In *The Iliad*'s sixth rhapsody, Helenus urges Aeneas and Hector to stop the Trojans' panicked flight. He asks Hector to go to the city and order his mother to assemble the Trojan women, who should take presents and votives to Athena to pray for her to save the city from Diomedes. Accounts written after Homer claim Helenus had predicted that Paris would bring disaster on Troy. When Helenus was captured by the Achaeans, he revealed to them that he would never be able to conquer the city without Philoctetes. Helenus was subsequently kept at the Greeks' camp or, according to a different account, was granted his life and freedom by the Achaeans after the sacking of Troy. He then left for Epirus with Pyrrhos, and after Pyrrhos's death married Andromache.

Laocoon, a priest of Apollo and brother of Anchises, and his sons struggle with two giant snakes sent by Poseidon to strange them after the Trojan hero tried to prevent his fellow Trojans from admitting the Trojan Horse into the city. (First century composition by Agisandros, Athinodoros, and Polydoros, Vatican Museum.)

carried it off. He then sent Sarpedon back to Lycia with Hypnos (Sleep) and Thanatos (Death) so that the hero could be buried with honor.

The Odyssey

The Odyssey narrates the tale of Odysseus's return to his home, Ithaca, after the sacking of Troy. It also tells of his struggle to regain his throne and his faithful wife Penelope from the suitors vying for both during his twenty-year absence.

Homer's epic poem has 12,110 verses, which the Alexandrian scholars divided into 24 rhapsodies or books. The epic combines tales of heroic feats with various folk tales and seafarers' stories. It revolves around the universal themes of love of one's homeland, love, friendship, and love of life; it is also a tribute to the resilience of the human spirit and humans' ability to rise to challenges and conquer danger and difficulty.

After the sacking of Troy, Odysseus set sail for home with twelve ships and his companions. The winds brought his

Odysseus escapes the Cyclops's cave by hugging the belly of the finest ram (pottery drawing, late sixth century B.C., Munich Archaeological Museum).

fleet to Thrace, land of the Ciconians, who had been the Trojans' allies and had settled the area between the mouth of the Evros River and Lake Vistonida. Odysseus and his companions laid waste to the city of Ismarus. But the Ciconians enlisted the help of their neighbors to mount a counter-attack on the Achaeans, defeating them and forcing them to abandon their land. Odysseus lost six companions from each of his ships in this battle. Reaching Cape Malea at the southeastern tip of the Peloponnese, a storm tossed the ships far from Greece. Nine days later, Odysseus and his companions arrived in the land of the Lotus-Eaters.

The Lotus-Eaters

The Lotus-Easters were a peace-loving and hospitable tribe who inhabited the small island of Mikri Syrti, off the coast of northern Africa. They lived off the fruit of the lotus, which they also used to make wine. The Lotus-Eaters were a placid people, who did not wish anyone harm. They welcomed Odysseus and his crew by offering them lotus fruit to eat, but anyone who tasted it forget about his homeland and was context to remain on the island. Odysseus forcibly removed his crew from the island and set sail for open sea.

Polyphemus, the Cyclops

From the land of the Lotus-Eaters, Odysseus and his men landed next in the land of the Cyclopes which, according to the ancient texts, was somewhere in Sicily. The Cyclopes were powerful giants with a single, round eye in the middle of their forehead (hence their name, from the Greek *cyclos*, or circle). According to Homer, each of the Cyclopes lived separately with their families in a primitive society with no formal structure, laws, agriculture, or shipping. Across from their land was an unexplored island with lush forests. Odysseus decided to explore this lost paradise and, against the urgings of his companions, landed on the island with twelve of his sailors and a flask of wine. Once ashore, they discovered that the island was inhabited by a man-eating Cyclops named Polyphemus, who was a son of Poseidon.

The blinding of Polyphemus, one of the oldest drawings on pottery (circa 670 B.C.). The Cyclops holds a deep kylix with wine as Odysseus puts his eye out with a lance (Elefsina Museum).

THE ODYSSEY

Odysseus tied to a ram's belly escapes the Cyclops's cave (late sixth century B.C., Delphi Museum).

Odysseus told Polyphemus that he and his men had been shipwrecked and requested that the Cyclops extend his hospitality. Instead, the Cyclops ate two of Odysseus's companions. The next morning, he ate two more for breakfast, then took the rest prisoner in his cave, blocking its entrance with a huge boulder. Odysseus realized that the situation was critical and devised a plan. When the giant returned at night, he ate two more of Odysseus's companions for dinner. Odysseus then plied the Cyclops with wine and got him drunk. He then introduced himself as *Outis* (Nobody) and blinded the Cyclops. The next morning, the crewmembers who had survived left the cave clinging to the belly of a ram, grateful to be free and enjoy the sun again.

Odysseus, however, committed a fatal error. He mocked Polyphemus's father, Poseidon, saying that the sea-god could not heal the Cyclops. His taunts provoked Poseidon's ire, who relentlessly persecuted Odysseus. The adventure of his long journey home had only just begun.

The island of Aeolia

From the land of the Cyclopes, Odysseus and his companions reached the island of Aeolia, island of Aeolus, who was the keeper of the winds. According to Homer, Aeolus was the son of Hippotas and Melanippe. Aeolus was not a god, but was a friend of the gods. With his wife, six sons, and six daughters, he inhabited a floating island surrounded by a copper wall.

Aeolus extended his hospitality to the travelers for a month. As they left, he gave Odysseus a pouch in which he had placed all the winds, except for the mild Zephyrus, or west wind, which would lead them to Ithaca. The ships set sail and nine days later the coast of Ithaca was visible. Weary, Odysseus fell asleep. Thinking that the pouch contained some treasure, his sailors opened it and let out all the winds, which whipped up a storm that carried Odysseus and his crew far back to Aeolia. Aeolus, realizing that Odysseus had incurred the wrath of one of the gods, sent them away.

The Laestrygonians

Six days later, the travelers arrived once again in an imaginary land, Telepylus, home of the inhospitable, man-eating Laestrygonians who were descendants of Lamus. These savage giants lived in organized communities. In summer, the days in their land were so short that the shepherd coming home at the end of a day's work would run into the shepherd leaving for work.

Odysseus sent three of his companions to find out who was the king of this land. Unsuspecting, they arrived at the palace of Antiphates. The king ate one of the men, then roused thousands of Laestrygonians to attack the strangers. They giants tossed enormous boulders at Odysseus's fleet, destroying eleven ships and devouring their crews. Only the hero's ship managed to evade the attackers because Odysseus had had the foresight to moor his ship at the edge of the harbor.

The island of Circe

With his one, remaining ship, Odysseus landed on Aeaea or Aea the island of the powerful sorceress Circe, daughter of Helius and the oceanid Perse. According to an older tradition, Aeaea was located on the eastern half of the earth and separated from the Underworld by Oceanus. Later myths, however, located the island at Tyrrhenia, about midway down the Italian coast.

Odysseus dropped anchor at Aeaea. Two days and two nights later, he divided his companions into two groups. After drawing lots, a team of 22 men led by Eurylochus set out to explore the island. Odysseus's companions reached the palace of Circe, where they were changed into swine. Eurylochus escaped unharmed because he had not entered the palace. He alerted Odysseus, who rushed to his men's aid. On the way, he encountered the god Hermes, who had taken the form of a youth. The god gave Odysseus a magic herb that was an antidote to Circe's spells. Odysseus thus managed to elude her sorcery and force Circe to vow that she would send him home and restore his companions to their human form.

The travelers remained on Aeaea for a year, enjoying Circe's wonderful hospitality. Odysseus became her lover, but later reminded her of the promise she had made to show him the way home. Circe told him that if he wanted to return, he would have to descend into Hades and seek guidance from the Theban seer Teiresias. Just before Odysseus and his men set sail, one became drunk, slipped off the palace roof, and fell to his death. His body remained unburied.

Odysseus in the Underworld

Following Circe's instructions and taking advantage of a favorable wind she sent, Odysseus's ship reached the far end of Oceanus and arrived in the land of the Cimmerians, who lived in the darkness of eternal night. After disembarking, Odysseus offered funerary libations and sacrifices. The souls of the dead approached the funerary pit to drink the blood of the slaughtered animals, but Odysseus did not let them drink until the shadow of the seer Teiresias appeared. After drinking the black blood, the seer told Odysseus that his troubles had been caused by Poseidon's rage and warned him not to touch Helius's cattle when they landed on the island of Thrinacia if they wanted to arrive home alive. The seer also told Odysseus what was happening at his palace where the princes were frittering away his wealth and wooing his wife Penelope. The seer told Odysseus he would destroy these suitors, and advised him to seek people who did not know the sea and live with them if he wished to have a long and peaceful old age.

Odysseus then spoke with the shadow of his dead mother Anticleia, daughter of Autolycus. She assured him of Penelope's fidelity, as well as of the just and responsible behavior of their son Telemachus. She also told him of the bitterness of his father Laertes, who lived isolated on his farm.

In the Underworld, Odysseus also encountered his unburied companion Helpinor, who asked his friend to bury him so that his soul could rest. He also encountered Agamemnon, who related his tragic end and advised him not to trust women.

Achilles told Odysseus of the beauty of life, stating bitterly that he would have preferred to have lived a humble life without fame, even as a slave, rather than being the most honored hero in Hades. He also asked for news of his aged father Peleus and his son Neoptolemus.

In the kingdom of the souls, Odysseus also met Ajax, who remained silent because of their fight over Achilles's armor that had resulted in Ajax's suicide. He also encountered other heroes and important people who now lived as shadows in meadows thick with asphodels.

The Sirens – Scylla – Charybdis – The cattle of Helius

It was nighttime when Odysseus and his companions returned from Hades. The next morning, they buried Helpinor's body with full burial rites.

The next day, Circe gave her lover the necessary travel directions to reach Ithaca but warned him of the dangers he would encounter: the Sirens, who charmed men with their song; the hideous Scylla, a twelve-headed monster who devoured sailors who veered too close to the rock she inhabited; Charybdis, another monster who swallowed up, then spit out the sea three times a day. Circe also told Odysseus about the island of Thrinacia where Helius's cattle grazed, and warned him and his men not to touch the animals if they wished to return safely to the island of Ithaca.

The next day, Odysseus set sail for open sea. He told his companions about the dangers they lay ahead. Having sealed his companions' ears with wax, he tied himself to the ship's mast with ropes so that the ship sailed past the island of the Sirens.

The company lost six members to Scylla, then approached Thrinacia. Odysseus asked his companions to continue past the island, but they were exhausted and asked to land, even for a single night. Odysseus made them take an oath that they would not touch Helius's cattle and would only eat the provisions supplied by Circe.

A huge storm erupted that night, and the men were stranded on the island for a month. They ran out of food, and the men soon forgot their oath as well as the warnings of Teiresias and Circe. While Odysseus was asleep, they slaughtered Helius's cattle and ate them.

The sun-god's daughter Lampeto told her father what had happened. Furious, Helius asked Zeus to punish Odysseus's crew.

Tied to the ship's mast, Odysseus listens to the song of the Sirens, which are depicted with a bird's body and a woman's head (pottery drawing, British Museum).

Odysseus on Ogygia

Odysseus battled the rough seas for nine days and nine nights, managing to squeeze past Charybdis while being pushed towards her by the southern winds. On the tenth day, he swam ashore to Ogygia, the island of inhabited by Calypso in the middle of the Mediterranean Sea. Ancient texts claim Calypso was the daughter of Pleione, and she was considered a nymph, either one of the oceanids-atlantidae or one of the Hesperides. According to mythology, she was the mother of Nausithous, Nausinous, and Auson, after whom southern Italy was named Ausonia.

Odysseus remained on Ogygia with the beautiful nymph for seven years. But her beauty, kindness, and promises of immortality were not enough to make Odysseus forget Ithaca, his wife, or his son, and he sat by shore lamenting his loss all day.

The gods decided that it was time for him to return home. Zeus sent the herald Hermes to Calypso to announce their decision and order her to free Odysseus so he could return home. Despite her anger, she acquiesced. She then helped her lover build a raft, gave him the necessary provisions, then bid him farewell. Odysseus was once again asea, but could not escape the notice of Poseidon. The sea-god was on his way back from the Ethiopians and whipped up a storm that shattered Odysseus's raft. The hero fought the waves; at a critical moment, Leucothea, daughter of Cadmus, appeared by him in the form of a duck. While mortal, Leucothea had been known as Ino. She gave Odysseus her magic kerchief, which he used to reach Scherie, land of the Phaeacians.

The land of the Phaeacians

Scherie, the land of the seafaring people known as the Phaeacians, has been identified with the island of Corfu. In *The Odyssey* it is described as a pleasant and prosperous land that hovered between legend and reality. Its king, Alcinous, was the son of the first settler of Scherie, the handsome Nausithous. This island was Odysseus's last stop before finally reaching Ithaca.

The hero lay asleep on the bank of a river where he was found by the king's daughter Nausicaa, who had gone to the river with her friends to wash their clothes. Hospitable and sympathetic, the young princess followed Athena's guidance in bringing Odysseus to the palace. There, he followed her advice and became a suppliant to her mother Arete whose assistance and mediation he sought to return home.

The Phaeacians extended their hospitality to the stranger. They held a symposium in his honor, followed by games and dances. The bard Demodocus entertained the banquet with songs narrating the Trojan campaign and the city's sacking by the Achaeans. Unable to hide his emotions, Odysseus revealed his identity to Alcinous and related his adventures. Alcinous then honored his promise. After the customary exchange of gifts, parting libations and wishes, Odysseus boarded a ship that brought him home.

Odysseus at Ithaca

When the ship arrived at Ithaca, Odysseus was asleep. The Phaeacians lay him on the beach, left Alcinous's gifts by the trunk of an olive tree, then returned home.

Odysseus awoke in a fog and did not recognize his homeland. Athena then appeared before him disguised as a young shepherd boy and told Odysseus where he was. The goddess then revealed herself to the hero. Together, they hid Alcinous's gifts and made plans to destroy Penelope's suitors. On Athena's advice, Odysseus disguised himself as a beggar and went to the hut of his faithful swineherd Eumaeus. He stayed there for four nights. There he met his son Telemachus who was returning from a trip to Pylos and Sparta at the behest of Athena. Taking advantage of the swineherd's absence, Odysseus revealed himself to his son and the

Odysseus disguised as a beggar grasps the hand of the grieving Penelope. The figures behind her are likely Telemachus and two old men, Laertes and the swineherd Eumaeus. (Melian relief, circa 460-450 B.C., Metropolitan Museum of New York.)

two began to plan how to punish the suitors.

On the fifth day after his arrival on Ithaca, Odysseus –still disguised as a beggar– went to the city and his palace, where he was taunted and beaten by Antinous, one of Penelope's suitors.

The following day, Penelope followed Athena's suggestion and declared an archery contest with Odysseus's bow. She said that the man who could shoot an arrow through twelve axes would become her husband. All of the suitors failed. Only the beggar-Odysseus managed the feat. Then, with help from his son Telemachus and his faithful servants Eumaeus and Philoetius, he killed the suitors. Order had been restored. Odysseus purified his home with sulfur and fire to cleanse it from the miasma of the massacre. He then reunited with his wife, who recognized him. Together, they finally enjoyed their love during a night that Athena made longer.

The next day Odysseus met his aged father Laertes, who recognized him. But in the city, the suitors' relatives sought revenge.

Led by Eupeithes, they armed themselves and headed towards Laertes's farm. Athena headed off the confrontation by using her booming voice and one of Zeus's thunderbolts to stop them. Odysseus's enemies were forced to retreat under the gods' command and take oaths of conciliation.

The death of Odysseus

With a war between Odysseus and Ithacans averted, the hero made a sacrifice to the nymphs and left for Elis where his herds were grazing. He was received by King Polyxeinus, grandson of Augeias, who gave him a valuable krater.

Returning to Ithaca, Odysseus offered sacrifices to all the gods. Following the advice he had received in Hades from Teiresias, he shouldered an oar and set off to find a people who did not know the sea or marine tools and who ate their food unsalted because they did not know salt. He thus arrived in Thesprotia in Epirus. After offering a sacrifice to his old enemy Poseidon, Odysseus settled in Thesprotia.

There, Odysseus had a son, Polypoetes, by queen Callidice. He also led the Thesprotians against the Brygi, whom he defeated with Athena's help.

After Callidice died, Odysseus handed over the throne to Polypoetes, and returned to Ithaca seeking peace. But he was destined to die asea.

Circe had given birth to a son, Telegonus. When the boy grew up, he went on a quest to find his father. His boat eventually arrived at Ithaca. Hungry and exhausted, his sailors slaughtered some animals they found grazing nearby and ate them. The Ithacans panicked, believing that the strangers were pirates. They notified

Odysseus, who raised an army and rushed to the coast to face the invaders. In the battle that followed, Telegonus unknowingly killed his father with the spear he had fashioned from a skate's poisonous barb. Odysseus, who had survived the sea and its monsters, was killed by the wound inflicted by his son, thus fulfilling the prophecy of Teiresias.

Grief-stricken over the accidental murder he had committed, Telegonus took his father's body, Penelope, and Telemachus, and returned to Aeaea to his mother. Circe gave Penelope and Telemachus immortality. She then married the son of her former lover, while Penelope married Telegonus.

And this is how fairy tales usually end...

Penelope's suitors try to protect themselves from the arrows shot by Odysseus (440 B.C., Berlin Museum).

Pronunciation

Acacallis	⇒	Akakal'lis		Alcinous	⇒	Alkin'oos
Acarnan	⇒	Akarnan'		Alcippe	⇒	Alkip'pe
Acastus	⇒	Ak'astos		Alcmaeon	⇒	Alkme'on
Achelous	⇒	Ahelo'os		Alcyone	⇒	Alkyo'ne
Acheron	⇒	Ahe'ron		Aloeus	⇒	Aleos'
Achilles	⇒	Ahile'as		Althaea	⇒	Althai'a
Acrisius	⇒	Akris'ios		Amphiaraus	⇒	Amfia'raos
Actaeon	⇒	Aktai'on		Ancaeus	⇒	Ankai'os
Admetus	⇒	Ad'metos		Andromache	⇒	Androma'he
Adonis	⇒	Adon'is		Anticleia	⇒	Antik'lia
Adrasteia	⇒	Adras'tia		Arachne	⇒	Ara'hne
Adrastus	⇒	Ad'rastos		Aristaeus	⇒	Aristai'os
Aeacus	⇒	Ai'akos		Arsinoe	⇒	Arsino'e
Aeetes	⇒	Aie'tes		Ascalaphus	⇒	Askal'afos
Aegaeon	⇒	Aigai'on		Astydameia	⇒	Astida'mia
Aegeus	⇒	Aigeus'		Atalante	⇒	Atalan'te
Aegina	⇒	Ai'gina		Boeotus	⇒	Voe'tos
Aegisthus	⇒	Ai'gisthos		Boreas	⇒	Vore'as
Aegle	⇒	Ai'gle		Busiris	⇒	Vou'siris
Aeneas	⇒	Ainei'as		Butes	⇒	Vou'tes
Aeolus	⇒	Ai'olos		Cabeiri	⇒	Kab'iri
Aerope	⇒	Aero'pe		Callidice	⇒	Kallidi'ke
Aeson	⇒	Ai'son		Callirrhoe	⇒	Kalliro'e
Aether	⇒	Aither'		Callisto	⇒	Kalisto'
Aglaea	⇒	Aglai'a		Calyce	⇒	Kal'ike
Aglaurus	⇒	Ag'lauros		Cecrops	⇒	Kek'rops
Agrius	⇒	Ag'rios		Celaeno	⇒	Kelaino'

Celeus	⇒	Keleos'	Graeae	⇒	Grai'ai
Ceto	⇒	Keto'	Harpies	⇒	Har'piai
Chalciope	⇒	Halkio'pe	Hebe	⇒	I'vi
Charites	⇒	Har'ites	Hecate	⇒	Ek'ati
Charon	⇒	Ha'ron	Hecatoncheires	⇒	Ekaton'heres
Cheiron	⇒	Her'on	Helle	⇒	El'e
Chimaera	⇒	Himai'ra	Herse	⇒	Er'se
Chronus	⇒	Hron'os	Hippocoon	⇒	Ipoko'on
Cilicia	⇒	Kiliki'a	Hippolyte	⇒	Ipolyte
Circe	⇒	Kir'ke	Hippolytus	⇒	Hipol'itos
Clytie	⇒	Klit'e	Hippothoon	⇒	Ipoth'oon
Coeus	⇒	Koi'os	Horae	⇒	O'rai
Coroebus	⇒	Kor'oivos	Hypsipyle	⇒	Ipsip'ile
Cronus	⇒	Kro'nos	Iacchus	⇒	I'akhos
Curetes	⇒	Koure'tes	Ialmenus	⇒	Ial'menos
Cybele	⇒	Kive'le	Iole	⇒	Io'le
Daedalus	⇒	Dai'dalos	Jocasta	⇒	Iokas'te
Danae	⇒	Dana'e	Kore	⇒	Ko're
Danaus	⇒	Danaos'	Labdacus	⇒	Lav'dakos
Daunus	⇒	Dav'nos	Lacedaemon	⇒	Lakedai'mon
Deianeira	⇒	Deian'ira	Laertes	⇒	Laer'tes
Deucalion	⇒	Defkali'on	Lampeto	⇒	Lampeto'o
Dictys	⇒	Dik'tis	Leucippus	⇒	Lef'kipos
Dike	⇒	Di'ke	Melicertes	⇒	Meliker'tes
Dioscuri	⇒	Dioscou'ri	Menoeceus	⇒	Menoikeus'
Dirce	⇒	Dir'ki	Menoetius	⇒	Menoi'tes
Echidna	⇒	Eh'idna	Mnemosyne	⇒	Menemosy'ne
Eeriboea	⇒	Eeri'via	Moerae	⇒	Me're
Eileithyia	⇒	Eili'thia	Neaera	⇒	Ne'aira
Eirene	⇒	Iri'ni	Neleus	⇒	Nelefs'
Eos	⇒	E'os	Nereus	⇒	Nerefs'
Ephialtes	⇒	Efial'tis	Niobe	⇒	Nio've
Erebus	⇒	Er'evos	Ocyrrhoe	⇒	Okiro'e
Erinyes	⇒	Erini'es	Oenomaus	⇒	Oinom'aos
Eurydice	⇒	Evridi'ke	Oreithyia	⇒	Orei'thyia
Eurypylus	⇒	Evripil'os	Paean	⇒	Pai'an
Glauce	⇒	Glaf'ke	Parthenopaeus	⇒	Parthenopai'os
Glaucus	⇒	Glaf'kos	Pasiphae	⇒	Pasifa'e

Peirithous	⇒	Pirith'os	Schoeneus	⇒	Schoineufs'
Penthesileia	⇒	Penthesil'ia	Scieron	⇒	Skir'on
Phaeacians	⇒	Fai'akes	Scylla	⇒	Skill'a
Phaedra	⇒	Fe'dra	Stheneboea	⇒	Sthene'via
Phaethon	⇒	Fethon'	Sthenelus	⇒	Sthen'elos
Philoetius	⇒	Philoi'tios	Taygete	⇒	Taige'te
Philonoe	⇒	Philono'e	Teiresias	⇒	Teiresi'as
Phorbas	⇒	For'vas	Teucer	⇒	Tef'kros
Phorcys	⇒	For'kis	Teuthras	⇒	Tuf'thras
Poeas	⇒	Poi'as	Thaumus	⇒	Thav'mas
Polydectes	⇒	Polydek'tes	Thriae	⇒	Thri'ai
Polydeuces	⇒	Polydef'kes	Tityus	⇒	Tityos'
Polyhymnia	⇒	Polyhimni'a	Tlepolemus	⇒	Tlepol'emos
Polyneices	⇒	Polynik'es	Tydeus	⇒	Tydefs'
Procrustes	⇒	Prokrous'tes	Typhoeus	⇒	Tifo'us
Proetus	⇒	Proi'tos	Urania	⇒	Ourani'a
Pyrrha	⇒	Pir'a	Uranus	⇒	Ouranos'
Pyrrhos	⇒	Pir'os	Xanthus	⇒	Ksan'thos
Rhadamanthys	⇒	Radha'manthys	Xuthus	⇒	Ksu'thos
Rhea	⇒	Re'a	Zeuxippe	⇒	Zefxip'e
Rhesus	⇒	Res'os			